fP

THE FREE PRESS
New York London Toronto Sydney Singapore

THE NATURE OF HORSES

Exploring Equine Evolution, Intelligence, and Behavior

Stephen Budiansky

Illustration credits follow the index.

fP

THE FREE PRESS
A Division of Simon & Schuster Inc.
1230 Avenue of the Americas
New York, NY 10020

Art direction and design by Kim Llewellyn and Trish Parcell
Illustrations by Diana Salles
Manufactured in the United States of America
10 9 8 7 6 5 4 3 2 1

Library of Congress Cataloging-in-Publication Data
Budiansky, Stephen.
The nature of horses / Stephen Budiansky.
Includes bibliographical references (p.) and index.
1. Horses. 2. Horses—Behavior. I. Title.
SF285.B798 1997
636.1—dc21 96-47004

ISBN 0-684-82768-9

For Rachael and Andrew

Horses and poets should be fed, not overfed.

—CHARLES IX

I know two things about the horse
And one of them is rather coarse.

—NAOMI ROYDE-SMITH

CONTENTS

Foreword by Franklin M. Loew, D.V.M. — *xi*
Introduction — 1
Chapter 1 The Improbability of the Horse — 9
Chapter 2 From the Brink of Oblivion — 39
Chapter 3 Equine Nature, Human Nature — 61
Chapter 4 Socioecology — 79
Chapter 5 Seeing and Perceiving — 109
Chapter 6 Horse Talk — 127
Chapter 7 Horse Sense — 147
Chapter 8 The Mechanics of Movement — 175
Chapter 9 Assume a Spherical Horse — 211
Chapter 10 Nature or Nurture? — 235
Conclusion The Fate of the Horse — 263
Further Reading — *267*
Acknowledgments — *273*
Index — *275*
Illustration Credits — *287*

FOREWORD

I was eight years old when I first got on a horse, a little brown mare barely fifteen hands, named Chatterbox. That was my introduction to horses and the human culture that has grown around them.

There were many others, and I can remember virtually all their names: Sunshine, Thunderhead, Golden Orchid, Skylark, and my two favorites, Stock Market and General. They became my friends, companions, heroes. I just couldn't understand why so few of my human friends cared much about horses back in the 1940s and '50s.

Today, however, there are more horses (perhaps seven million) in the United States than at any time since the U.S. Cavalry ceased being an effective fighting force between the two world wars. Americans have rediscovered the horse on the eve of the twenty-first century.

"God forbid that I should go to any heaven in which there are no horses," wrote Robert Bontine Cunningham-Graham to Theodore Roosevelt in 1917. Listen to what Stephen Budiansky has to say in this marvelously informative book:

> *The domestication of the horse as a mount and a chariot horse was an event so overwhelming in the history of mankind that it was virtually impossible that man could have looked upon it with cool and sober detachment . . . Humans would inevitably see horses through their own eyes, their dreams and ambitions, myths and fears, vanities and fashions.*

And from biology, anthropology, veterinary medicine, and agricultural science, Stephen Budiansky extracts the information that applies to our understanding of the horse. I know of no more complete source of the latest interpretations and newest findings from these fields than *The Nature of Horses.* But a warning here: this is a tough-minded book, one that does not accept without critical evaluation many of the romantic myths surrounding *Equus caballus.*

Some of the questions this book will help the serious horse person to answer:

- How "intelligent" are horses?
- How do horses "play"?
- Where—really—did horses come from?
- What is the role of endorphins—the body's own type of morphine—in common equine vices?
- Just how well can horses see?
- Do horses "talk" to each other?
- Can horses *really* find their way home unassisted?

The Nature of Horses has the best discussion of equine vision I've seen, and the material covering genetics (including the genetics of behavior and racehorse "speed") is superb. The reader who invests in this book will be amply rewarded by an unsurpassed understanding—in modern terms—of the horse.

—*Franklin M. Loew*
DEAN OF VETERINARY MEDICINE
CORNELL UNIVERSITY

INTRODUCTION

Horses have been enveloped in human dreams, myths, ambitions, and sentiment for so long that the story we have come to think of as theirs is often but a distorted reflection of our own desires, and then not always our most noble desires.

It takes a harder heart and a stronger mind than I, for one, possess not to be dazzled by the pure beauty of man and horse working together. The almost magical cooperation of horse and rider is testimony both to the inventiveness of man and to the remarkable learning ability and physical prowess of the horse. It is art as much as science, a product of pure imagination as much as it is any predictable outcome of evolutionary biology. The thrill of watching the performance of a superb racehorse or jumper or cutting horse or polo pony or dressage horse comes from the sense that these are creatures at once of nature and transcendent of nature.

But the character of these all too human endeavors has perhaps made us forget that even after 6,000 years of domestication the horse still has its own story to tell. It is a story worth knowing for its own sake; but it is also a story worth knowing if we are to be better riders and trainers and keepers of this species that is now wholly dependent upon us for its survival, its well being, and its future.

We ask horses to do many things that build upon their instincts—especially their well-developed social instincts, their acute sensitivity to social hierarchy and to subtle cues of dominance and submission. But we also expect them to do many things that are not instinctive at all, or actually counter to their instincts—to walk into a dark horse trailer or, for that matter, to carry 175 pounds of weight on their backs. The latter they come to do through learning; and of course an ability to learn *is* a part of their nature, too. But that does not alter the fact that we have all too often confused the horse's willing nature in the company of man with its inherent nature. Those who claim it is "unethical" to ask a horse to do anything it would not do of its own inclination are being naive and foolish; but equally naive and foolish are those who expect to teach a horse to do their bidding without taking into account its natural inclinations.

Science is now beginning to allow the horse to tell its own story. And indeed I would argue that at this late date in the shared history of man and horse it is *only* the objective tools of science that can sort out what millenniums of tradition, lore, and wishful thinking have sometimes muddled. Training and riding a horse is hard work, and it is inevitable that all the mental tricks, practice, and athleticism that go into getting ourselves to sit right and balance and relax and keep our heels down and look up at the jump sometimes make us forget to see things from the horse's point of view. Horsemen have always been susceptible to one great foible, and that is the belief that the categories and terms and concepts they apply to their art are ones their horses hold, too. The art of riding is just that—an art—and it has evolved its own language and techniques that contain a whole suitcase full of assumptions. As seen from the lofty peaks of the high school of equitation, the hands may be a "natural" aid while the voice is an "artificial" one, but it would be hard to contend that a horse having a metal bit stuffed in its mouth but possessed of a highly evolved ability to respond to varying tones of vocalization views the world in such categories. Twenty-four centuries ago Xenophon advised that horses be taught the prancing leap known as the curvet, for "such are the horses upon which gods and heroes are depicted riding, and men who manage them well will present a magnificent appearance." Magnificent, no doubt. But to describe such accomplishments as noble, or brilliant, or (in Xenophon's words) "the finest actions proper to a horse" is to say more about human culture than equine nature.

It has only been in the last ten years or so that basic science has begun to focus intensively on the horse, and the resulting explosion of research into the evolution, behavior, biomechanics, energenetics, perception, learning, and genetics of horses has yielded remarkable insights into the true nature of the beast.

It may seem odd that an animal of such cultural and economic importance had escaped scientific inquiry for so long. But historically the people who studied horses had other concerns. Veterinary medicine quite naturally focused on disease and its treatment, while the animal-science departments of agricultural universities tended to emphasize practical matters of livestock production. There is much in the animal-science literature on how to feed dairy cows, but relatively little on horses, especially in the half-century since tractors arrived on the scene in large numbers. Neither discipline is especially given to asking the "why" questions that are at the heart of basic science.

Meanwhile, the zoologists, ecologists, evolutionary biologists, and animal behaviorists who have revealed so many fascinating things about wild animals have tended to look down their noses at their domesticated counterparts. There is a long (though scarcely justifiable) tradition in zoology and ecology of viewing domesticates as "degenerate" forms, unworthy of serious biological study. This may conceivably have something to do with the fact that scientists, being only human, would rather catch an airliner to the tropics to study an exotic rain forest parrot than catch a bus to the nearest chicken farm. But the upshot, in any case, is that only recently have domestic animals begun to get their due from basic science. For 60 centuries man has ridden upon the backs of walking, trotting, and galloping horses; for nearly as long horse doctors of varying degrees of scientific pretension have sought and found ways to bring horses back to soundness when their legs suffer injury. But it was only in 1981 that anyone was finally able to explain *why* a horse uses its legs the way it does in the first place.

For this thanks are partly due to the arrival on the scene of a host of scientists from disciplines not traditionally associated with the study of animals: acoustics, optics, mechanics, computer science, even engineering. Another factor has been the growing number of research veterinarians who have acquired Ph.D. degrees in specialized areas of basic science in order to pursue questions more fundamental than matters of disease and treatment. Together, these researchers have begun to apply the tools of physics, engineering, mathematical modeling, biotechnology, and other sciences to questions about the horse that the traditional disciplines either failed to answer or failed even to ask. Applying the analytical methods of structural engineering and materials science to the study of bones and muscles has yielded a wealth of data about the way animals move and breathe, how they convert energy into motion, and what factors ultimately limit their performance. Evolutionary ecology has offered powerful insights into why animals behave the way they do, in everything from their social structures to their means of communication. Archaeology has revolutionized the story of how and why animals such as the horse came to associate with man, rewriting the traditional tale of human invention into one of mutual gain in the evolutionary struggle for survival. Optics and acoustics and neurophysiology have made enormous strides in allowing us to see the world through the eyes of other creatures, and have even given us a crack at that most elusive of questions, what an animal thinks.

Learning why and how a horse is what it is and does what it does has added a new dimension to my enjoyment and appreciation, as a rider, as a student of animal behavior, and as a naturalist. If science does not always support our sentimental dreams and myths about the horse, it offers something more durable, more practical, and often no less beautiful. To me, the real story of how the modern horse was saved from extinction by a hair's breadth through its domestication by Eurasian steppe dwellers 6,000 years ago is far more thrilling (and certainly more revealing) than any of the romantic tales that have cluttered the story of the modern horse's origin. Learning how scientists have tried to tease out the secrets behind the amazing homing sense that animals possess has given me an infinitely richer perspective on my own horse's behavior than I had when, like so many horse owners, I just chalked up their direction-finding skills to some vague and mysterious "instinct." The deep evolutionary roots that lie beneath the emotional and social bonds that we forge with our horses give substance and meaning to what we might otherwise dismiss as mere human sentiment. The scientific story of the horse is full of wonder and surprise, and I suspect that some of the findings I describe in these pages will come as a surprise even to those who have devoted their lives to horses.

But, lest anyone get the wrong idea, I definitely do not presume to present here some "scientific" system of riding or training. By one published estimate, there have been 40,000 books written about the horse since Xenophon penned the first, and there are plenty of how-to books available (probably about 40,000, in fact) that can tell you how to hold your reins and turn on the forehand, how to cure bad habits or bad feet, or (increasingly these days) how to win blue ribbons with the aid of acupuncture, herbs, or Zen imagery. Let me be the first to admit my total lack of qualifications to hold forth on any of these subjects. I do own a horse, a big and mostly well-meaning quarter-horse/thoroughbred palomino, and I have spent many happy and wonderful hours upon his back fox hunting across the fields and hills of my neighborhood in Virginia; but he knows far more about riding and hunting than I ever will, and I have no illusions about my amateur status. While it was my love and admiration for horses that motivated me to write this book, I have written it emphatically in my capacity as a science journalist, not an equestrian. I would not presume to tell another person how to pick out his horse's hooves, and if in places I seem cautious about drawing practical lessons from the discoveries of basic science, it is out of deference to and enormous respect for the skills of horsemanship that belong to those who are far more talented and experienced than I will ever be. I would prefer to allow the science to speak for itself; horsemen can draw the appropriate conclusions without my help.

Successful training and schooling of a horse in any event has always relied as much on intuition, experience, and unconsciously honed instinct as on anything that science (much less any book) can tell us. And so it will always be. One does not need to know thermodynamics to fix an air conditioner; or, to draw perhaps a better analogy, one does not need to understand the physics of acoustics to play a Beethoven sonata beautifully.

That said, the beauty of science is that it can sometimes reveal to us things that all the intuition and experience and instinct in the world cannot. Scientists are sometimes easy to make fun of on this score, but one of their most admirable traits is their refusal to take anything on faith. Putting old assumptions to an objective test has time and again yielded up wonderfully counterintuitive discoveries. The delight that a true scientist takes in proving even himself wrong is a lesson for us all.

But most of all, science, as the great naturalist Aldo Leopold observed, is what has truly given human value and meaning to the creatures and other "wild things" we share the world with—a meaning that goes deeper than sentiment, and a meaning that comes only when we have learned the story of where these wonderful animals come from, and how they live.

CHAPTER 1

THE IMPROBABILITY OF THE HORSE

Of the more than 4,000 species of mammals that have occupied the earth during the last 10,000 years, the horse is one of fewer than a dozen that have achieved widespread success as domesticated animals.

That low success rate was certainly not for want of trying on our part. The ancient Egyptians attempted to domesticate hyenas, antelope, ibex, and gazelles (figure 1.1). The American Indians kept pet raccoons, bears, and even moose. The Australian aborigines even kept wallabies and kangaroos. Yet none survive as domesticated animals today.

If it were simply a matter of human will, it would be hard to explain why we should have domestic dogs, sheep, goats, cows, pigs, horses, asses, camels, rabbits, and cats—but not deer, squirrels, foxes, antelope, or even hippos and zebras.

The answer is that it was not a matter of human will. The successful domesticated species were largely "preadapted" to their role through quirks of adaptation and evolution that had nothing whatever to do with human intentions or needs, but that turned out to be vital to their future success in our homes and fields. The horse was no exception. Among the myriad ways of making a living that evolution has cast up, a few—a very few—turned out to be compatible with human ways.

The horse, like the other animals that were to enter into domestication, was a generalist, able to survive on a variety of widely available foods. (An animal such as the giant panda, which eats nothing but bamboo leaves, would surely have been a nonstarter.) These generalists were able to exploit their new domesticated niche with a high potential reproduction rate. They had relatively simple courtship patterns, typically harems in which one male readily mates with multiple females. They were social animals, instinctively given to understanding signals of dominance and submission. They were relatively

FIGURE 1.1
The ancient Egyptians were experienced horse-keepers; they also tried—and failed—to domesticate a number of other animals, including antelopes and hyenas.

nonterritorial, not given to disruptive intraspecies combat over fixed bits of ground. In other words, the first step toward domestication was one that nature took millions of years before we even arrived on the scene.

The second step also seems to have been more the doing of the animals than of us. It was animals who discovered the mutual compatibility of our species, and it was they who chose to act upon this discovery. Recent archaeological and animal behavior studies strongly support the idea that domestication was not the human invention it was long supposed to have been, but rather a long, slow process of mutual adaptation, of "coevolution," in which those animals that began to hang around the first permanent human settlements gained more than they lost. Some were killed and eaten, but for every cow or sheep or horse killed, many more flourished on the crops they robbed from our fields and the incidental protection they gained from other predators in the proximity of human habitations. Like the starlings, mice and rats, and chimney swifts that invade our homes today for the food and shelter that are a by-product of our domestic habits, those forebears of our domestic stock took the initiative. We followed.

In the process, these semidomesticated but still free-living animals acquired still more of the characteristics that would make full domestication possible. Those individuals that were more curious, less territorial, less aggressive, more dependent, better able to deflect human aggression through submission, were the individuals that had the edge in this new niche.

It was only in the third stage of domestication, when humans began breeding animals in captivity, that human "invention" began to play a predominant role. But in consciously selecting and emphasizing those traits that appealed to our fancy or our needs, we could still only draw upon what nature provided. If the horse had not existed, we most definitely could not have invented it. The species upon which agriculture and indeed civilization have been built were a remarkable gift of evolutionary chance and opportunism.

The Disadvantage of Being a Horse

A number of species that expanded their range throughout the world during the respites that punctuated the Ice Age glaciations of the Pleistocene epoch (15,000 to 2 million years ago) may have acquired "domesticated" traits as a package deal. The twin pressures of climatic upheaval and massive hunting by humans placed specialist feeders at a decided disadvantage; it was the generalists, which could adapt to a wide variety of climates and circumstances, that flourished. Moreover, it was those species that were migratory, curious, adaptable—as opposed to territorial, suspicious, and conservative—that thrived on upheaval. Sheep, wolves, cattle, goats, camels, and horses all fit this bill. Thus in at least one sense the coincidence of domestication seems a bit more comprehensible: there were sound evolutionary reasons that made horses ripe for domestication. Even tameability may have been part of this package. The pressures that placed a premium on adaptability favored the retention into adulthood of juvenile characteristics, an evolutionary process known as neoteny. Juveniles are curious and adaptable, traits that were in demand in the Pleistocene; they are also playful, submissive, and dependent, traits that proved valuable to man in domestication.

Yet horses possessed a number of other remarkably convenient characteristics—convenient from our point of view—

that make the existence of the modern horse seem all the more astonishing. To begin with, its very survival to modern times was practically a fluke. Many things worked against the horse ever making it. The speed, size, and weight-bearing capacity of the modern horse, all vital to its utility to humans, are extraordinarily unusual among mammals. An animal the size of the horse is in fact a prime candidate for extinction, a fact borne out repeatedly in the fossil record of life on earth. Large animals are long-lived as a rule, but they are also slow to reach sexual maturity, require long gestation periods, and rarely bear more than one young at a time. A drought, an insect outbreak that strips vegetation bare, or any other climatic or ecological disturbance can deliver a blow to a population of large-bodied animals that it takes years to recover from—if it recovers at all. A population of small animals that reproduce quickly and in large litters, on the other hand, can bounce back from repeated calamities.

Large animals face other evolutionary risks, not least of all gravity. Thomas McMahon, a biomechanician at Harvard University who has made an extensive study of the biology of size, notes that when an animal falls the damage it does to itself is directly proportional to its height, or length. (McMahon's argument in a nutshell: The strength of bones is proportional to their cross-sectional area. An animal twice as tall or twice as long as another will have bones that are twice as thick in all of their dimensions; their cross-sectional area will thus be 2 x 2 = 4 times as great [see figure 1.2]. If an animal's body length is proportional to L, the cross-sectional area of its bones will be proportional to length squared, L^2. On the other hand, the energy of a falling body is proportional to its mass, and mass typically increases with the cube of an animal's length, or L^3, because an animal twice as long as another will, roughly speaking, also be twice as wide and twice as tall, so its total volume will be eight times as great: 2 x 2 x 2 = 8. So if the energy of an impact is proportional to length cubed, and the ability to resist damage is proportional to length squared, the ratio of the two is $[L^3/L^2]$, which equals just plain L. The old adage is true: the bigger they are, the harder they fall.) As the renowned British zoologist J. B. S. Haldane observed, "You can drop a mouse down a thousand-yard mine shaft; and, on arriving at the bottom, it gets a slight shock and walks away, provided the ground is fairly soft. A rat is killed, a man is broken, a horse splashes."

FIGURE 1.2 *As the height (or length) of an animal doubles, the cross-sectional area of its bones increases four times (the square of the length) and its total mass increases eight times (the cube of the length).*

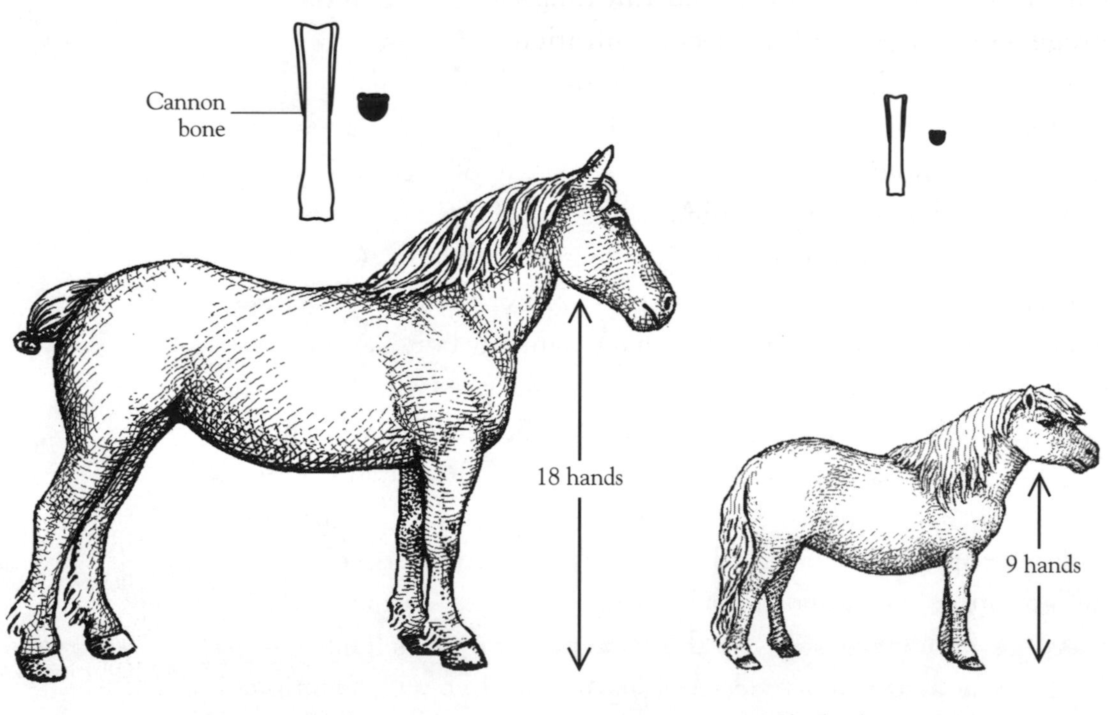

As we shall see, there were some compensating evolutionary virtues that made large size attractive, but that does not alter the initial fact of the relative rarity, and improbability, of animals the size of horses.

The speed of the horse is a rarity, too; indeed, it has few equals in speed over long distances. The cheetah, the fastest land animal, can hit 100 kilometers per hour for extremely short bursts over a distance of a hundred meters or so; a horse's sustained racing gallop is nearly 70 kilometers per hour.

At the same time, the horse's dietary needs are astonishingly easy to meet for such a large animal. The black rhino, an animal whose body weight is comparable to that of a large draft horse, requires huge quantities of green twigs and legumes. Large carnivores of similar weight, such as polar bears or lions, will eat up to 40 kilograms of meat in a single meal. Yet the horse has adapted to eating the poorest-quality forage, containing the lowest concentration of protein, of any large herbivore. It thrives on grasses that a cow would starve to death on.

And unlike many large grazing animals, horses break down the otherwise indigestible cellulose of stems and leaves in a digestive organ known as the cecum. While ruminants such as sheep and cattle have to rest for hours after eating, the hoofed herbivores that possess a cecal digestive system (horses, tapirs, and rhinos) can eat and run.

It is another remarkable and happy coincidence that the horse possesses a diastema, or gap between the front incisors and the rear grinders

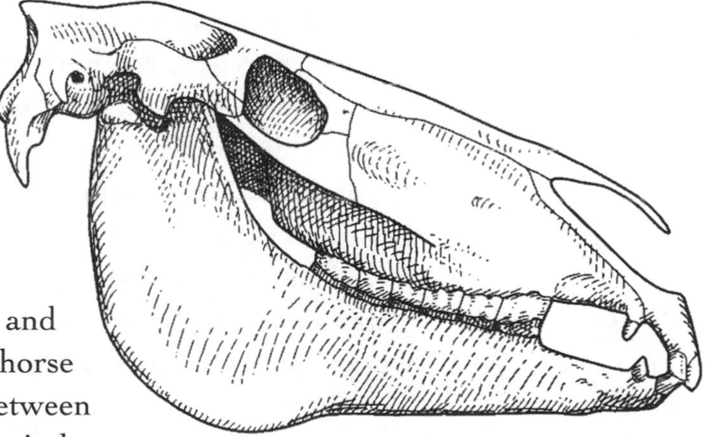

FIGURE 1.3
A long muzzle allows the horse to keep an eye out for danger while grazing. An evolutionary side effect of the lengthened muzzle is the diastema, the gap between the incisors and premolars that makes the placement of a bit possible.

(figure 1.3). Control of the horse by man would have proved far more difficult without this anatomical convenience, which allowed the effective placement of bridle and bit.

Horses possess one final anatomical convenience from our point of view: almost unique among hoofed animals, they lack horns or antlers.

The Nature of Evolution

The sheer abundance of horse bones, and especially horse teeth, in the fossil record has made the horse the single most frequently cited paradigm of evolution. There are more than half a million specimens of fossil horses in museum and academic collections in North America alone.

Explaining evolution has never been easy, and educators and museum curators quite naturally seized on the well-documented fossil history of the ever popular horse as Exhibit A. Practically everyone who has visited a science museum or taken an elementary biology course has seen the evolutionary sequence of fossil horses from tiny eohippus (more properly known by its scientific name, *Hyracotherium*) to modern *Equus*. Starting as a small, squat, dog-sized, four-toed creature 55 million years ago, the horse step-by-step turned into the tall, fleet, elegant, single-hoofed animal of modernity.

But this simple, linear picture of evolution has led to a couple of unfortunate misunderstandings. One is the idea that evolution really does run in a straight line. This notion, known technically as orthogenesis, was assumed by many early biologists, and is still the popular conception of how evolution works: each species in an animal's fossil family tree gives rise to a (presumably superior) replacement. "The orthogenetic template has . . . influenced millions of lay people, many of whom visit natural history museums with turn-of-the-century exhibits that convey 100-year-old ideas," says paleontologist Bruce MacFadden, an expert on fossil horses. In fact, paleontologists now know that evolution is full of branches, dead ends, and blind turns.

The recent history of modern equids is no exception. Analysis of the similarity of mitochondrial DNA among the seven modern species of the genus *Equus* (three zebras, two asses, the horse, and the now-extinct, zebralike quagga of South Africa, which was hunted to its death in the late-nineteenth century) has allowed scientists to reconstruct a branching family tree that is surely far more paradigmatic of evolution than any straight-line model (plate 1). Mitochondrial DNA is the genetic material found in a portion of the cell known as the mitochondria, which is responsible for generating energy and which has the peculiarity of reproducing itself separately from the rest of the cell. Mitochondrial DNA is inherited solely from the mother. Thus, changes in mitochondrial DNA can occur only slowly, by accumulated mutation, not by the recombination of male and female genes through mating in every generation. By comparing this DNA in related species and estimating the mutation rate at 2 percent every million years, biologists have calculated when the various modern *Equus* species diverged from one another. (The extinct quagga's mitochondrial DNA was extracted from a bit of muscle tissue in a preserved hide at the Museum of Natural History in Mainz, Germany; it appears to have diverged from *Equus zebra* 3 to 4 million years ago.)

The other, related misperception that the orthogenetic model of evolution has engendered is that evolution has a purpose, or goal. It is commonplace, and perhaps inevitable, for people in love with horses to see this 55-million-year history as a process of "perfecting" the horse. We often read that the horse is "perfectly" adapted to running, for instance, and it is hard for us not to see modern *Equus* as superior to its forebears.

In fact, the evolutionary explosion of the horse in North America beginning some 20 million years ago gave rise to a multiplicity of other branches, too, with as many as 13 genera existing simultaneously. Some species were larger than their predecessors, but some were smaller (figure 1.4). Some moved toward the "modern" horse diet of grasses, but others specialized in the "primitive" diet of browse (figure 1.5). Some showed a trend toward the one-toed hoof of the modern equid, others did not.

The first step toward understanding how evolutionary forces shaped the modern horse is to understand that the purpose of evolution is not progress or perfection in the long run, but survival in the short run. And that in turn involves a

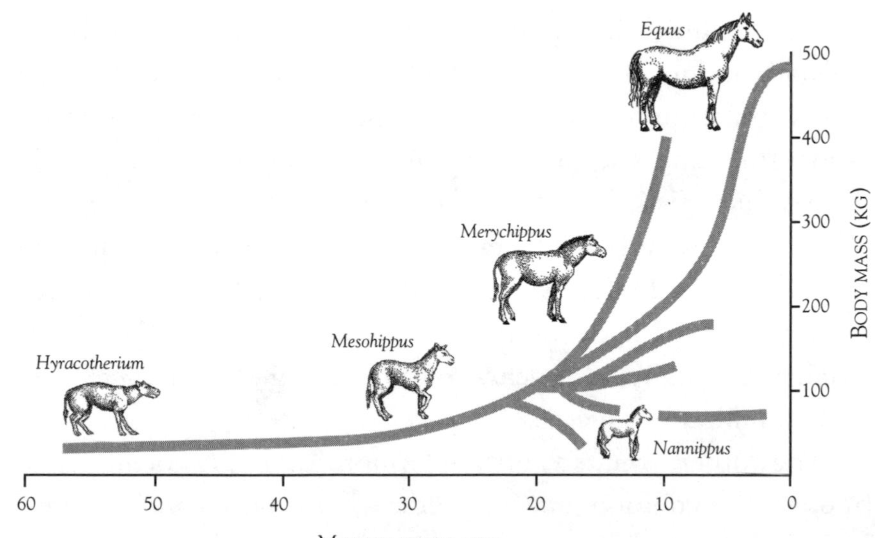

FIGURE 1.4
Rather than increasing steadily over the course of evolution, the body size of equids remained nearly constant for 30 million years, then diverged into both larger and smaller branches starting around 20 million years ago. The survival of the one branch that led to Equus was more a matter of chance than "progress."

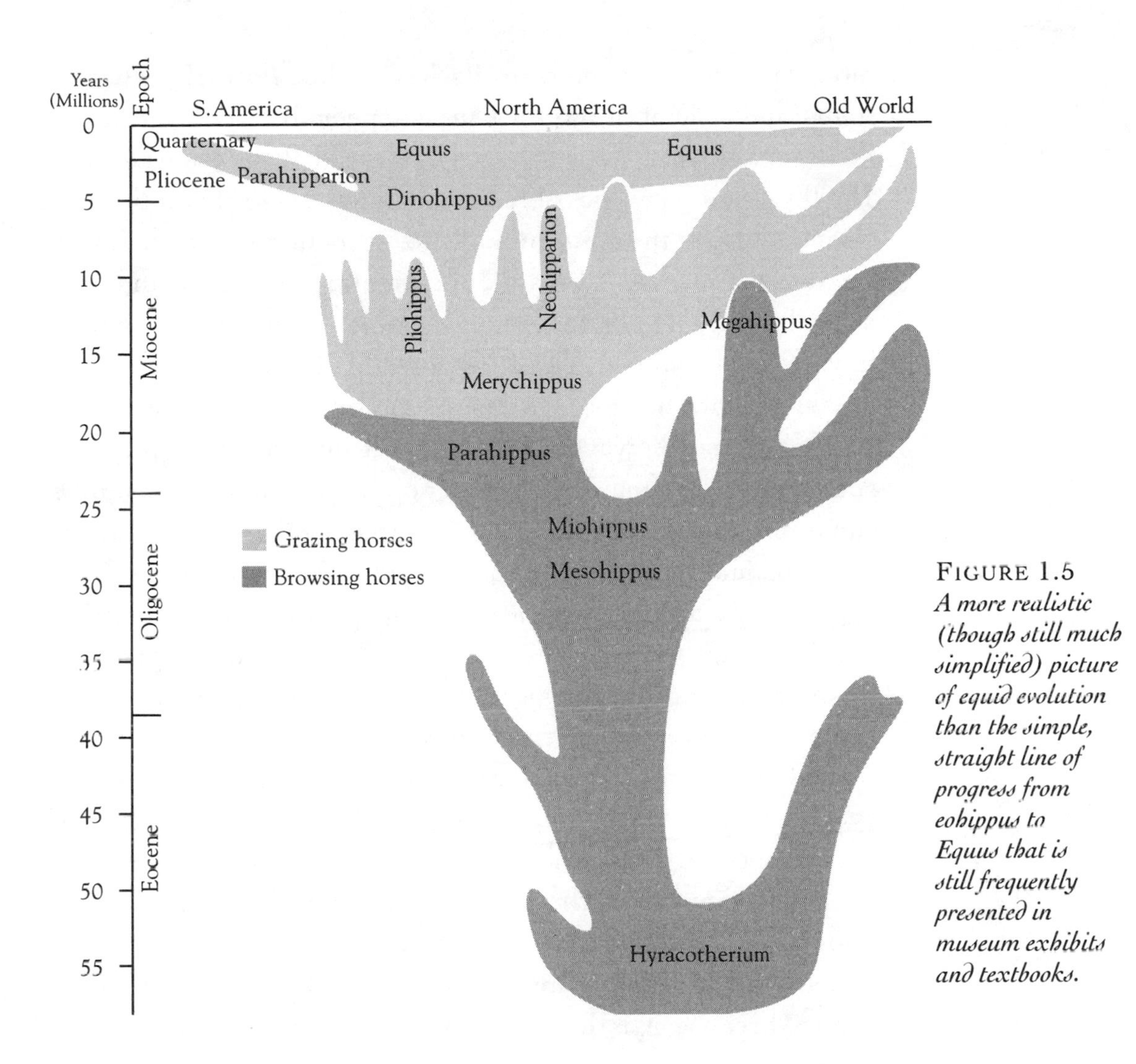

FIGURE 1.5
A more realistic (though still much simplified) picture of equid evolution than the simple, straight line of progress from eohippus to Equus that is still frequently presented in museum exhibits and textbooks.

complex interaction of genes and the environment. It is simply wrong to say that the modern horse is "superior" to its extinct predecessors. Many of those predecessors that we so cavalierly dismiss as failures, or as inferior stepping stones on the path to perfection, were in fact brilliant successes that flourished for millions of years—until an unpredictable change in climate finally did them in. The evolutionary success of the modern horse owes more to its having been a lucky guesser than a pinnacle of progress. That is especially borne out by the fact that abrupt climatic changes at the end of the Ice Age some 15,000 years ago (possibly exacerbated by overhunting by humans) drove the modern horse to extinction in North America and within a hair's breadth of extinction in Europe and Asia as well. Were it not for domestication, *Equus caballus* would have gone the way of *Hyracotherium* and all the other ancestral horses that are testimony to the inevitability of extinction.

A new trait, however meritorious it may prove in the long run, cannot become fixed in a population unless it confers some immediate advantage. A trait that increases the odds of an individual's surviving to the age of sexual maturity, successfully finding a mate, and bearing a large number of offspring will be a trait that is preferentially passed on to the genes of the next generation. A trait that is less efficacious in achieving these ends will be preferentially weeded out of the population.

Still, there *are* general trends that can be traced in the evolution of what paleontologists call clades—large families of related species. All species that survive today are descendants of species that defied the dead end of extinction. And we also know that evolution can be very conservative. Some traits, selected for at some point in the course of evolution, tend to persist because it is in effect too costly or difficult to weed them out. To change the metaphor, they are trap doors: once evolution has passed through them it is very hard to go back. In each generation, natural selection can only use the raw materials that previous generations of selection have left it. Thus, over long periods of time, certain branches will prove more successful than others; certain trends will emerge. But again, it is always worth remembering that these trends reflect what are in effect the sum total of lucky guesses or accidents. They are the long-term consequences of short-term "decisions," consequences that could not have been anticipated at the time those choices were made. Most extinct species were victims of their own success—they had the misfortune of being supremely adapted to a niche that did not last.

The Nature of Luck

One general trend that appears early on in the evolution of horses, and which sets them apart from their fellow herbivores in the Eocene epoch (55 million years ago), was a significantly larger brain. In particular horses developed an expanded neocortex—the part of the brain unique to mammals that is responsible for learning and for correlating multiple sensory inputs.

But if horses were smarter than dinosaurs, it was not because of any inherent tendency toward progress in evolution. There are plenty of phenomenally stupid creatures that make a remarkably fine living these days, and plenty of perfectly smart creatures that ended up in the dustbin of evolution.

Evolutionary biologists look for more narrow selective forces to explain the trends they see in the fossil record. And *Hyracotherium*'s development of a larger brain may initially have been related to a need for increased tactile sensitivity of the lips, important to a grazer or browser's ability to efficiently select desirable forage.

The earliest equids were uniformly browsers; that is, they ate the shoots and leaves of trees and woody plants, which are relatively higher in nutritive value than grasses. At this time in the earth's history, such food was also much more abundant. A remarkable fossil specimen of the equoid *Propalaeotherium* from the late Eocene epoch was found complete with fossilized stomach contents, which included grape pits. These were forest dwellers well adapted to the lush, moist conditions of this period.

"You are what you eat" may not be a strictly accurate nutritional statement but it certainly has a lot of merit as an evolutionary principle. Much of the evolution of the modern horse—including its speed, size, and intelligence—can be explained by diet and changes in diet. As the global climate became drier, savannas and grasslands began to displace forests. After millions of years of relatively slow evolution, the equids showed a sudden burst of diversification beginning about 18 million years ago, just as these sweeping climatic changes began. The browsers began to decline—though they by no means vanished, holding on for another 9 million years. The key word here is diversification. New niches made many more successful options available. Equids had all been confined within a relatively narrow body type up until this point; body weight of the various equid species ranged only from about 25 to 50 kilograms for the first half of their evolutionary history. The climatic changes of the Miocene epoch beginning about 18 million years ago gave rise to branches that ranged in size from 75 to 500 kilograms. Of 24 ancestral-descendant pairs that paleontologist Bruce MacFadden examined from this period, 19 showed an increase in size, while 5 decreased.

Many of the distinctive and, from our point of view, useful traits of the modern horse first arose in this epoch within those branches of the equid family that would ultimately survive to modern times. The grass-eating branches faced a number of new problems that required new adaptations. Grass is not only tough; the cellulose that contains most of its available nutrients is locked in the plant's cell walls and is basically indigestible to mammals without special tricks (more on this below). To start with, it requires a lot of chewing. While fruits are designed to attract animals as part of a plant's strategy for spreading its seeds and reproducing by offering a tempting (and discardable) appendage, the leaves of a grass are its all. Plants subject to herbivory have therefore evolved an array of defenses, one of which is the incorporation of tough silica particles, known as phytoliths, into their cell walls. And food eaten off the ground is already full of dirt, all of which means herbivores need to have much tougher teeth than browsers.

The grazing horses begin to show rapid adaptations to this problem. The compressive action of the jaws and teeth of the browsing horses is replaced in grazers with a transverse shearing action that acts to grind the food. The depth and the size of the jaw increase to make room for more powerful muscles. The problem of tooth durability is solved by several tricks (figure 1.6). Premolars change to full molars, increasing the surface area available for grinding. Teeth become cement-covered, higher-crowned (hypsodont), and eventually ever-growing (hypselodont).

Interestingly, the initial change toward hypsodonty may

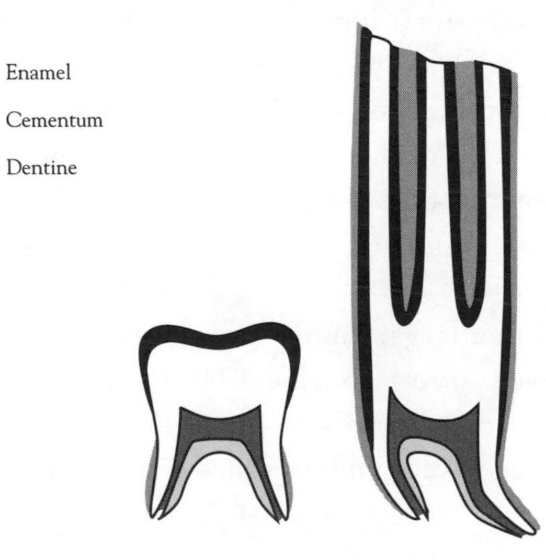

FIGURE 1.6
Compared to a human molar (left), the horse's molar reflects several adaptations that grazers acquired to deal with tough plant tissues and sandy grit, including a high crown and multiple folds of enamel.

have been not so much an adaptation to grasslands as to dirt. At at least some sites in the interior of North America, it has been shown that the early Miocene brought a change to coarser sand in place of finer clay soils. When the grasslands later began to spread in the middle Miocene, those clades that had already evolved toward tougher and bigger teeth were better positioned to exploit this new niche.

This is also the period when the "springing" foot appears in the equids and when the trend toward substantially larger size is first seen, at least in the clade that would lead to the modern horse. The springing foot (plate 2) is basically an arrangement of tendons that allows elastic energy to be stored and reapplied with each stride, making for more efficient locomotion (more on this in chapter 8). And larger size is one way (though as we shall see, only a relatively modest way) to increase top speed.

Size and Speed

The usual explanation for these changes, and for the eventual appearance of the single-toed foot in Pliocene horses (beginning 5 million years ago) is that, as grassland animals, these grazing horses were more exposed to predators and had to be able to flee. The evolution of the diastema may well be related to this fact, too; a long distance between the front of the mouth and the eyes allows an animal to graze and keep an eye out at the same time.

There is no doubt that larger animals are faster, and that the springing hoof allowed for a faster gait. The almost unbelievable discovery of fossil footprints of three *Hipparion* horses from the middle Pliocene (3.5 million years ago) has provided ample confirmation of the speed and agility of these grasslands-adapted horses (figure 1.7). Although *Hipparion* still had three toes on each foot, it had already developed the springing foot mechanism; and in spite of its relatively small size (about 1 meter in length), its overall proportions—leg length relative to body size, for instance—are quite similar to those of modern horses. The two side toes in *Hipparion* species, while able to help balance the foot and even add some to the locomotive effort, were already much reduced in size compared to those of their ancestors, and clearly most of the work was done by the large central toe.

The *Hipparion* footprints, made in soft lava subsequently

FIGURE 1.7 *Fossil footprints left by three Hipparion equids 3.5 million years ago closely match the running walk of modern "gaited" horses.*

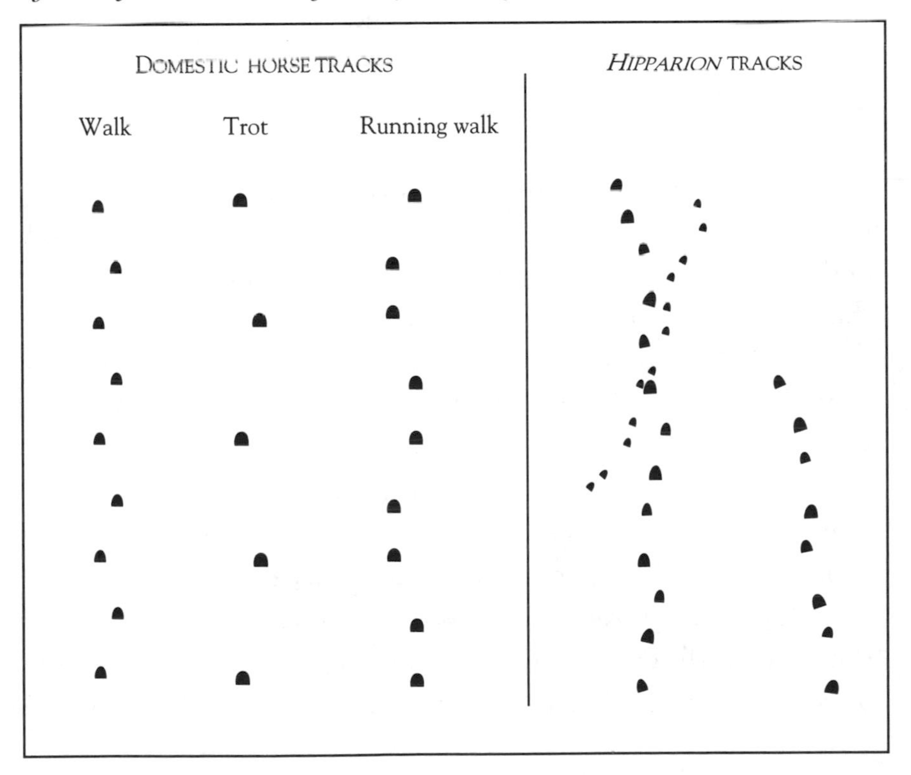

covered with volcanic ash, were discovered in Tanzania by Mary Leakey in 1979, along with trails of a number of other mammals, including early hominids. A subsequent analysis of the horse footprints makes a convincing case that these *Hipparion* horses traveled at a good clip utilizing the gait known as the running walk—the characteristic gait of Tennessee walking horses, Icelandic ponies, and paso finos, in which the length of stride is extended and only one or two feet are in contact with the ground at any given time. Comparison of the fossil footfalls with the footfall patterns of Icelandic ponies suggests that one of the *Hipparions* was traveling at 15 kilometers per hour. The other two trails appeared to be those of a mother and foal, the latter crisscrossing the path of its mother in much the same fashion as is observed in modern horses. The finding incidentally provides at least some suggestive evidence in support of the contention that the running walk, though associated with only certain breeds these days, is nonetheless an instinctive and natural gait, rather than (as is sometimes argued) one that is artificial and man-taught.

If there was a selective pressure for speed, then getting bigger might seem one of the more direct ways to achieve that end. It seems obvious that bigger things run faster. But in fact that ain't necessarily so. A 700-kilogram horse does run faster than a 26-kilogram greyhound, but not 27 times as fast—or even 3 times as fast, which is what one would expect if speed were proportional to the length of the legs or the body of an animal. (If mass is proportional to a linear dimension cubed, then an animal 27 times the mass of another would be 3 times its size in any given linear dimension, since $27 = 3^3$.)

In fact, the top racing speeds of greyhounds and horses are not much different—about 70 kilometers an hour for a horse, 60 kilometers an hour for a greyhound. Obviously a horse is faster than an ant, and there is indeed some correlation between speed and size that has been established both by observation and by calculation (based on fundamental mechanical principles of how muscles and limbs work). But it is a relatively modest correlation, which suggests that top speed increases only by approximately length to the three-eighths power, or mass to the one-eighth power (figure 1.8). Thus, to double in speed, an animal would need to be about 6 times as long or 250 times as heavy. By this yardstick, a 500-kilogram *Equus* would have a potential top speed only about 30 percent faster than that of a 50-kilogram *Hyracotherium,* a rather modest gain for a lot of evolution.

FIGURE 1.8 *Speed increases with body size, but not dramatically so. The top speed of a horse is hardly greater than that of a greyhound or a fox.*

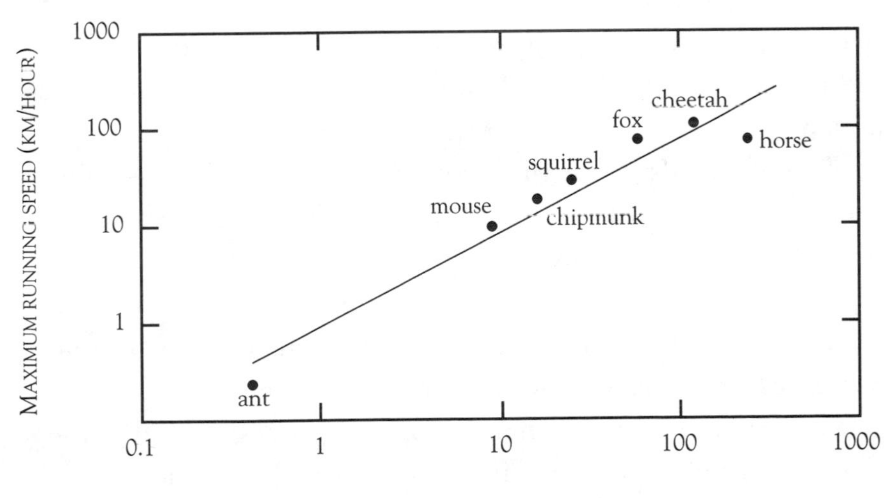

Size and Diet

There may have been a more important selective force driving up the size of grazing equids, of which speed was merely a by-product. In fact, one school of thought suggests that speed and the need to escape from predators have been greatly exaggerated in the interpretation of equid evolution. Zebras, for instance, rarely try to flee from predators at all, instead forming a tight group defended by an aggressive herd stallion. Size itself is of course one defensive mechanism—large animals are hard to attack. Rhinos, for instance, are generally safe from predation by virtue of their sheer bulk, as are elephants.

A more important consideration in explaining why horses got bigger may be the nature of the horse's diet and digestive system. As we have already observed, mammals are fundamentally incapable of breaking down cellulose, the complex sugar found in the cell walls of the structural parts of plants, such as stems and leaves. Many herbivores avoid the problem altogether by concentrating on the reproductive products of plants—fruits, berries, and seeds. The earliest equids probably did the same. But all modern hoofed animals (except for pigs) depend more or less on a diet heavy in cellulose.

These animals solve the problem by forming a symbiotic relationship with gut bacteria that break down the cellulose into a form that the animals' own enzymes are then able to digest. It is a lengthy process, requiring that the host animal provide a fermentation chamber where large amounts of plant matter can be stored while the bacteria do their job.

There are two basic schemes for this process found among the hoofed mammals, or ungulates (figure 1.9). One is rumination, the method that sheep, cattle, goats, deer, camels, and hippos have evolved. Ruminants have four stomach chambers; the first two, the rumen and reticulum, are where fermentation takes place. Only when the plant matter has been broken down to a sufficiently small size through bacterial action, assisted by regurgitation and further chewing ("cud-chewing"), can it pass through a sievelike passage that separates this forestomach from the omasum and abomasum—the stomach proper.

Horses, rhinos, and tapirs have a different fermentation apparatus. This consists of an organ known as the cecum, a large, dead-end alley at the junction of the small and large intestines. Careful study of the bacterial, physical, and biochemical properties of ruminant and cecal digestion has found that their basic mechanism of action is indistinguishable. Rumination, however, makes more efficient use of the food matter taken in. A horse extracts only 70 percent as much energy from a given amount of food as does a cow. This appears to be mainly because the ruminant digestive system holds the food in its "fermenting tank" for a longer time—it takes 70 to 90 hours for food to pass through a cow, versus 48 hours in a horse. In ruminants, the small orifice between the reticulum and the omasum acts like a valve, shutting off the flow until every last bit of cellulose has been broken down.

For this reason, animal scientists long believed that ruminants were more efficient than cecal digesters in making use of plant food. And in one sense that is true. But animal behavior studies have consistently shown one extremely curious fact: wild equids in competition with ruminants invariably choose the very worst, lowest-protein, highest-fiber roughage. *Equus burchelli,* the plains zebra, for instance, were observed to eat the same plants as wildebeest, but they consistently ate the stems while the wildebeest ate the leaves. Wild asses and the

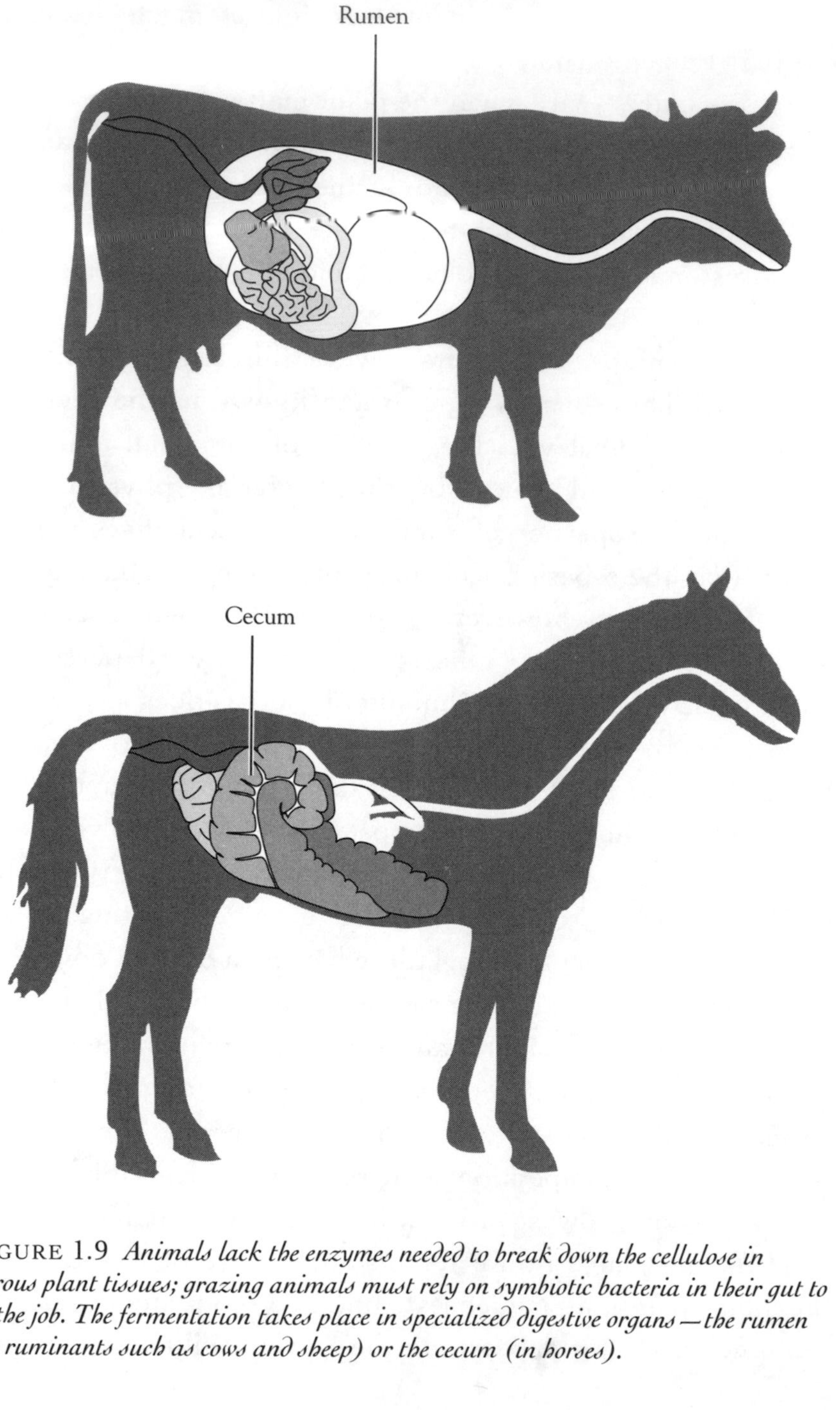

FIGURE 1.9 *Animals lack the enzymes needed to break down the cellulose in fibrous plant tissues; grazing animals must rely on symbiotic bacteria in their gut to do the job. The fermentation takes place in specialized digestive organs—the rumen (in ruminants such as cows and sheep) or the cecum (in horses).*

wild Przewalski's horse live in regions containing only very poor-quality vegetation that is apparently unable to support any of the native ruminants. As researcher Christine Janis has noted, this was precisely the diet that the rumen was supposedly evolved to deal with, yet here were horses thriving where ruminants feared to tread. Experiments with domestic cattle and sheep have also confirmed that a diet containing more than a certain level of fiber cannot support a ruminant.

The reason for this apparent contradiction turns out to be quite simple. Ruminants are indeed more efficient than horses in extracting usable energy from a given weight of food. But there is a limit to how much food a ruminant can move through its system in a given period of time. As the quality of the forage declines, a ruminant's digestive system actually slows down further, giving the food more time in the rumen to be broken down. A ruminant's intake is limited by how much food it can stuff into its rumen; after that, it has to sit back and wait for fermentation to run its course.

A horse, on the other hand, can—and does—respond to a poor-quality diet by eating more. It may only be 70 percent as efficient in extracting usable energy from its food, but it can push a lot more food through its digestive system in a 24-hour period than a cow can. Per unit of *time,* if not per unit weight of food, a horse can get more energy out of a low-quality diet than can a cow of the same weight. In fact, as Janis writes, "this digestive strategy enables horses to exist on a diet on which ruminants of similar body size simply cannot maintain themselves."

What does all this have to do with body size? Like all animals, equids have chosen an ecological niche that allows them to avoid competition from other species. Their niche is the poorest-quality vegetation. For animals that start down this road, an interesting law of energy consumption dictates that the pressure to increase size becomes irresistible. Small animals need a lot more energy compared to their body weight than do large animals (figure 1.10). Thus, hummingbirds spend every second of the day feeding while lions spend hours snoozing. This is because (to a first approximation) the metabolic energy a warm-blooded animal expends just in staying alive is proportional to the heat it loses through its exposed surface area. Surface area increases with increasing size in proportion to L^2. Body weight, though, increases much faster, in proportion to L^3. An animal that weighs eight times as much as another has only four times as much exposed surface area. Another way to think about it is this: in a small object, all of the interior is close to a surface; in a large one, there's lots of stuff inside that's packed away far from the surface. Thus, it is easier for a larger animal to retain its body heat than a smaller one. Each cell in a sheep's body needs to run at a higher rate, and thus needs more energy, than each cell in a horse's body.

So, having adopted a strategy that depends on eating the lowest-quality, most energy-poor stuff, equids continue to gain a further competitive advantage over ruminants by getting bigger. This general principle relating body size to dietary strategy among herbivores seems to hold up well—those species of African antelope that are predominantly grazers (such as the topi) are large, those that browse are medium-sized (Grant's gazelle), and those that eat fruit and only the leaves and young shoots of plants are the smallest (Thomson's gazelle). Once body size drops below about 5 kilograms, calculations suggest that the energy requirements of the diet are so high that it doesn't pay to ruminate at all, since nearly all of the animal's food intake would have to come from high-quality foods such as fruits and seeds. This is very close to the weight of the smallest ruminants, such as the dik-dik.

During the Eocene, the tiny, forest-dwelling *Hyracotherium* would have been able to find a diet with abundant high-quality forage and very little fibrous cellulose. In the tropical climate of this epoch, young plant shoots would grow all year round. But as the climate cooled and growth became seasonal, a fibrous diet would have been all that was available at certain times of the year, making fermentation a necessity. Cecal fermenters are generally at a competitive disadvantage against ruminants in the medium-fiber diet range; the horse's strategy was thus to avoid competition by choosing a diet too fibrous

FIGURE 1.10 *Large animals lose heat more slowly than small ones; because the energy demands of each cell in the body are correspondingly less, getting big is one way to cope with a high-fiber, low-protein diet.*

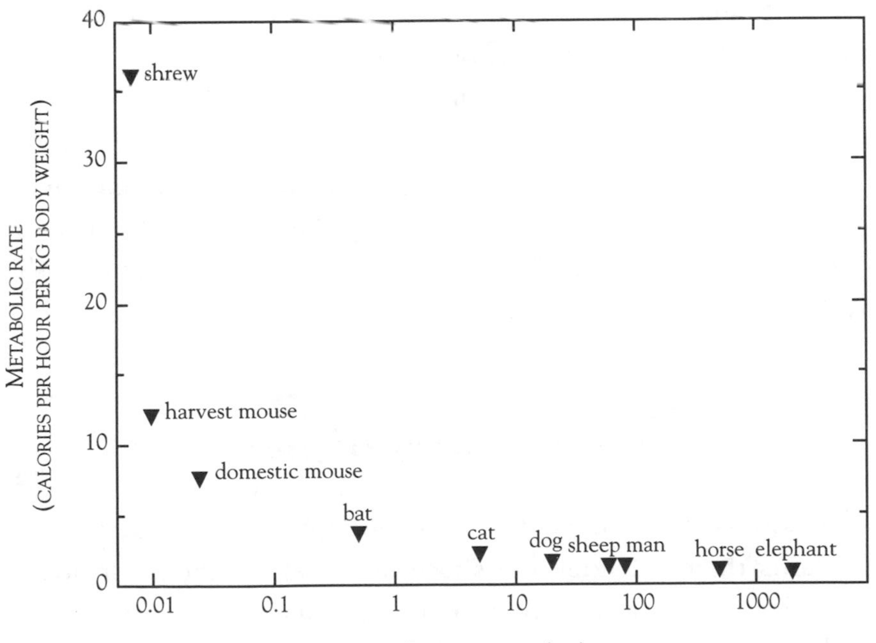

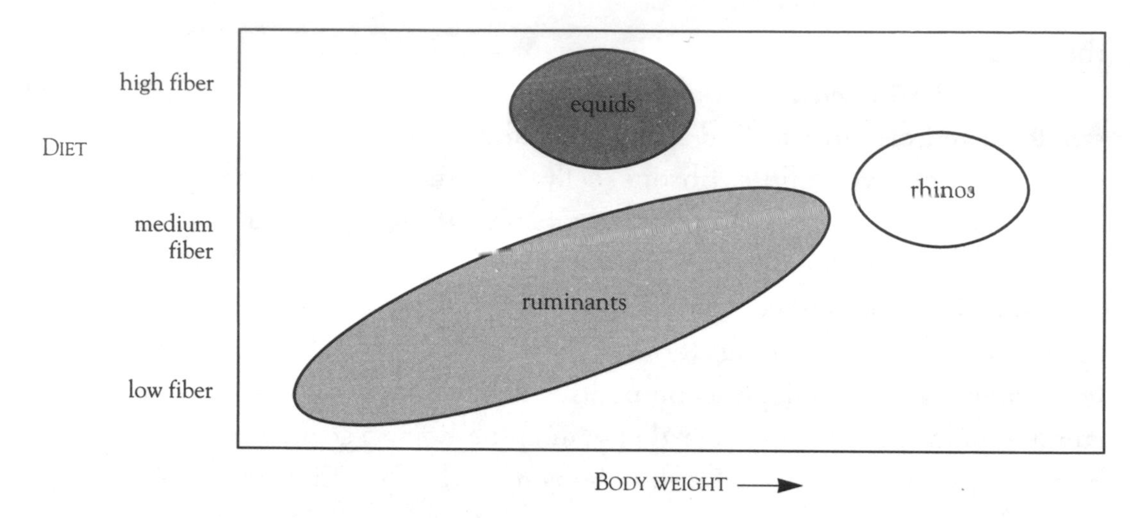

FIGURE 1.11 *Equids avoid competing with the more efficient ruminants by specializing in a high-fiber diet. Rhinos use a different approach: they are so large, and their energy need per body weight so low, that rumination offers no advantage.*

for ruminants to cope with at all (figure 1.11). And that made getting big a necessity. (The other possible strategy is to continue consuming a medium-fiber diet and also to get very big. Calculations suggest that once an animal reaches 1,800 kilograms, rumination provides no further advantage over cecal digestion even in the consumption of a medium-fiber diet. The black rhino, a browser, in fact weighs almost exactly 1,800 kilograms.)

Side Effects of Bigness

The equids' position at the high end of the fiber diet scale explains their considerable success as well as their considerable size. But it also may explain why, as the climate cooled and became more arid and as grasslands replaced forests, the overall diversity of equids began to narrow. There are but 6 species of living equids worldwide today, compared to some 200 species of ruminants. The number of genera of equids began to drop rapidly beginning about 13 million years ago, from a peak of 13 genera to the single extant genus.

Other consequences followed from this selection for size in response to dietary and energetic factors. Speed, as we have already seen, was one. Another was longevity, which is also closely correlated with size. It is a remarkable fact that virtually all mammals live an average of 1.5 billion heartbeats. Since small animals, as we have already seen, have faster metabolisms, their lifespans are correspondingly shorter. (Biomechanician Thomas McMahon says that this size-independent limit of 1.5 billion heartbeats may simply be a coincidence, and that other factors, such as the death and replacement of individual cells in the body, may be more proximate limiting factors in an organism's lifespan. One theory of aging holds that death is the result of accumulated genetic errors in cells as they divide and reproduce. Both cell replacement rate and heart rate might plausibly be related to an animal's size in the same proportion, thus providing the seeming correlation between heartbeats and lifespan. In either case, lifespan is roughly proportional to an animal's mass raised to the one-fourth power. The calculated lifespan for humans by this yardstick would be 33 years, which is about what it was before the Industrial Revolution.)

MacFadden has estimated the lifespan of fossil equids by measuring the height of unworn crown left on the teeth and making a reasonable guess at the wear rate per year, and his figures support the theoretically predicted trend of increasing longevity with increasing body size. *Hyracotherium* would have lived about 4 years; the *Protohippus* of 12 million years ago would have lived about 12 to 15 years; the first members of the genus *Equus* some 4 million years ago would have had a lifespan of 20 or more years.

Another consequence of the increasing size of equids was the evolution of mechanisms to cope with bigness. As we have seen, large animals suffer many disadvantages, not least of which is gravity. Getting up and down is hard work; a large herbivore subject to predation would not want to lie down too much, given the time it would take for it to get to its feet in a moment of danger. But standing is hard work, too, when you're big. The fossils of Pliocene equids begin to show another of the modern horse's remarkable coping mechanisms, the so-called passive stay apparatus (plate 2). Unique to equids, this arrangement of tendons and bones allows both the forelimbs and hindlimbs to lock in place while the horse is standing, obviating the need to expend muscular energy in resisting gravity. In the forelimbs, the tendons have a groove that locks into the humerus; in the hindlimbs, the patella locks into a crest on the femur. A rudimentary form of this apparatus appears first in *Dinohippus* about 5 million years ago and is fully developed in the first *Equus*. A careful measurement of energy expenditure in two domestic horses found that they actually burned about 10 percent *less* energy standing up than lying down. By contrast, cattle and sheep use about 10 percent more energy standing up than lying down.

The bigness of the horse is an oddity among mammals, but almost more than any other big mammals the horse has evolved means to compensate for the many disadvantages that come with size. The important lesson of all this is that its size and swiftness are most likely accidental by-products of the its ecological niche—at the low end of the herbivore diet.

Paleoecology

With surprising accuracy, it is also possible to predict an animal's social structure from its habitat and diet. Small animals that are selective feeders in resource-rich forests tend to spread out and defend individual territories. Males who hope to find mates under these circumstances are forced to follow suit, which means that the mating system tends to be monogamous.

When females live less far apart, a single male may be able to defend a territory that includes two females, but still he is forced to go where the females are, and to defend that territory against other males. That in turn tends to select for sexual dimorphism—differences between the sexes, such as males with larger horns or larger body size.

Larger grassland animals that rely on patchier and scarcer food sources, by contrast, tend to form into herds. This gives males the opportunity to hold harems, and so these animals tend to be polygamous.

These principles, which work well when applied to living ungulates, allow for some interesting speculation about the evolution of social organization in horses. A quarry site in Colorado known as Castillo Pocket yielded up a huge find of *Hyracotherium tapirinum* fossils—a large enough sample (24 individuals) to get some meaningful statistics about the social structure of these small, primitive, forest-dwelling equids. They fit the pattern well. The ratio of males to females was between 1:1.5 and 1:2. There was a distinct sexual dimorphism; the males' skulls were on average 15 percent larger than the females', and the canine teeth of the males were 40 percent larger.

The body-size dimorphism begins to disappear in the middle Miocene grazers, and vanishes entirely after about 15 million years ago. The failure of equids ever to develop horns or antlers may be explained in part by their relatively early specialization in fibrous, low-quality forage, which made it necessary for them to cover vast ranges in search of food—areas far too large to effectively patrol and defend as a territory. On the other hand, competition between males for control of harems does occur in modern equids, even if there is no territorial combat involved; this has led to some sexual selection for canine teeth, which stallions use in fighting and in threat displays with one another. The ratio of the male canine to molar size has increased steadily over the last 20 million years, while the ratio of the female canine to molar has declined.

The horse, like all living things, is a product of its evolutionary history. However clever it may have been for man to recognize the potential of the horse in harness or under saddle, it is to dumb luck—and mainly to a several-million-year-old choice of diet—that we owe the gift of the modern horse.

CHAPTER TWO

FROM THE BRINK OF OBLIVION

Domestication, for those animals lucky enough to fit the bill, proved a brilliant evolutionary strategy. As the Pleistocene came to an end, the large mammals that had evolved to exploit the open tundra and grasslands started vanishing at a staggering pace. In North America, the end of the Ice Age, probably combined with vigorous hunting by Indians, led to the total extinction of 35 genera of "megafauna"—mammoths, mastodons, stagmoose, giant elk, saber-toothed tigers, and equines. North America had been the evolutionary cradle of the equids for 55 million years, giving rise to successive waves of new species that crossed the land bridges to colonize the Old World. But in the end the New World turned on its once favored offspring. By 10,000 years ago the equids of North America were gone. No depiction of horses appears in any known pre-Columbian art of the New World. They left their traces only in the rich trove of fossils that would be discovered by scientists thousands of years later.

The horse would not return to North America until January 2, 1494, when Columbus arrived at Hispaniola on his second voyage to the New World, bringing with him 24 stallions and 10 mares. The Indians, lacking a word for these unknown creatures, called them "big dogs."

The extinct Ice Age equids, like countless species that preceded them into oblivion, had been victims of their own success. They were too well adapted to a niche that was rapidly disappearing as the climate changed at the end of the Ice Age. In Europe and Asia, the same fate was rapidly overtaking the horses of the Old World. As the climate warmed and forests overtook the open grasslands, the herds fled ever eastward, vanishing from the British Isles and from France and Spain, where they had been depicted over and over in paintings drawn by Neanderthal men crouching in torchlit caves tens of thousands of years ago (figure 2.1), until all that remained were remnant herds in the still-open grassland steppes of Ukraine and Central Asia.

But for domestication, the Eurasian wild horse would likely have shared the fate of its New World cousins. This rescue of the horse follows a pattern that has been repeated time and again in domestic species. The aurochs, the wild progenitor of the domestic cow, is gone; wild sheep and goats teeter on the brink of extinction throughout the world; the last remnant of the Asian wild horse, Przewalski's horse, survives only in captive and artificially managed populations rescued from oblivion at the end of the last century.

Yet from the moment of its domestication around 6,000 years ago in Ukraine, *Equus caballus* makes an explosive

FIGURE 2.1
Cave paintings by Neanderthal humans in France and Spain depict a horse similar in appearance to the modern-day Przewalski's wild horse of Asia.

reappearance in the fossil record of Eurasia, sweeping back through the regions it had only lately vanished from. By 4,000 years ago, horses were once again common in archaeological sites from West Asia to the British Isles. A comeback from the brink of extinction to a present-day population of 60 million is rare indeed in the annals of endangered species. The horse's remarkable recovery is matched only by a handful of other domestic animals that similarly defied extinction through their opportune alliance with man, particularly domestic cows, sheep, and pigs, which each number about 1 billion in the world today.

Life on the Fringe

Romantic tales about the origins of horses appeal to something deep in the hearts of horse lovers. The feral horses of the western United States are sometimes claimed to be survivors of a prehistoric line that somehow evaded extinction, rather than the descendants of escaped Spanish horses (as they almost certainly are). The feral horses of the barrier islands of Virginia and the Carolinas, abandoned by nearby farmers not too many generations ago, have acquired a fanciful history as the descendants of castaways from shipwrecked Spanish galleons. The Andalusian horses brought by Columbus and the conquistadors have somehow been transformed into Arabs. And the Arabs of the North African desert are often held to have evolved there in a distinct, ancient lineage, from a primitive and now extinct wild horse that was sleeker and more delicate than its heavy northern counterparts.

The search for separate races or species of wild horse that separately gave rise to particular modern-day breeds seems to be an especially absorbing pastime, but one for which science offers little or no encouragement. (One skeptical scholar recently—and aptly—complained about this passion for "making horses out of thin air.")

Although the actual evidence may dash some of the romantic myths about the origins of the horse, it points to a story that is if anything more fascinating. For it appears that the modern horse was likely snatched from the jaws of extinction by a single act of human daring and inspiration in a remote corner of a barely civilized world. The domestic horses that populate the world today may well *all* be descendants of the horses domesticated in Ukraine 6,000 years ago.

This evidence matches well with general theories of how and why the domestication of various plants and animals happened when and where it did. A precondition for domestication was an animal whose evolutionary history preadapted it to approaching man, and geographic and environmental circumstances that allowed for a period of close association and coevolution between man and animal. It was only after evolution had fashioned an animal that was tamable that man could tame it and begin deliberate, captive breeding.

The rude hunters and farmers who would first begin to domesticate the horse were not neophytes. For the horse arrived relatively late in the history of domestication, and as early as 7,600 years ago the inhabitants of the forest-steppe zones north of the Black Sea were keeping cattle, pigs, and sheep. The immigrants from the lower Danube valley who introduced these animals to the region, along with wheat, barley, and the technology of copper working, had an even older tradition of herding. The first domesticated livestock animals, the sheep and the goat, had entered into full domestication as many as 9,000 years ago. Thus, the people who were destined to become the first horse herders were already well versed in the skills needed to handle animals. The fact that to perform useful work horses must be "broken" anew in each generation also implies that human innovation may have played a larger role in the domestication of the horse than in that of its domesticated predecessors.

But it is always worth remembering that there are considerable limits to human ingenuity where animals are concerned, even today, after thousands of additional years' worth of experience under our belts. In her reminiscence of growing up in Africa, Elspeth Huxley relates how a hard-bitten hunter named Jock Cameron succeeded, after a great many failures, in training four zebras that he had raised up from foals to pull a buggy. None but Cameron could control them, and not even he at times; at best, the zebras would stand with ears pinned back, teeth bared, biting and kicking at one another, alternately setting off at a full gallop and digging in their heels and refusing to move.

For the small number of species that came equipped with the potential to be domesticated, the question still remains why humans took the final step toward captive breeding and stock raising, when and where they did. There is a growing body of archaeological evidence and theory that supports the notion that this transition from a long, loose association between species to full domestication is most likely to occur in marginal areas, outside the principal range of the animal species and far from the center of the local human culture. Stock tending in the long run allowed for a civilization that could support a much higher-density human population than did hunting and gathering. But that was only in the very long run. Agriculture did not increase wealth, longevity, leisure time, or health for average workers until the Industrial Revolution freed them from the menial, accident-prone, and exhausting toil of agricultural labor. Raising animals in captivity was something that people did in desperation, not triumph; it was the response of people living on the fringes of ancient society, in the most resource-poor areas, struggling to maintain a standard of life that eluded them as game grew scarce, as forests were cut down, as soils were exhausted.

Likewise, it was in the remote, resource-poor reaches of an animal's natural range that it was most likely to be forced into intimate contact with humans. Herds that could no longer make a living in the familiar niche that millions of years of evolution had adapted them to exploit began to seek out a new niche, one that exploited the grain fields and garbage dumps of human habitations. This niche may also have exploited the natural care-giving instincts of humans toward animals that exhibit what animal behaviorists call care-soliciting behavior. In many parts of the world even today, free-roaming populations of feral dogs thrive around villages, not because they serve any useful purpose, but because they are so successful at deflecting human aggression with cringing, submissive behavior that brings out our soft side.

As far as horses and men were concerned, the region north of the Black Sea seven millenniums ago was precisely such a fringe area (figure 2.2). From about 7,100 to 6,600 years ago, the human population there focused its attention on the forest-steppe, an intermediate zone some 200 kilometers wide between the dense forest and the open steppe. The broken forest provided a perfect habitat for abundant game. Wild boar, red and roe deer, and aurochs were hunted. The rich, loess soils that underlay the forests supported fertile crops. Cattle and other livestock were raised.

But as the human population grew, local pressures mounted. The forests were cleared for grain fields and pasture. The forest game dwindled. At archaeological sites in the region dating from 6,600 to 6,100 years ago, bones of boar, deer, and aurochs become much scarcer. And in their place begin to appear vast numbers of bones of horses.

This was a total change, for horses were animals of the steppes. For the first time, the hunters of the region were beginning to tap this previously unexploited and far less hospitable zone.

By the end of this period, settlements appear on the steppes themselves. Heaps of bones found on sites of the Sredni Stog culture show that nearly 50 percent of the inhabitants' meat came from horses.

FIGURE 2.2 *The domestication of the horse was centered in places like Dereivka in modern-day Ukraine, a marginal area where horse and man were forced together some 6,000 years ago.*

Eat or Ride?

Intimate association, isolation, desperation—all the ingredients for domestication were present. But were those thousands of horses whose bones lay heaped upon the steppes domesticated—animals captively bred as a source of food? Or were they still-wild animals that were hunted—and whose descendants were to become truly domesticated only after man discovered their utility as mounts or draft animals?

A case can be made for each theory. The horse is not the most efficient meat-producing animal in captivity. It has a long gestation period and mares rarely produce more than one offspring at a time. Traditional Mongolian nomads studied early in this century (before they were forced onto collective farms and had to abandon their old way of life) would only slaughter horses for meat that were too old to breed or be used for work—typically at 15 or 16 years of age. Throughout the world today, horse meat is produced either as a special and expensive luxury item (as in Japan) or as a by-product of horses kept primarily for other purposes (including draft, transport, and milk). It therefore seems unlikely that people would go to the trouble of breeding and rearing horses in captivity just for meat.

On the other hand, horses are able to shift for themselves in a way that cattle and sheep cannot. When snow covers the ground, cattle and sheep must be fed, surely a considerable challenge to early agriculturists. Horses will paw through snow to forage on their own. That makes them potentially valuable as a low-maintenance source of winter food to a human population living on the edge.

The archaeological evidence tends to favor the theory that

horses were hunted for food, but domesticated as mounts. Archaeologist Marsha Levine examined 151 horse teeth from the Sredni Stog site known as Dereivka and calculated the age at death of the animal from which each one came. (The wear patterns of the teeth are an indication of age.) She then was able to reconstruct the population structure of the Dereivka horses—that is, what proportion of the animals fell into different age groups.

As shown in figure 2.3, it is possible to predict how different hunting and domestication patterns lead to different population structures. In a wild population where deaths occur from natural causes, remains will include a lot of teeth from young animals, which are especially vulnerable to disease and predation, many fewer teeth from mature adults, and then another peak as the animals reach old age.

A herd kept by humans primarily for purposes other than meat production (following the traditional Mongol practice, for instance) would show much the same pattern, with relatively few deaths among animals in their prime breeding and working years, and an increase among horses 15 years or older.

A herd raised in captivity primarily for meat production will have a similar pattern, but with an added bulge in the curve at 2 to 3 years old, corresponding to the slaughter of surplus animals that have reached full adult weight but will not be kept for breeding—and whose flesh is still tender.

By contrast, the remains of wild animals taken by hunters will show quite a different age distribution, especially in the case of "stalking"—the selective hunting of prime-age adults (5 to 8 years old). Adolescents (2 to 3 years old) will be rare, as will old animals (more than 15 years), who would have already died from natural causes in the wild.

Levine's analysis of the Dereivka teeth fits well with the

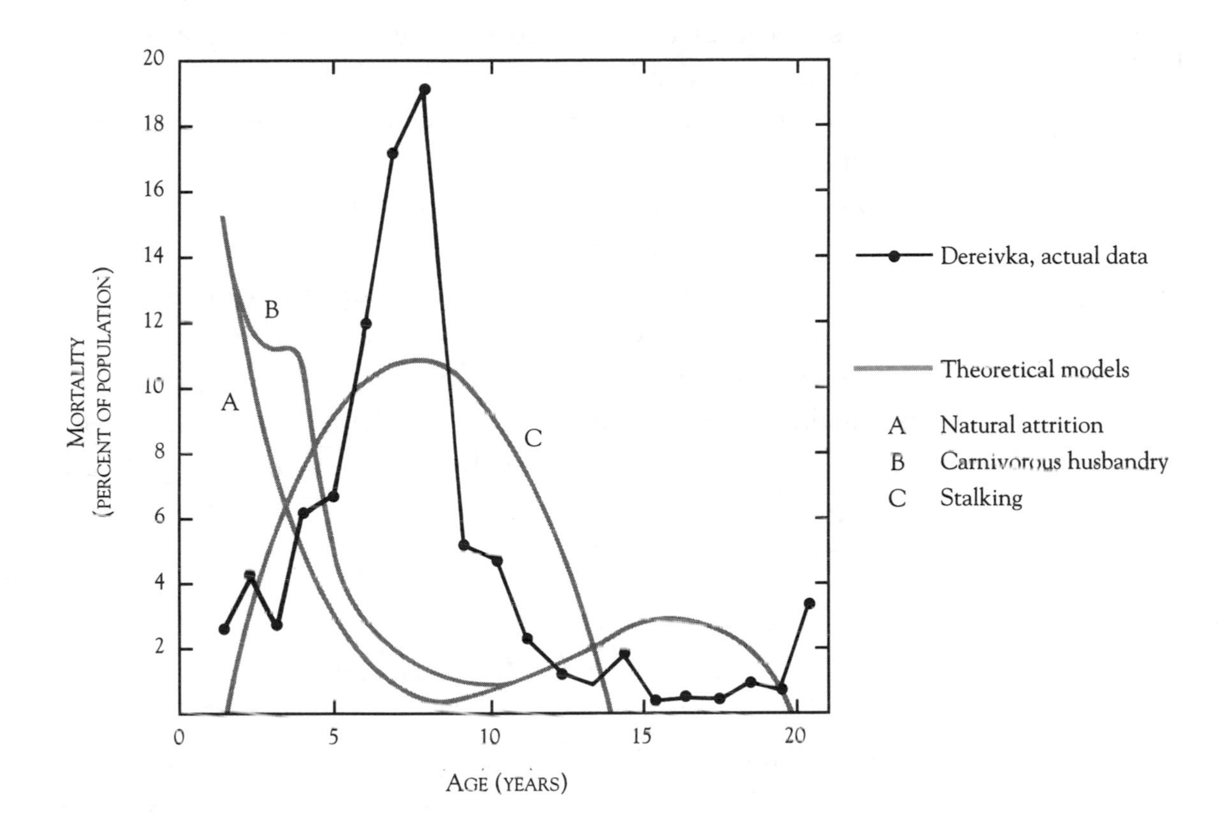

FIGURE 2.3 *In a wild population of horses, deaths occur mostly among the very young and very old (natural attrition model). In a population raised for meat (carnivorous husbandry), the slaughter of two- to three-year-olds for consumption skews the curve. The selective hunting of prime-age adults (stalking) produces a very different pattern, with a sharp central peak. The age distribution of horse teeth found at Dereivka most closely matches the stalking model.*

pattern of a hunted population, and poorly with the pattern of a domesticated population raised for meat. She notes it is extremely unlikely that herders raising horses for meat would have slaughtered as many 5-to-8 year-old horses as the

Dereivka people did; likewise, the absence of many older horses in the Dereivka sample argues strongly against other forms of domestication. Levine concluded that the Dereivka horses were still predominantly wild animals, hunted and killed for meat.

But more evidence will be needed to settle the issue. For one thing, a large number of teeth from Dereivka were discarded by the Ukrainian archaeologists who originally excavated the site, which may have skewed Levine's sample. Moreover, there is an odd preponderance of males (which can be distinguished by their canine teeth) in the sample. The culling of young males would be a clear sign of a captively bred population.

The Cult Stallion

Whether most of the horses slaughtered at Dereivka were wild or captive, one Dereivka horse was very different from the rest. Archaeologists found the skull of this horse in what appeared to be a ritual grouping of bones and artifacts. Along with the skull, which belonged to a stallion 7 or 8 years old, were the skeletons of two dogs, clay figurines, and, most striking, two pieces of antler tines pierced with carefully bored holes (figure 2.4). These antler tines closely resemble objects that are known from later archaeological sites to have served as cheek pieces in a horse's bit; and indeed actual experiments have confirmed that they work effectively in that role.

The first human to have ridden on the back of a horse must have been a very brave person indeed. Domesticating the horse even as a source of meat would have been a daunting prospect, for the animal's speed, alertness, and capacity for inflicting injury made it qualitatively different from the sheep, goats, and cattle that the Dereivka farmers knew. Riding a horse was a total departure from anything in previous human experience. The ritual treatment of the Dereivka "cult stallion" in death is a hint of the awe with which these first riders must have regarded it in life.

Painstaking analysis of the wear patterns on the teeth of the cult stallion's skull have offered further proof that this horse carried a bit in its mouth. Although a properly adjusted bit is

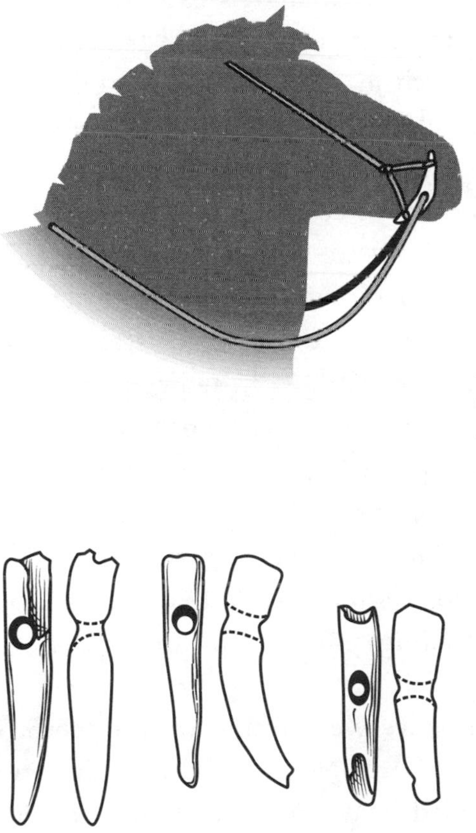

FIGURE 2.4
Perforated antler tines found at Dereivka may have been used as cheekpieces, with a rope bit.

supposed to rest on the soft tissue of the horse's mouth in the gap between its front incisors and back molars, in fact that isn't always the case. X-ray pictures of horses show that they often try to evade the bit by lifting it out of place with their tongue, pulling it back onto the forwardmost premolars. Because the sides of the bit push into the corners of the mouth in this position, it takes a strong grip to keep the bit between the teeth. A horse's jaws are nothing if not strong. But as anthropologist David Anthony found, the enormous pressure applied to the bit in this position leaves distinctive marks and wear patterns on the premolars.

The trick in analyzing the Dereivka cult stallion's teeth was to distinguish between wear marks caused by a bit and wear marks caused by the normal wear and tear of chewing tough plant matter and grit and grinding the teeth together. Anthony took scanning electron micrographs of the teeth of 20 feral horses from Nevada and Assateague, Virginia—horses that he knew had never carried a bit. He did the same with 10 specimens from domestic horses that had been autopsied at veterinary hospitals. The patterns left by the bits were remarkably distinctive and consistent. The bits tended to wear down the front edge of the premolars, leaving a beveled surface; they tended to cause repeated microscopic chips in the same spot, resulting in a stair-step pattern of cracks; and they caused spalls, or a small radiating fracture on the enamel surface of the tooth. The location of the damage was also consistent and distinct from that caused by the normal side-to-side grinding patterns produced by normal chewing.

All of these characteristics were found on the teeth of the cult stallion (figure 2.5); further comparison with modern domestic horses suggested that the cult stallion must have carried a bit in its mouth for at least 300 hours to produce the degree of damage found. Among all the other teeth found at Dereivka, there were four other premolars; none showed bit wear. Premolars from other sites dating from 1,000 to 25,000 years ago told a consistent story: none dating from more than 6,000 years ago showed any evidence of bit wear.

Anthony's findings argue for a major change in thinking about the origins of horseback riding. Archaeologists traditionally believed that the first use of the horse was to pull chariots or other wheeled vehicles—that this was the "reason"

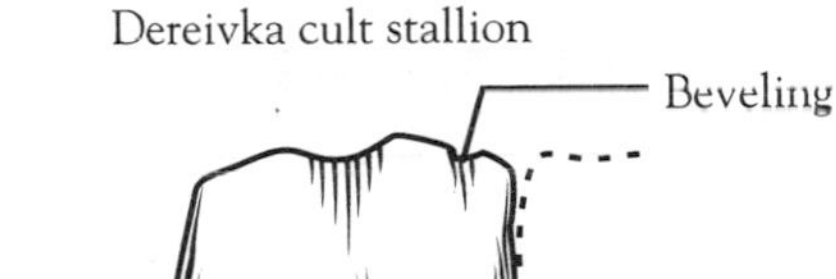

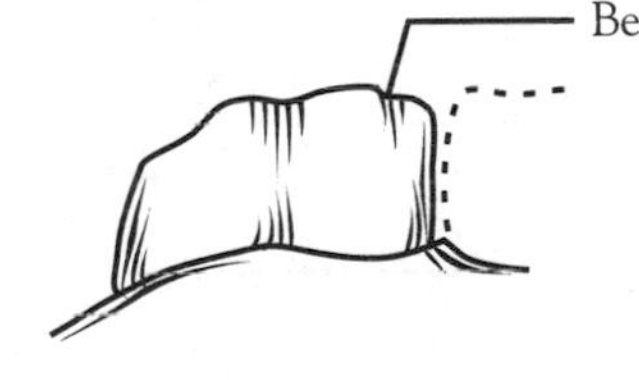

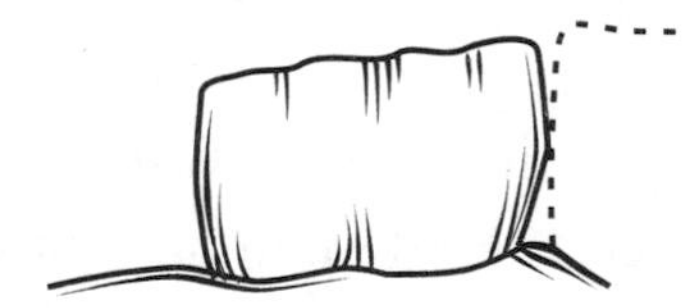

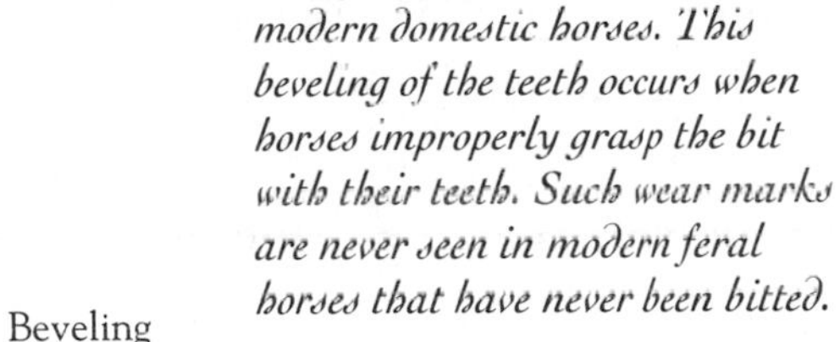
FIGURE 2.5 *The premolar of the Dereivka "cult stallion" shows wear patterns similar to those of modern domestic horses. This beveling of the teeth occurs when horses improperly grasp the bit with their teeth. Such wear marks are never seen in modern feral horses that have never been bitted.*

man domesticated the horse. (The chariot would assume an undeniable and enormous importance in the Near East as a weapon of war with the arrival of the horse there, but that was not until much later—about 3,800 years ago.) The findings from Dereivka, however, strongly suggest that horses were first ridden: the 6,000-year-old evidence of a horse that carried a bit in its mouth is 500 years older than the oldest known wheel. To ride a horse before the wheel or ox cart existed, and before humans conceived of riding on the back of any other beast, was a total leap of imagination. It was surely more an act of daring, bravado, curiosity, and yearning than of necessity. One cannot need what one cannot conceive of. To have ridden upon the back of this powerful and dangerous animal at the dawn of its domestication must be ranked more as a sacrament than an invention.

Yet it did not take long for the Dereivka farmers to grasp the implications of what they had done. From the earliest days of its domestication, the horse quickly began to transform warfare and human society. By 5,000 to 4,500 years ago, horse remains suddenly begin to reappear in the archaeological record at sites from which they had long before vanished, sweeping first through the Caucasus and then into Hungary, Romania, and farther west into Europe. Depictions of chariots and mounted riders appear, first in crude petroglyphs (figure 2.6) and then in ever more elaborate artwork (plate 3). Exotic trade items and materials begin to appear at Sredni Stog sites—elaborate copper ornaments and carved horse figures on porphyry, a stone not available locally. Some of these items appear to have been traded over distances of almost 1,000 kilometers. And very soon after the Dereivka stallion was first ridden some 6,000 to 5,500 years ago, humans began to penetrate the deep steppes, equipped for the first time with the means to carry their goods with them, to exploit the shifting and scattered resources of this barren realm, and to bring sudden, ferocious warfare upon their less mobile neighbors. Their settlements became larger, household size increased, and social hierarchies become apparent in burials—all signs, Anthony argues, of the dramatic change brought about by horse transportation.

Even if horses were in the first instance domesticated as a source of meat, it was the horse's value as a mount, not as a meal, that quickly came to dominate its relationship with man.

FIGURE 2.6
Bronze Age rock carvings from Central Asia depict horses being ridden and pulling chariots.

A Question of Ancestry

The Dereivka stallion appears to have been a horse of about 14.2 hands; most of the Dereivka horses were 12 to 14 hands. There is nothing about these horses' physical appearance, or indeed that of later domesticated horses from the Caucasus region, that reliably distinguishes them from the modern wild Przewalski's horse. A silver vase from a chieftain's grave in the north Caucasus dating from about 4,300 years ago depicts a short-legged, chunky, large-headed animal with an upright mane, very similar in appearance to the Przewalski's horse.

There has been a running debate among archaeologists over whether horses were domesticated once, by the Copper Age peoples in and around Dereivka—from whence they spread to the rest of Europe and Asia—or whether domestication of wild horses occurred separately in several different places in Europe, at several different times. A closely related question is whether the domestic horse is in fact of the same species as Przewalski's horse, or whether it is descended from a separate, now-extinct, European species of wild horse.

Those who champion a non-Ukrainian origin of at least some domestic horses point to the fact that small, remnant populations of wild horses survived in many isolated pockets well after the end of the Ice Age, even in parts of Europe from which they had largely vanished as the forests began to overtake the open tundra. The bones of wild horses appear, in small numbers, among the remains of animals killed by human hunters as late as 3000 B.C. in the marshlands of northern Germany and the mountainous, semialpine regions of southern Germany, and until about 2500 B.C. on the plains of the Iberian peninsula. (Claims that wild horses survived in Poland

and Ukraine as late as the nineteenth century have generally been viewed with skepticism by experts; these so-called tarpans were probably feral descendants of domestic horses, much like the "wild" horses of the American West, rather than a remnant prehistoric population.)

Further support for the non-Ukrainian theory comes from an analysis of mitochondrial DNA, which implies that the ancestors of the modern domestic horse and the ancestors of Przewalski's horse diverged as many as 250,000 years ago. Another key difference appears in the chromosome numbers of the two branches of the family: Przewalski's horse has 66 chromosomes, all domestic horses have only 64.

But calculations based on mitochondrial DNA remain theoretical and iffy, and they are not universally accepted. Paleolithic cave paintings of wild horses found in France depict an animal indistinguishable in any meaningful way from Przewalski's horse. The domestic horse can interbreed with Przewalski's horse and produce fertile offspring; the behavior of the two is virtually the same; and domestic horses frequently show "atavistic" traits, such as dorsal stripes and dun color, which are characteristic of Przewalski's horse.

The difference in chromosome number poses a tougher challenge to the notion that Przewalski's horse and the domestic horse are the same species, though not an insurmountable one. Although their chromosome numbers differ, two of the chromosomes in the domestic horse appear to be simply fused versions of four smaller chromosomes in Przewalski's horse. The basic genetic information they carry is the same.

Such a fusion in chromosomes can result from a well-understood mutation. A horse with 66 chromosomes would, after two of its chromosomes fused, have only 65 chromosomes; since chromosomes come in pairs that are split to form the egg or sperm cells, such a mutant horse would have germ cells that carried either 32 or 33 chromosomes. If two 65-chromosome horses mate, there is a one-in-four chance that their offspring will receive 32 chromosomes from each parent and become a 64-chromosome horse.

In a small, genetically isolated population of wild horses, such a mutation could readily occur and become locked in. In the wild, there is one interesting mechanism that could maintain genetic isolation among even neighboring bands of horses. For reasons that no animal behaviorists have yet been able to explain, stallions will sometimes favor mares of a particular color. In one study of feral horses in Nevada, a black stallion was observed to assemble a harem consisting entirely of reddish-brown mares with black manes; most of the horses in the region were yellow buckskin and blue grulla. Thus a small population of horses that acquired the 64-chromosome mutation through chance might retain its separate genetic identity, especially if the subpopulation was marked by another trait, such as color, that encouraged group cohesion through mating choice.

The difference in chromosome number between domestic horses and Przewalski's horses may thus have been just a coincidence. A mutation that happened to arise within the small band of horses that was to become domesticated in Ukraine would be passed on to all of the world's domestic horses.

Once this population was domesticated, its genetic isolation from its wild counterparts may have increased as the wild ancestors of Przewalski's horse retreated into ever more inhospitable reaches of the steppe. Indeed, the very survival of Przewalski's horse as a wild, free-living population into the twentieth century was a result of its ability to survive where humans could not.

If this account is correct, it strongly implies that horses were domesticated once and only once, since it is unlikely that the very same mutation occurred repeatedly in separate, isolated populations in Ukraine, Germany, and Iberia. All domestic horses today have 64 chromosomes, without exception.

It also certainly calls into question the fanciful efforts by some scholars to derive a dozen and a half separate species of ancient wild European horses on the basis of subtle differences in cave-painting depictions (variations much more likely attributable to artistic license or artistic ineptness)—or the chauvinistic claims of some horse fanciers that modern-day breeds can be traced to distinct prehistoric ancestors. It seems more likely that all the world's horses today have a common ancestry that goes back to a single point, perhaps even to a single event of human inspiration, on the Ukrainian steppes some 6,000 years ago.

CHAPTER 3

EQUINE NATURE, HUMAN NATURE

When cultures meet, they usually clash. The culture of horses and the culture of men were no exception, especially when the men in question were superstitious, anthropomorphic, warlike, and intensely status conscious. (Some might argue that nothing much has changed in the several thousand years since the cultures of man and horse first met.)

Equine society and human society had enough in common to make domestication possible—a common "language" of dominance and submission that was intuitively and mutually intelligible, a common evolutionary adaptation to a grasslands habitat, and, as we shall explore in greater detail in the next chapter, a common social fabric built upon both subordination to authority and trust.

But while this common ground brought us together, it hardly ensured understanding. The domestication of the horse as a mount and a chariot animal was an event so overwhelming in the history of mankind that it was virtually impossible for man to have looked upon it with cool and sober detachment. Domestication ensured that horses as we would come to think of them would not be horses in their natural setting, nor behaving in their natural fashion. Humans would inevitably see horses through their own eyes, through their dreams and ambitions, myths and fears, vanities and fashions.

The die was cast early in the culture that man quickly fashioned around the horse. Xenophon, in his instructions on teaching parade horses to curvet, emphasizes the importance of using subtle aids so that "to the beholders he may appear to be doing [it] of his own free will." The horses that the beholders of ancient Greece beheld conformed admirably to human ideas of the horse's nobility and power, just as dressage horses today match our notions of grace and racehorses our notions of athletic competitiveness and boldness. There is nothing wrong with any of these things per se, and it is not a condemnation of dressage or racing to say that they are not wholly natural. But it is often hard for us to remember what part of these sports and arts reflects the horse's fundamental nature and what part is the unique product of the blending of our two species' cultures. Coming to a clear understanding of the horse's true nature is not just a matter of calling upon science, but of shutting the door, at least for a moment of quiet contemplation, on 6,000 years of accumulated legend, myth, and sentiment.

The myths that man has attached to the horse, and the motives we impute to it, continue to form a set of unconscious and often unexamined assumptions about equine nature. So it is worthwhile to examine briefly how these myths came to loom so large in our minds—to look at how the very early history of the horse in the company of man has colored our perceptions of the beast ever since.

A Warrior and a Foreigner

"The horse is a warrior and a foreigner." Thus said the soothsayer to King Croesus of Lydia; thus did the horse burst upon the consciousness of the ancient world. David Anthony's studies of the transforming role of the horse in the steppe cultures of Ukraine and Central Asia tell a story that was repeated wherever the horse made its appearance.

There is much scholarly debate over the connection between the spread of the horse and its related accoutrements on the one hand, and the spread of the Indo-European language on the other, but it is clear that at least in the ancient Near East the appearance of the horse (which the Sumerians called the "horse of the mountains," distinguished from the ass, the "horse of the deserts," which they had earlier domesticated and broken to harness) coincides with the invasion of barbarous warrior nations speaking a group of related Indo-European languages. These were the Hittites, the Mitanni, the Kassites, and the Aryans, and it was as a terrifying and unprecedented weapon of war in their hands that the horse made its entrance at the gates of the civilized world.

Whether the civilized world, which already possessed wheeled vehicles drawn by oxen and asses, viewed riding upon horses as hopelessly barbarian (something for "bumpkins," as Anthony ruefully suggests), or whether it was more a matter of military calculation, the chariot quickly displaced the ridden horse in warfare in the ancient Near East. By 2000 B.C. chariots were well established as the quintessential weapon of terror.

The massed chariot attacks of Hollywood are alas fiction, but the way the horse and chariot were actually used was if anything more terrifying. The chariot was an instrument of pure intimidation on the battlefield, flanking the enemy and unleashing a flight of spears or arrows without warning. This new weapon of warfare bolstered the near-mythical status of the horse at the dawn of its association with man. Wherever the horse and the light two-wheeled chariot spread—to Egypt, Greece, India, China, Rome—it is represented in art with a barbarian warrior crushed beneath the animal's hooves (figure 3.1). This was heady stuff. (To the Aryans we must credit the invention of a word not just for chariot—*ratha,* which forms the root of the modern-day English words *roll* and *rotate*—but also the first known word for chariot wreck, *rathabhresa,* no doubt a not uncommon occurrence in this intense and hair-raising form of combat.)

FIGURE 3.1 *Riding down the natives: a recurrent theme in depictions of the horse in war. From a Roman relief in Bridgeness, Scotland, 142 A.D.*

It is worth reminding ourselves that the horse as warrior *was* the horse for thousands of years. Horses were not farm animals or hacks or children's pets; until quite recently oxen remained far more common even as draft animals. To humans, the image of the horse was the image of the horse in combat, and no other. Thus, reminding Job of his creations, God says:

Do you give the horse his strength?
Do you clothe his neck with a mane?
Do you make him quiver like locusts,
His majestic snorting spreading terror?
He paws with force, he runs with vigor,
Charging into battle.
He scoffs at fear; he cannot be frightened;
He does not recoil from the sword.
A quiverful of arrows whizzes by him,
And the flashing spear and the javelin.
Trembling with excitement he digs up the land;
He does not turn aside at the blast of the trumpet.
As the trumpet sounds, he says, "Aha!"
From afar he smells the battle,
The roaring and shouting of the officers.

The Affinity for Heroic Measures

Just as its military role shaped thinking about the horse, military necessity shaped its treatment. Charging into battle on a chariot behind a pair of nervous, barely controllable animals may in time have come to be a natural act to an elite warrior class, but it could never have been natural to the animals in question. The routine employment of what to us now seem horrifyingly drastic measures to control horses in harness may have been inevitable under the circumstances; but their use is a measure of the gulf that separated the cultures of man and beast from the start—of the gulf between human expectations and equine nature.

The problem of control was not made any easier by the routine practice of leaving stallions intact; the Greek geographer Strabo noted in 44 B.C. that the Scythians had the "peculiarity" of castrating their horses to make them more manageable. Apparently this was a strange enough practice at the time to merit comment.

Drastic measures were inherent in the way chariot horses were harnessed. The reins were passed through rings near the end of the yoke that acted to increase the leverage the driver could exert, but it was leverage that could be exerted effectively only in a straight backward direction. This arrangement allowed for effective braking but no steering to speak of, as there was no way to exert an outward pull, or "leading" rein. There were several solutions, all of them more or less drastic. One was the use of bits with spiked cheekpieces (figure 3.2). A pull on one rein would force the spiked inner edge of the opposite cheekpiece against the outside of the mouth. Such bits are abundant in the archaeological record from the earliest days of the lightweight, maneuverable two-horse chariot; they were adopted, too, by the sixth century B.C. Greeks, whose infatuation with the new sport of chariot racing apparently created a corresponding demand for effective steering control. (Such bits were consistently misinterpreted by many early archaeologists, who thought the burrs must have been intended for attaching a leather cheekpiece; it took the amateur archaeologist and professional horse trainer Mary

Aiken Littauer to make the correct identification, based, as she put it, on her knowledge of the "seamy side of the horse world"—variations of such severe bits having continued a sub-rosa existence in certain shadier racing and training circles into modern times.)

Another drastic form of control was afforded by dropped nosebands. Bridles found in Egyptian tombs, and depicted on bas reliefs, often have no bit at all but simply a low noseband, sometimes with the reins attached directly to either side. The very low position of these nosebands on the horse's muzzle would have exerted pressure directly on the sensitive tissue around the nostrils. In some of these bridles a bar bit was used, but probably not as a bit per se; rather, it served primarily to stiffen and reinforce the whole apparatus, and so more effectively transmit the force of a single rein pull directly to the opposite side.

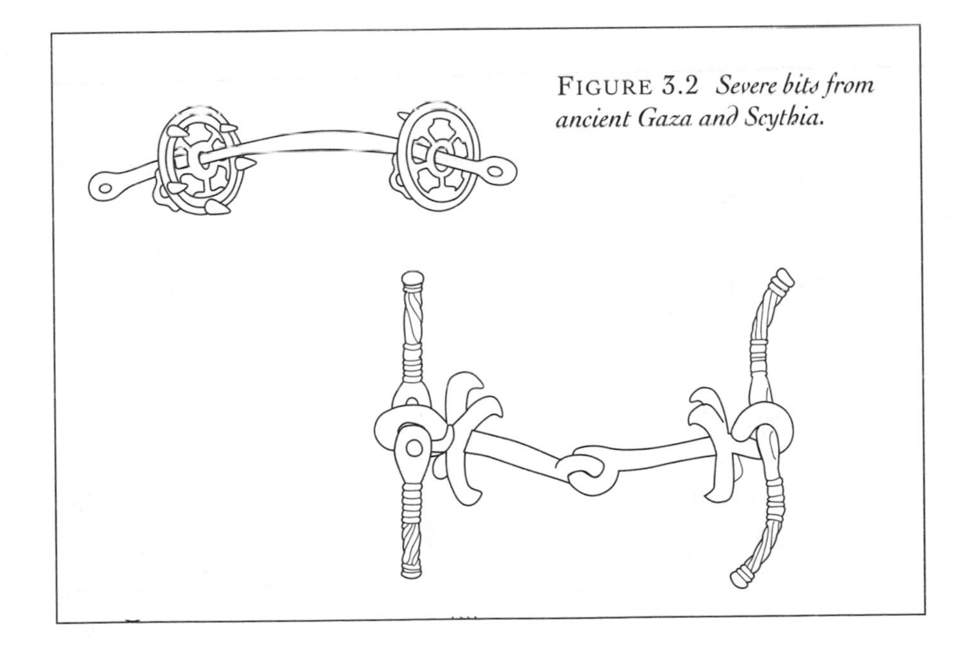

FIGURE 3.2 *Severe bits from ancient Gaza and Scythia.*

The low position of the noseband in turn necessitated another drastic step: because horses cannot breathe through their mouths, and because the low noseband interfered with the nostrils, an apparently quite common practice was to slit the nostrils of the horse in an effort to compensate. Horses with slit nostrils appear on a relief from Eighteenth Dynasty Egypt (around 1450 B.C.). Slit nostrils also show up in a number of other places and times when the use of a noseband was common to control horses and asses; both paintings and literary accounts document the practice in fifteenth- to seventeenth-century Europe, where rigid and brutal cavessons were frequently used in training.

The need to control nervous and fiery horses in the heat of battle by extreme means clearly suited the ancient warriors' conception of themselves, the nature of battle, and the nature of their war-horses. Not a little of that conception survives today, even in the mainstream equestrian world. Bits with spikes may generally be a thing of the past, but the attitude behind them still colors our conception of the horse. A rider whose horse goes quietly on loose reins through the thick and thin of the hunting field never seems to evoke quite the same attention and admiration as the one wrestling heroically with a foaming bundle of nerves barely held in check by a gag bit. How much of a "spirited" horse's spirit is the consequence of our whipping it into a frenzy remains a valid question. "Many of us still derive sincere pleasure out of a brutal mastery of the horse," noted the famous twentieth-century riding instructor Vladimir Littauer, who recalled pupils spending months learning to get the most artistic performance out of a horse by mastering the subtleties of its natural cooperativeness under their hands, only to derive the greatest pleasure from "the emergency subduing of a bucking or rearing horse." As

Littauer observed, "for our romanticizing of ourselves on his back the horse has continuously suffered."

The military necessity that created the ideal of the "high school" of riding is another distorting lens that still affects our notions of what constitutes not only the natural behavior but also the natural movement of the horse. Xenophon spoke of the thrill of seeing a horse curvet, and the precise movements of a superbly trained dressage horse continue to be a breathtaking sight. The close-order drill—the execution of precise maneuvers in tight formation—was a necessity in massed cavalry actions; thus the emphasis on training a horse to keep its balance to the rear, with tightly collected gaits, to permit rapid turns and close placement. The "prancing" horse pose—chin in, neck tightly arched, feet lifting high—became an ideal admired not only for its military utility but for its supposed "brilliance" as well. Not incidentally, this is also something that is hard to do, or at least hard to do well, requiring years of daily work before a rider achieves the coordination between seat, legs, and hands necessary to ride a horse under such precise control. Of course, this difficulty was considered only another virtue by the self-romanticizing practitioners of classical horsemanship, as indeed it remains today. It is significant that when Napoleon created the first modern army, its vast cavalry too large to be filled by aristocrats, the French abandoned the high school and adopted an easily learned method of riding on loose reins. "It is with this, so unscientific riding, that our armies made the tour of Europe," said the Comte d'Aure.

By the second half of the nineteenth century a romantic revival had brought back the *haute école,* along with all sorts of theories about the natural balance of the horse to justify it, the common notion being that a horse is naturally balanced when its weight is evenly distributed over all four feet.

To suggest that there is something unnatural about dressage is to risk bringing upon oneself a torrent of abuse from its devotees, but the truth of the matter is that these collected gaits are not ones that a freely moving horse, or a green horse, or a wild horse, will ever select on its own—unless it is highly emotionally aroused. A nervous horse may prance, but a freely moving, calm horse shifts its weight forward in a dynamically maintained balance. (As we shall see in chapter 8, all animals at the walk move their legs as inverted pendulums; the center of mass arcs up and falls forward. What keeps a horse—or a human—from falling flat on its face is a continual shift of the balance point forward to match the forward movement. The same is all the more true at the trot or gallop, which involve an actual jump through the air for part of the stride.)

Through steady schooling a horse can be taught to move at a collected gait perfectly calmly, just as a police horse may be taught to overcome its natural nervousness at the sound of a gunshot. But the enshrinement of the high school as an ideal continues to do great mischief to our understanding of the natural movements of the horse.

The heroic mentality of horsekeepers is alive and well today in one other context whose ancient roots are worth a brief mention. The earliest known equine veterinary text, a cuneiform tablet of the fourteenth century B.C. from the ancient city of Ugarit, located in modern-day northwest Syria, offers this advice: "If a horse discharges a putrid liquid, grain and bitter almond should be pulverized together, and it should be poured into his nose." Thus began a long tradition of the drastic and heroic cure. Recent technological advances in veterinary medicine notwithstanding, the tradition remains unbroken to this day, witness the continued favor of such practices as "firing" and "blistering"—the application of hot irons or chemical irritants—as supposed cures for lameness.

Status Symbols

The connection of horses to wealth and aristocracy is as ancient as the connection of horses to warfare. The nature of the horse and its special role in human society guaranteed that, alone among domesticated animals, it would be a consumptive luxury rather than a productive resource.

The British archaeologist Stuart Piggott has admirably described the considerable cost of what he terms the "chariot package deal," for in ancient times as now, the acquisition of a horse was just the beginning of the expenses a horse owner could expect to entail. To begin with, chariots were pulled by matched pairs, which necessitated extensive training; Hittite horse-training texts from the fifteenth century B.C. make clear just how extensive such training could be, with a detailed day-to-day tally of how many laps horses were made to run. Payroll lists from Mesopotamia in the eighteenth century B.C. record the considerable staffs required to support such an establishment: horse buyers, trainers, grooms, stable hands. The feed bills an ancient horsekeeper faced must have seemed even more staggering than they do today. Piggott estimates that feeding a pair of chariot horses in prehistoric Britain would have required the entire annual crop from 10 acres of barley. The arrival of the chariot in China in the twelfth century B.C. led directly to the importation and planting of an entirely new crop, alfalfa, to provide needed fodder for the horses. Finally, the building and maintaining of the chariots themselves placed huge demands on the services of wood, leather, and metal workers and wheelwrights.

This was something for kings and aristocrats, and from Egypt and Israel or Greece and Rome to China and "barbarian" nations such as Britain that later adopted the chariot, it was kings and aristocrats who exclusively commanded them. Akkadian texts from around 1500 B.C. and Egyptian texts from the time of Ramses IV (1166 B.C.) stipulate a two-man crew for chariots, a nobleman "chariot-warrior" and a "chariot master" or driver of equal or even greater status. The chariot was not just an accoutrement of power and wealth but a symbol of them: When Pharaoh wishes to show the people that he has placed Joseph in charge of all the land of Egypt, he dresses him in robes of fine linen, puts his signet ring upon his finger, and has him ride in the chariot of his second-in-command.

The pattern remained unbroken when cavalry began to replace chariotry as the elite corps in the first millennium B.C. In ancient Athens only the wealthiest members of society formed the cavalry, as they did in ancient Rome, in China, and of course in medieval Europe, where the knight on horseback became symbol and cornerstone of the Age of Chivalry. And from this grew the icon of the warrior-king on horseback, which would survive, at least in heroic equestrian statues of sovereigns, through the nineteenth century.

Equestrian games further tightened the link between horses and human wealth, pomp, and prestige. (It surely is not a coincidence that we have so many makes of car named after horses, or that a line of clothing called Polo can generate instant cachet.) The *Iliad* contains an account of chariot racing at the time of the Trojan War in the thirteenth century B.C.; four-horse chariot races were introduced at the Twenty-third

Olympiad in 684 B.C.; and in the Near East, Greece, and China, chariots appear early on in ostentatious display by monarchs during royal hunts (figure 3.3). More and more the horse was seen through the distorting lens of wealth, status, and privilege.

"No animal is more noble than the horse, since it is by horses that princes, magnates and knights are separated from lesser people," wrote the knight-farrier to Emperor Frederick II in 1250 A.D.; his words might just as easily have been written at any time during the preceding 2,000 years. The unavoidable expense of horses made them something only the richest members of society could afford; given the nearly universal belief that wealth equaled nobility, and given what Piggott calls "the ever latent anthropomorphism of antiquity," the association with nobility made the horse itself a Noble Animal.

Perhaps there is no surer sign of the part that the horse so quickly began to assume in the mind of man than its invocation by the Hebrew prophets as a symbol of luxury and apos-

FIGURE 3.3
The aristocratic associations of the horse are as ancient as its association with man. This scene of a royal lion hunt appears on Assyrian reliefs from the ninth century B.C. The Granger Collection, New York.

tasy. Amos and Isaiah and Micah, those voices in the wilderness ringing with righteous denunciation, equate horses with gold and silver and the idolatry of wealth:

For they are full of practices from the East,
And of soothsaying like the Philistines;
They abound in customs of the aliens.
Their land is full of silver and gold,
There is no limit to their treasures;
Their land is full of horses,
There is no limit to their chariots.

Thus does Isaiah denounce the corruptions of the House of Jacob. And when God wreaks his vengeance upon Israel for its sins, he not only sends the plagues that he set upon Egypt at the time of the Exodus, but also slays its captured horses.

Horse Gods and Household Gods

Deification is the ultimate distorting mirror that man has held up to the horse in the course of our shared history. While the ancient elevation of the horse to the status of a god is hardly a tradition that endures to affect modern-day attitudes toward the horse, it is nonetheless a reflection of the intense emotions that the horse was—and still is—capable of evoking. When the ancients were overwhelmed they found an outlet for their feelings in religious and magical terms; in our more competitive age we are perhaps more likely to impute our motives more crassly, for instance in wishing to believe that our horses love to win ribbons at horse shows. We may not literally worship horses anymore, yet the religious awe that the horse once evoked is testimony to a basic inability to see straight on this subject, which endures.

The most obvious evidence of deification is the elaborate horse burials that appear continuously from the cult stallion at Dereivka through early medieval pagan Europe to modern times in Central Asia. Often, of course, these burials reflect not so much deification of the horse as deification, or at least exaltation, of the horse's owner; the sacrifice and burial of the king's horses (and concubines, slaves, chariots, etc.) along with the king were examples of what Piggott nicely terms "conspicuous consumption"—a way to show off status and wealth and to maintain the special and even mystical nature of the king's possessions by putting them permanently out of circulation. Herodotus describes the ritual sacrifice and burial of 50 horses along with the dead king of the Scythians on the Dnieper River in the Crimea; the horses were killed, disemboweled, stuffed, and set upright in a circle about the tomb. The hecatomb of a Chinese prince of the fifth century B.C. contained 600 horses sacrificed and buried in similar fashion; terra cotta figures take the place of real horses in later burials (figure 3.4).

More suggestive, perhaps, are the simpler "hide burials" of the pagan horse cults of medieval Europe and of the Central Asian steppe peoples, the former well documented by travelers and the latter having continued into modern times recently enough in Soviet Asia to be photographed by early anthropologists (figure 3.5). The head, feet, tail, and hide of the horse were mounted on a pole to mark a burial or other sacred location, after the flesh was consumed in a ritual feast.

And then there is the account from the twelfth century A.D. of the "barbarous and abominable" pagan ceremonies by which a local ruler was installed in a province of Ireland, involving

the ritual mating of the king with a white mare, which was then slaughtered, cut up, and boiled. The ceremony culminated in what must have been the considerable spectacle of the king climbing into the cauldron, squatting in the horse broth, and consuming some of the soup.

Science is no magic elixir, but after 6,000 years of distorting myth, it may be the purgative we need if we are to approach the horse with a clear head.

FIGURE 3.4 *The third century* B.C. *tomb of the First Emperor of Qin in Xian, China, contains thousands of lifelike terra cotta sculptures of soldiers, servants, and horses.* © Earl Dibble/FPG International Corp., 1983.

FIGURE 3.5 *The deification of the horse is suggested by a widespread Indo-European rite, recreated here, in which horse hides were mounted on poles to mark sacred sites.*

CHAPTER 4

SOCIOECOLOGY

Animal trainers—the successful ones, at least—have an intuitive sense, honed from long experience, of what makes an animal respond. The unabashedly anthropomorphic terms and concepts that nearly all good animal trainers use are not strictly speaking "wrong." They offer a way of thinking about an animal's motivation and behavior that makes intuitive sense to us, and more important, that works in practice. To say that a dog responds to praise because it wants to please us is, in fact, a more useful way of thinking about it in the practical, day-to-day business of training than describing it as appeasement behavior in response to a threat from a dominant member of the social hierarchy would be.

But even the best trainers may be hard pressed at times to explain *why* an animal behaves as it does. The "why" questions belong to the realm of evolutionary ecology: only by looking at the environment and circumstances that an animal, through long evolution, has adapted to, can we begin to understand the fundamental reasons it does what it does.

Horses in domestic settings are obviously doing something very different from what they evolved to do in the wild. Much of this is the result of learning, which might be considered one form of specialized behavior (and which we will examine more closely in chapter 7). But even the most stereotyped and seemingly rigid forms of behavior are, after all, an evolved means for an animal to mediate between itself and its environment; behavior is by its very definition adaptable to new circumstances.

Many popular books about domestic animals (especially dogs) assert as a simple truth that we take on the role of the pack leader or herd leader in our relationship with animals. That is true only in a small way. The dog's natural instinct to respond to gestures of dominance or submission is part of the template of natural behaviors that permits it to live in peace with humans, and to respond to our wishes. But a little reflection ought to make us realize that it is only a template, on top of which human society and human behavior, as far as the dog is concerned, are superimposed. It is probably true that a dog views us as a dog more than it views itself as a person, but we are clearly a very funny sort of dog; we don't act like any pack leader in the history of dogdom. We exert our dominance in extremely selective ways. We do not fight over food like a normal member of the pack would. We engage in mutual grooming, but only up to a point. We don't go around sniffing rear ends or letting ourselves be sniffed. We most definitely do not engage in canine sexual behavior. In short, we exhibit only a small fraction of the social behavior that a dog "expects," as a result of millions of years of evolution, of a fellow dog.

On this same point, it is interesting that foals taken very

early from their mothers and raised solely in the company of humans—so that they really do view us as "other horses"—do not fit in well with human society. They often exhibit inappropriate sexual behavior toward humans and are difficult to train and manage. What we are exploiting in our relationship with horses is a well-developed set of equine behaviors, developed within the context of the equine social structure, which we then tap into and redirect.

But however much we modify and redirect it, still it is the domestic animal's innate behavior, especially its innate social behavior, that provides the raw material we of necessity must work with; this is the basis for the bonding and subordination that makes learning even possible. And in an intensely social animal such as the horse, whose survival for millenniums has depended upon the cohesion and effectiveness of its social structures, it is the animal's highly evolved social behavior that is key to understanding why it does what it does.

Why Bond?

The fundamental business of any animal is to survive and reproduce. As we saw when we looked at the evolution of equid social structures in chapter 1, an animal's habitat is a powerful force in determining what type of organization will be most effective in carrying out that business. Animals form groups for a variety of reasons, including defense against predators and cooperative hunting or foraging. But in horses, as in many group-dwelling animals, the overriding factor is sex. Once the availability of resources determines how a population distributes itself across the landscape, the inexorable demands of sex dictate what sort of social structure will follow. Where food resources are stable, animals tend to be solitary and territorial, and mating occurs according to territorial lines. The distance between individuals means that males mate with only one or a few females; there are no permanent bonds between individuals and no harems.

But where resources are sparse and constant migration is a necessity just to find enough to eat, harems become both a possibility (because individuals are not tied down to a specific patch of ground) and a necessity (because males cannot claim females simply by holding a patch of ground). Another way to look at it is that by establishing a stable reproductive unit bound together by permanent social ties, animals that live in harems are free to move as a unit as the available grazing shifts; migration to meet food needs does not threaten the social structure built to meet reproductive needs. Sex is dissociated from territory.

Both types of social organization occur in modern-day equines. Grevy's zebra *(E. grevyi)* and the African wild ass *(E. asinus)* are highly territorial. This "type II" social structure in equines may be a vestigial holdover from the primitive equids that lived in forests. Grevy's zebra stallions will keep the same territory for years on end. Although the stallions will vigorously defend their territory against intrusion by neighboring stallions, once a mare enters a stallion's territory that settles the matter: they will mate without challenge from other nearby males. Territory rules.

The significant point is that, having evolved this territorial mating structure, Grevy's zebras and African wild asses simply never had any need to develop a social instinct for bonding with other individuals. Adults are either solitary or live in loose associations that can shift from hour to hour; the only social bonds of any lasting character are between a mare and her young foal while they remain together.

The horse, the plains zebra *(E. burchelli),* and the mountain zebra *(E. zebra)* by contrast form harems. Stallions will rarely tolerate sexual behavior by other nearby stallions without a fight. Mating is determined by social structure, not territorial lines. Social organization rules where territorial ties are ephemeral.

These "type I" equids show a strong fundamental instinct—under a wide variety of circumstances—to form long-lasting attachments to specific individuals. This basic instinct toward bonding with other individuals is the glue that holds harems—the fundamental social structure of the horse—together. Both mares and stallions will select their mates, a mutual attraction that gives the harem its long-term stability.

But so general is this drive to bond that it appears within horse society in many contexts that have nothing to do with mating. Mares within a farm herd or a harem in the wild will almost invariably pair off, forming fixed "friendships" with particular horses whom they will groom more often than others and whom they will permit to stand nearby, within the boundaries of a "personal space" that they will otherwise defend against intrusion (plate 4). In the wild, young bachelor stallions who have not yet been able to establish their own harems will band together themselves, usually in groups of two to four. (The average size of bachelor groups in a study of feral horses in the western United States was 1.8.)

Other evidence points to how basic the instinct to bonding is in horses. Horses that have formed an attachment lose their drive to form new social attachments; for example, a stallion will only rarely seek new mares once it has formed a harem.

(The average harem among the feral horses studied in the western United States consisted of only five horses in all: one stallion, one to three mares, and their immature offspring.)

By the same token, horses deprived of their familiar equine companionship will readily form a strong attachment to any horse they are placed with. It is possible to create new "friendship" bonds between horses by placing two together in an unfamiliar location; after about two weeks they will invariably form an attachment that will survive even after they are turned out with a larger, established group of horses. Horses removed from a herd will also readily form attachments to surrogates, including their human owners or even a barn cat. It is this instinct that humans draw upon in establishing their relationship with domesticated horses. An extreme, but extremely effective, method used by some trainers to deal with recalcitrant or aggressive horses that refuse to accept human control is to deprive them of any social companionship for as much as 23 hours a day; social contact (even with a nonequine) becomes so valuable to a socially deprived horse that it very quickly comes to accept and bond with its trainer.

I have often noticed the same phenomenon, on a less dramatic scale, in my horse's behavior at my home farm, where he has only a single pony for equine company, compared to his behavior at a large riding stable where he is sometimes boarded with 40 or 50 other horses. At home he is normally quite affectionate and even eager for human contact, often following me or my children around the field and coming up to the fence when he catches sight of one of us; when he is at the riding stable, or just back from a stay there, he is markedly less so. Our horses' affection for us, their owners, is unquestionably real, grounded in a basic instinct to form friendship bonds; it is slightly bruising to our egos, though, to realize that they bond with us only for lack of better company.

Friendship and Grooming

If bonding was originally an evolutionary adaptation that supported the harem social structure, this basic drive in horses was probably reinforced over the course of evolution because it proved to have additional adaptive value. In one study of domestic horses, friendship bonds were found to have the effect of superimposing a second social hierarchy upon the dominance pecking order; low-ranking horses that formed an attachment to a higher-ranking horse often gained better access to food than did horses that they regularly submitted to in aggressive encounters. Being tolerated by or attached to a high-ranking horse that spent a lot of time beating up on other horses, in other words, offset to some degree the cost of being picked on.

Other studies, of feral horses, suggest that horses tend to form friendship bonds with horses of similar age and dominance rank. But even so, the mutual social support of a pair bond is an advantage in deflecting aggression from other horses. The instinct to form attachments clearly has survival value, separate and apart from reproduction.

An ability to form bonds is meaningless if you cannot tell who you are forming the bond with, and who you aren't, so a corollary requirement for group cohesion is an ability to recognize individuals. Studies of feral herds show that horses unquestionably have a keen ability to recognize and remember individual horses—by sight, by smell, and by sound. Stallions immediately spot an intruder and readily single out members of their harems that have strayed into another group. Many instances have been observed of mares and foals recognizing one another by sound alone. The ability of horses to recognize individuals may also explain why some riding horses appear to know and put to the test by disobedience—unfamiliar riders, and why some horses can be successfully managed only by certain people.

At the most basic instinctive level, grooming may play a key role in creating—and certainly in maintaining—bonds between horses. Grooming occurs frequently between pairs of horses, and is almost always simultaneous and mutual. The two horses stand head to tail, pull the lips back, and scratch one another with their bared incisors. If one horse stops, the other does too. Mutual grooming in feral horses occurs only between members of a single band, never between bands.

Although any single horse will usually spend considerably more time grooming one or two friends than grooming other members of the herd, every horse will at one time or another groom all, or nearly all, members of its band; the only mutual grooming combination not observed in feral horses studied in the western United States was between the dominant stallion and foals. Grooming also frequently occurs as an "appeasement" gesture following an aggressive encounter between members of the group.

Grooming may have its roots in the removal of parasites from areas that an animal cannot easily reach itself—and mutual grooming in horses does concentrate on the neck, withers, base of the mane, back, and rump (figure 4.1). But in horses, as in many mammals, it has become ritualized as a way to cement social relations. Horses normally maintain a "personal space" against intrusion, engaging in threat displays against horses that approach closer than 1.5 meters. The necessarily close contact between pairs of grooming horses per force lowers these barriers and strengthens the social bond. The ritual nature of grooming is also apparent in the behavior of foals and young horses, who will frequently clap their teeth together with lips apart as a submissive gesture toward older horses. Foals will engage in "unilateral" grooming of adults in response to aggressive moves, and teeth clapping, which involves the same motions of the mouth that occur in grooming, appears to be a ritualized version of this behavior.

In the evolution of social signals this is quite a familiar pattern. Social signals in effect draw upon preexisting material. A lizard whose visual system and brain have evolved to detect fast-moving insect prey will use a rapid up-and-down head bob as a courtship signal—it is a gesture that the species is already "hard wired" to respond to. Grooming may have

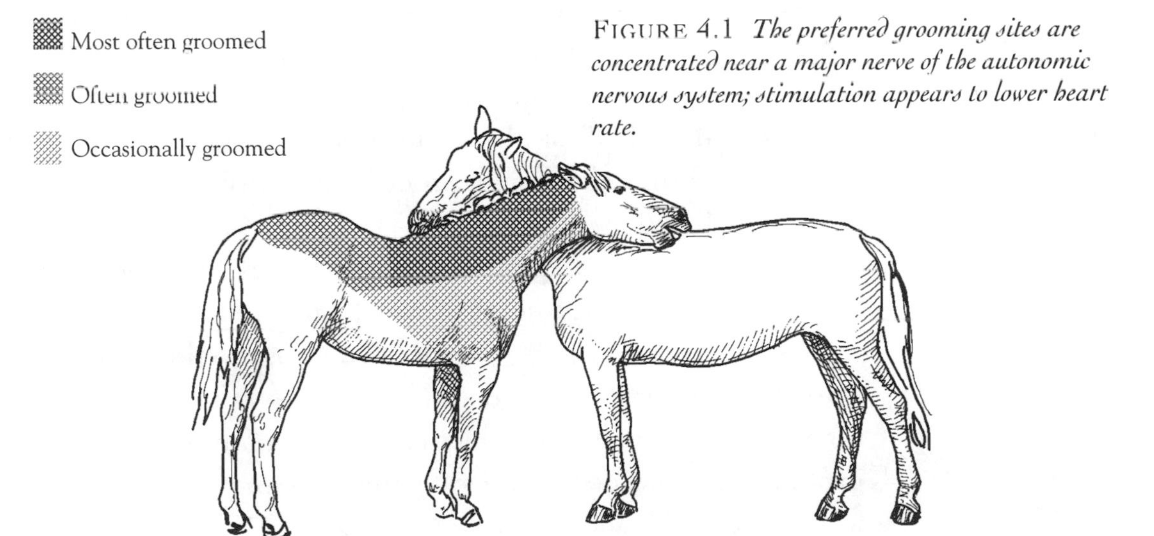

FIGURE 4.1 *The preferred grooming sites are concentrated near a major nerve of the autonomic nervous system; stimulation appears to lower heart rate.*

begun as a utilitarian matter of survival (removing harmful parasites), but its social consequences (facilitating the creation of pair bonds and reducing aggression within the herd) have over time led to its ritualization.

Interestingly, at least one line of evidence suggests that the ability of grooming to reduce tension between individuals may also have been hard-wired. A recent study by two French biologists, Claudia Feh and Jeanne de Mazières, found that when tame horses were groomed by humans at the site they most frequently chose when grooming one another (the lower neck), their heart rate decreased significantly—about 11 percent in adults and 14 percent in foals. Grooming at a site never chosen by horses themselves (the lower shoulder to elbow) had no effect on heart rate. The preferred site lies close to a major ganglion, or bundle of nerve tissue, which may account for the effect.

The point is not that the "purpose" of grooming is to lower heart rate; the point is rather that, because grooming happens to have this pleasurable, calming effect, it has naturally been drawn upon in the course of social evolution as a means of both cementing pair bonds and appeasing aggression. The physiological roots explain why grooming was "chosen" as a social signal in the first place; but it was the adaptive value of grooming within the horse's social structure that led to its being ritualized.

The importance of grooming to horses is apparent in the passive behavior they show toward an unlikely companion, the cattle egret. These birds have been observed perching for up to 50 minutes at a time on the backs of feral ponies, picking off flies; egrets will also sometimes accompany ponies on the ground, and the ponies tolerate them as they strike at their legs, underbelly, and flanks.

Similarly, grooming is clearly an important ingredient in the bond between humans and horses; scratching and petting play an important part in "breaking" horses and gaining their trust, as well as in communicating praise.

Aggression Versus Violence

Although it may not seem obvious to anyone who has watched horses shoving, biting, kicking, and squealing at one another, the establishment of a dominance pecking order among horses is actually a way to avoid violence.

As with all group-dwelling animals, actual acts of physical aggression between horses are the exception. A new horse placed into a group will typically fight it out physically. But within two days its place in the hierarchy is usually well established. It has learned whom it may threaten with impunity and whom it had better give way to without a fight whenever there is a conflict over food, water, or personal space.

A study of free-ranging domestic ponies on the Isle of Rhum in Scotland found that more than 80 percent of aggressive encounters between animals consisted of threats with the head alone—pinning back the ears and extending the neck—and that kicks or even threats to kick were rare. Studies of feral horses in the western United States found this to be even more the case in dominance confrontations between a herd stallion and mares: 98 percent of the time the stallion had only to lower his head to get a mare to move.

Studies of domestic, feral, and Przewalski's horses all find remarkable consistency in the number of threats horses issue to their fellow herd members, an average of 1.5 per hour per horse. Although some authors have claimed that dominance contests only occur among horses in the stressful domestic circumstances of close proximity and competition for food, in fact even free-ranging and wild horses have been found to establish and maintain well-defined hierarchies. Horses at the top consistently issue the most threats. And although there may be some odd, circular dominance orders (A threatens B who threatens C who threatens A), in general there is a clear pattern in which each horse only threatens those below it in the order.

But the relative rarity of actual violence is testimony to the effectiveness and stability of the social hierarchy. And indeed the frequency of aggressive encounters would be even higher but for the fact that subordinate animals, once they learn and accept their position, will make a strong effort to avoid higher-ranking animals altogether so that even threats are unnecessary. The very purpose of a social hierarchy is to avoid the need for constant and bloody battles over access to resources, which would otherwise be inevitable among group-dwelling animals whose close proximity makes constant competition unavoidable.

Age, size, sex, motivation, and experience all seem to play a part in determining where in the hierarchy an individual horse will end up. Whether a horse will fight or submit when it encounters another horse seems to be a complex calculation that depends both on its inner motivation and on a subtle reading of social signals. For example, a hungry horse will be more keen to get at food than a well-fed one, and will fight more vigorously to defend its place at the feed bucket. A mare with a new foal will often become more aggressive out of its natural protective instinct, and as a result may temporarily move up the dominance hierarchy. Some studies have found different dominance hierarchies in the same herd in different contexts; some horses will be higher when it comes to access to the water trough, others when it comes to access to food. Stallions, which have a much higher intrinsic level of aggressiveness than mares, are generally higher in the dominance hierarchy. (But not always. A study of dominance relations among foals found that colts were by no means automatically dominant to fillies. The study also found that there was a significant correlation between the rank order of foals and the rank order of their dams; whether this was learned or genetically determined is not clear, but what is clear is that the intrinsically more aggressive foals were consistently at the top of the heap.)

All of this evidence suggests that an individual's internal motivation is a key factor in establishing where it ends up in the pecking order. In this sense the pecking order is an "honest" reflection of each animal's propensity for violence and its chances of prevailing in an actual fight. The aggression that maintains the dominance hierarchy is a surrogate for actual violence. In other words, aggression is actually a way to avert violence.

The Natural History of Bluffing

The necessarily symbolic nature of most of the threats used to communicate dominance and maintain the hierarchy means that horses have to have evolved an adeptness at reading subtle cues.

To be sure, the cues all bear a logical relationship to actual acts of violence. A lowered head and extended neck are preliminaries to a bite, and flattening the ears back is a natural way to guard a vulnerable part of the body in a fight; swinging the head toward another horse is an even more obvious prelude to a bite, as raising a leg or wheeling the hind quarters around are preliminaries to a kick.

Yet some of these gestures have become so attenuated and ritualized (some, indeed, are almost indiscernible to a casual human observer) that it is possible, as in any symbolic language, to lie. Or perhaps a better word is "bluff." A new horse that joins a herd will sometimes establish its position in the hierarchy with almost no discernible aggressive encounters. A sort of quiet confidence and the subtlest of threats are sufficient. It is a matter of eye, head, and ear carriage, of overall demeanor, of bearing—or what race handicappers have long called "class." It is a well-accepted fact in both human society and horse society that an individual with a don't-mess-with-me attitude usually doesn't get messed with.

Of course, if lying becomes too frequent the system breaks down; a bluff is only good if it can be backed up at least most of the time. The social code has to be a fairly honest measure of reality; if cheating becomes common, it will begin to pay for those lower in the hierarchy to call the bluff of those higher up. Losing in a violent encounter will become worth the risk, given the counterbalancing benefit of moving up the social hierarchy by challenging a false claim to dominance.

All of which means that for a social code to have stability it must remain mostly honest. Which in turn means that prudence demands that the society's members respect it, at least as a rule.

The keen ability of horses, as of all social animals, to "read" and correctly interpret symbolic social signals is perhaps the most important key to their surprisingly peaceful subordination to humans in the domestic relationship. When I was first learning to ride, I remember my astonishment at discovering that merely *carrying* a whip was all that was required to persuade one huge white gelding named Nicky to knock off his entire repertoire of nasty tricks that he employed to intimidate neophytes like me (bucking when asked to canter was his specialty). This was a lesson that all experienced riders of course learn: once a horse has learned to associate the whip with a dominance threat, the mere presence of a whip on the scene can be as effective—or even more effective—in reinforcing the dominance hierarchy than its actual employment.

The well-known ability of horses to "mind read" (see chapter 7 for more on mind reading) is neither so extraordinary nor so mythical as it is often made out to be; it is hardly surprising that an animal whose entire socioecology is based on an ability to read subtle social cues can pick up on the hesitations, uncertainty, and lack of self-assurance of one rider, and the confidence and resolution of another.

Many successful systems used today in "breaking" horses rely almost entirely on the use of subtle social "threats"—that is, bluffs—rather than force, restraint, or physical punishment. In so-called lungeless breaking, an untrained horse is brought into a closed, round pen and put through controlled paces solely by the body language of the trainer. Moving toward the horse's rear with waving arms or a lowered head makes the horse move away; moving toward its head slows or halts the horse; and inclining the head back or holding out a dropped hand, in mimicry of a horse's nose-to-nose greeting, encourages it to come in.

Some speculate, perhaps a bit fancifully, that horses so readily accept human dominance in part because our ears appear to them to be permanently pinned back in a threat posture. But such explanations are really not necessary. Watching a good trainer or rider at work, it is clear that human dominance is asserted and maintained largely through confidence and assurance, a language that horses through long evolutionary adaptation are well equipped to understand.

Do Dominant Horses Win Races?

Leadership is not always the same as dominance.

In cattle and sheep, it is usually a high-ranking, but not the highest-ranking, individual that walks at the head of a line of animals on the move. In feral horses, some studies have found the dominant stallion in the lead most of the time when the herd was traveling, though often a dominant mare took the lead. In socially stable groups of farm horses, leadership is often consistently taken by an older gelding or mare from the middle of the dominance hierarchy. (In plains zebras, too, it is the oldest mares that lead movements of the group.) If the movement of the herd is in response to an intruder, however, the stallion usually interposes himself between the herd and the intruder and drives his herd from the rear.

Significantly for those interested in the relationship between position in the dominance hierarchy and the winning of horse races, though, there is at least a rough correlation between rank and leadership. Although any horse may initiate movement in feral bands, a low-ranking individual who starts to lead the way will usually soon stop and allow a dominant horse to pass ahead. This tendency may explain the well-known handicapping dictum that "class will tell." (Or, as the veteran handicapper Tom Ainslie put it, "Cheap horses know it.") Handicappers have frequently noted that some seemingly slower horses will consistently beat horses that have recorded considerably faster speeds; it seems plausible that this is at least in part a reflection of subtle assertions of dominance that horses (especially mares) instinctively defer to when the herd is on the move.

But those who hope for a foolproof handicapping method would do well to consider one other observation of leadership in feral horses: in stampedes, it is usually the most nervous mares that are consistently out in front. Perhaps the question is whether a horse race more resembles a purposeful herd movement or a stampede.

Why Stallions Are Belligerent

Aggression has several different evolved functions in the horse; establishing and maintaining the social hierarchy within the herd is but one. Just as the affiliative instinct to form pair bonds is the basic instinct that gives rise to group cohesion and the equine social organization, so the aggressive defense of personal space is the basic instinct that gives rise to the dominance hierarchy. Basically all dominance challenges are fights over mutual violations of personal space, with one horse giving way.

In our relationship with horses, the human assertion of dominance—and, perhaps more important, the forging of a pair bond by which the horse accepts our routine violation of its personal space—deflects much of this social aggression. Aggressiveness will still sometimes be displayed, even by horses that are well adjusted to humans, in the form of muted threats—a toss of the head toward the person tightening a saddle girth, perhaps, or a foot stamp, which is probably an abbreviated strike threat. (Teeth clapping or "snapping" in young horses may appear to be a bite threat but is actually a submissive gesture derived from grooming, as noted earlier.) These, however, are probably all social threats that attempt to test the dominance relationship between man and horse, and can often be dealt with by a suitable dominance response—a stern tone of voice or a whack.

But aggression has other roots and functions in horses, which can pose complications in our dealings with them and in managing their behavior toward other horses in a domesticated setting. These aggressive behaviors occur mainly in stallions and serve several adaptive purposes. Stallions, as noted above, will "drive" or "herd" their mares and foals using the classic aggressive posture: ears lowered and pinned back and neck outstretched. This behavior is used in feral herds most often to move the harem away from another group or a lone stallion, or to start, stop, or slow the movement of the group in normal migrations to food and water sources. (In only about 4 percent of cases in one study was this herding behavior used to try to gather a mare into the harem. Harems maintain a dominance and submission relationship to other harems, and although confrontations between stallions do occur not infrequently, more often harems move so as to avoid encounters. Just as individual animals have a personal space, so bands try to maintain a distance from other groups, usually at least 100 meters.)

Stallions also regularly exhibit aggression toward their own adolescent colts and fillies; young horses in feral herds typically are driven off at around three or four years of age.

The aggression toward colts is a straightforward extension

of the instinct to keep the herd away from other bands and lone stallions that could threaten its integrity—that is, the group's spacing in relation to other groups. The aggression toward fillies is more complex, and must reflect at least in part a separate evolutionary selection against incest. In support of this interpretation is the interesting fact that stallions are not sexually aroused by estrous displays of fillies, especially their own offspring.

Finally, stallions have been found to exhibit another form of aggression that implies a different, special selective force at work. When a stallion takes over a harem from another male, it will frequently subject the mares to persistent harassment, including chasing and aggressive biting, and sometimes (though not always) forced copulations with the unreceptive mares. In these aggressive copulations the stallions do not engage in normal male courtship behaviors, such as sniffing and licking the female's genital area. Eleven pregnant mares taken over by a new stallion were studied by biologist Joel Berger in feral herds in Nevada; ten aborted their fetuses after forced copulations or some other form of violent physical harassment by the new stallion, who then reinseminated the mares.

Infanticide by males newly arrived on the scene has been observed in lions, domestic cats, and some primates. Apparently, male horses have adopted the only slightly less grisly strategy of forced abortion owing to a peculiarity of the equine reproductive cycle. Unlike mammals that remain anestrus while nursing, a mare will quickly go into estrus again after its foal is born. A new stallion thus has nothing to gain by killing foals that are not his. But by inducing abortion in a newly acquired mare, he can increase his reproductive potential by immediately rebreeding the mare, rather than waiting up to a year for the pregnancy to carry to term. Given that the average tenure of a stallion in the bands Berger studied was only a little over two years, that is time a stallion can ill afford to waste. Stallions that adopt this strategy are far likelier to maximize their number of offspring, and the inexorable laws of natural selection take care of the rest: stallions with these aggressive instincts will contribute disproportionately to the gene pool of the next generation, ensuring that the instinct is passed on.

Not surprisingly, most of these aggressive behaviors that are unique to stallions can be reduced or eliminated in captivity through castration. Studies have found that in problem stallions that show unacceptable aggressive behavior, castration eliminates aggressiveness toward people in 60 to 70 percent of the cases and aggressiveness toward other horses in 40 percent. A study of 140 horses found that the reduction in aggressiveness is the same whether the stallions are castrated before or after puberty.

The Uses of Play

Play is fundamentally a juvenile pursuit. Various theories, none entirely convincing, have been proposed in recent years to explain why animals play, but there is general agreement that it is especially important in the development of particularly complex adult skills in mammals, such as social behavior or hunting. Wolf pups, for example, will go through what looks almost like a graded series of how-to-hunt exercises, first playing with twigs or rocks, then chasing bugs or anything else that moves, then circling around a moving object to cut off its motion, and finally putting all of these skills together in an actual hunt.

Ungulates in their play concentrate on escape maneuvers, mock dominance encounters, exploration, and mating behavior. Lambs, for example, will butt and try to mount one another. Foals engage in mock fights with nips and shoves, charge about in groups, and seem to "practice" forming pair bonds (plate 4).

In the wild, play drops off sharply when an animal reaches adulthood. Adult Przewalski's horses at the Bronx Zoo were observed to spend less than 0.2 percent of their time playing, versus 1.5 percent for foals. Some studies of feral ponies have found essentially no play among adults.

Yet many domestic animals seem to persist in playing well into adulthood. Dogs are probably the best example; they seem to be perpetual wolf puppies, willing to spend hours playing with objects, chasing sticks, and stalking real or imaginary objects; adult dogs will play with one another and with their human owners much as wolf pups do, engaging in extended mock fights with much barking, snapping, and running.

The reason for this seems to lie in the fact that all domestic animals are more or less cases of arrested development. As we saw in chapter 2, domestic animals, through the course of their preadaptation during the Pleistocene glaciations, and then through their further coevolution with and selective breeding by man, preferentially acquired many "youthful" traits, including inquisitiveness, adaptability, docility, playfulness, and care-soliciting behavior. Neoteny, the retention into adulthood of juvenile traits, is a common feature of both the behavior and physical appearance of domestic species. And a relatively modest genetic change can bring this about; it does not require a trait-by-trait selection but simply a single change in the timing of puberty's onset. Consciously or (more likely) not, our breeding of domestic animals has selected for precisely this change.

Domestic animals retain not only juvenile behavioral characteristics but juvenile physical characteristics as well. Again, dogs are the clearest example; many breeds retain the rounded heads, short noses, and floppy ears characteristic of wolf puppies. In dogs there is also an interesting and suggestive correlation between the degree of puppylike appearance and the degree of puppylike behavior. Those with more puppylike heads, such as retrievers, tend to be "object players" even as adults; those with more adult features, such as Border collies and corgis, display more fully developed adult behavior that includes chasing and cutting off prey.

Horses show a much smaller change under domestication than other domestic species, which is probably in part a function of how recently they were domesticated compared to dogs, cattle, sheep, and goats. Most breeds of domestic horses do show some neotenic physical characteristics, however, such as long, coltlike legs relative to body size.

It is not clear whether adult domestic horses play more than adult wild horses do, though anecdotally that appears to be the case. And at least some speculative correlations can be drawn between the degree of physical neoteny and coltlike behavior in domestic horse breeds (figure 4.2). It is interesting that in terms of the ratio of the length of the foreleg to the torso, Arabs and thoroughbreds appear to lie closer to foals than do ponies, which much more closely match the proportions of the adult wild type (Przewalski's horse). There is no good evidence that horses are necessarily more playful than ponies, but they do appear to exhibit a comparatively greater proportion of some typically juvenile behaviors. Ponies as a rule seem to be inherently wilier and shrewder and less docile than horses.

The veterinarian and horse authority Andrew Fraser has suggested that some residual inclination toward play is activated in adult domestic horses in many horse sports. The movement, group activity, or variety of pace and environment involved in racing, jumping, dressage, hunting, and even driving in harness with other horses may be accepted by horses in part as "analogs" to natural play. The argument certainly has much appeal. Training and learning may explain why a horse can be made to perform these tasks, but seem inadequate to explain the undeniable enthusiasm that many horses show for these pursuits. Fraser says that it might make sense to think of these more as "work-games" from the horse's point of view.

FIGURE 4.2 *Domestic horses retain into adulthood the leggy proportions of a colt; domestic ponies are closer to the wild type.*

Przewalski's horse

Pony

Arabian

Foal

Abnormal Behavior and Evolution

An estimated 15 percent of domestic horses exhibit what their human owners, with only the usual degree of anthropocentrism, term "stall vices." Many of these annoying habits involve repeated, stereotypic rituals. A horse will weave back and forth, pace ceaselessly in its stall, drink abnormally huge

FIGURE 4.3 *Cribbing is a common form of self-stimulation that stabled horses engage in. The behavior reinforces itself by triggering the release of endorphins, natural opioids produced within the body.* Animals Animals © Renee Stockdale.

amounts of water all day long, bite repeatedly at its own flank or legs, or "crib bite"—grab hold of the edge of a board or other solid surface with the incisor teeth, arch the neck, and swallow a gulp of air (figure 4.3).

Although injury or disease that affects the nervous system can result in abnormal behavior in any animal, stall vices are so common in horses, and form such a clear and consistent pattern, that they appear to arise from some basic mechanism present in all horses.

This implies that there must be an evolutionary story at the heart of these abnormal behaviors. It seems unlikely that they are adaptive in themselves; none seems to help increase a horse's survival and most are frankly harmful. Horses that bite themselves can actually leave serious flesh wounds; cribbers can wear down the incisors to the point that they can no longer graze.

But evolution plays the averages. No trait is adaptive under all circumstances that an animal may encounter in its lifetime. The immune system that protects us from infection has also bequeathed to many of us the annoying tendency to sneeze at ragweed pollen. On balance, though, allergies are a small price to pay for not dying when we get a cold. Stall vices in horses may, by the same token, be an unintended side effect of a fundamentally adaptive behavioral mechanism.

That is precisely what recent evidence suggests. The striking thing about all stall vices in horses is that they are exaggerated forms of some of the horse's most basic, instinctive, and presumably hard-wired motor patterns—eating, moving, grooming. A number of similar human disorders (hyperactivity, obsessive-compulsive behavior, Tourette's syndrome) have been associated with the abnormally high activation of certain pathways used by the brain to send nerve signals out to the body. These pathways involve dopamine—a chemical messenger, or neurotransmitter, that causes certain nerve cells to fire when it attaches to a special receptor site on the cell surface.

Stimulant drugs such as amphetamines ("speed") likewise seem to owe their effect to an ability to trigger the release of excess dopamine within the brain. Experiments in which humans and various other animals are given large amounts of stimulant drugs produce precisely these same sorts of repeated, stereotyped behaviors. Cats move about incessantly, looking from side to side and sniffing. Monkeys pick and probe at themselves. Rats gnaw the bars of their cages. Humans, quite interestingly, engage in repetitive and compulsive acts of sorting and manipulating objects; women subjects often empty and rearrange the contents of their handbags over and over. Excessive stimulation of the dopamine pathway in different species seems to trigger activities that are in a sense characteristic of the fundamental behaviors of each.

Other experiments have shown that narcotics such as morphine seem to have a similar effect, either by increasing the release of dopamine in the brain or by making the receptors more sensitive to its presence. This led veterinarian Nicholas Dodman and his colleagues to wonder if perhaps the stereotypic behavior in stall vices was actually somehow triggered by the natural, opiumlike compounds known as enkephalins and endorphins that the body itself produces, especially in response to stressful stimuli. Dodman's results were nothing short of astonishing: seven crib-biting horses were given injections of chemicals known to block the effect of narcotics; in all seven cases the frequency of crib-biting dropped from several times a minute (and from a high of 15 a minute) to zero within 20 minutes. In some cases the effect of a single injection lasted for days. An experiment with a stallion who engaged in extreme self-mutilative behavior produced similar results; he went from striking at himself 69 times in a four-hour period to 4 times in four hours after receiving a dose of a narcotic blocker.

The body's natural ability to release endorphins in response to stress, and the ability of these natural opioids to stimulate the dopamine pathway, makes adaptive sense. In the natural environment, stress usually demands a fight-or-flight response; activating the basic motor instincts (via dopamine) and increasing tolerance for pain (via the opioids directly) is a prudent course of action. The well-known ability of soldiers in battle or football players in a game to carry on oblivious to serious injury is a good example of the effect of natural opioids released in response to stress.

A natural feedback mechanism may help to keep the whole system in balance. Eating, walking, grooming, and other basic activities appear to act on the so-called pleasure center of the brain, which in effect "rewards" these important activities with a release of endorphins. Przewalski's horses in natural settings will spend half or more of their time in a 24-hour period grazing, and nearly 10 percent of their time walking or running (figure 4.4). A horse denied the chance to engage in these activities (as are many stabled horses fed concentrated feeds and turned out for only an hour or less a day) may in effect fall into a vicious circle. Stress tends to activate the stereotyped motor patterns, which in turn stimulate the release of endorphins, which further stimulate the stereotypical behavior. At the same time, the pain-killing effect of the endorphins may inure the horse to the pain of self-mutilative behavior or the constant tensing of the neck muscles in cribbing, allowing the cycle to continue.

Of course, many horses kept under identical conditions

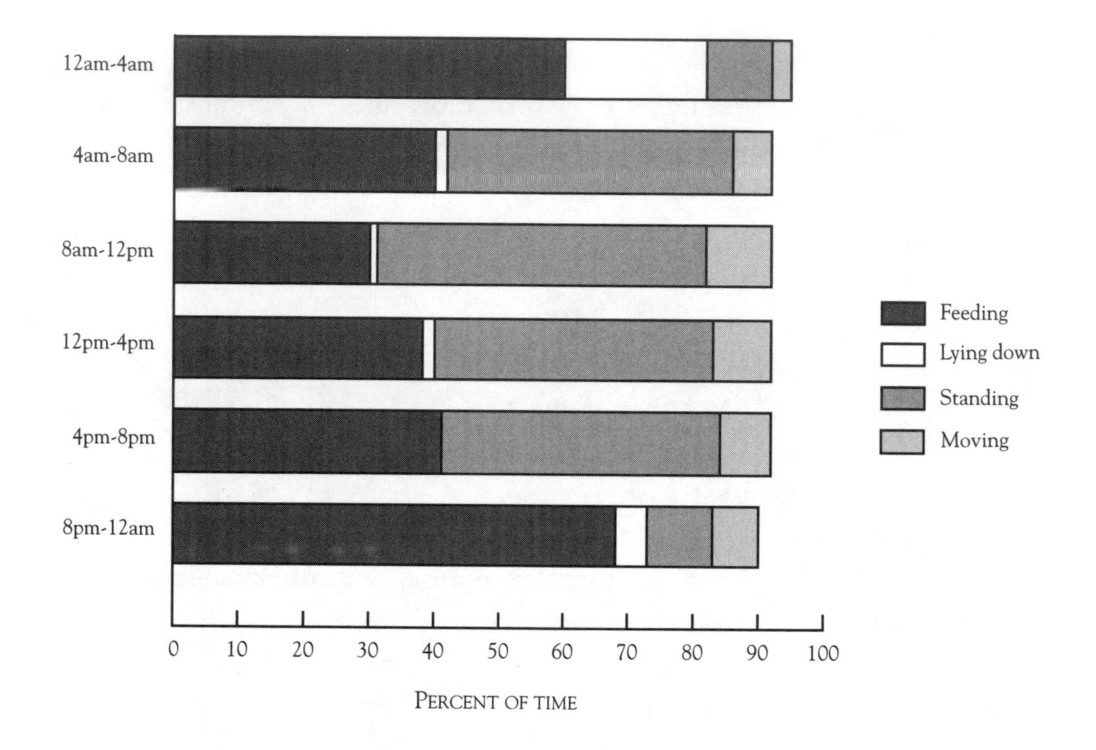

FIGURE 4.4 *Time budgets of Przewalski's horses show that eating and standing around are fundamental behaviors even of wild horses.*

never develop these abnormal behaviors, so stress is not the sole explanation. There is some evidence of a hereditary tendency toward stall vices: Dodman suggests that susceptible horses may start out with naturally low endorphin levels and initially engage in these behaviors in an attempt to raise them; in the end they become "endorphin junkies."

But this research suggests that a mechanism evolved to deal with the occasional stress of life in the wild can easily backfire under the stresses of artificial confinement in an animal adapted to a very different environment. The ability of most horses to tolerate what humans dish out to them is all the more remarkable testimony to their adaptability and learning ability.

CHAPTER 5

SEEING AND PERCEIVING

Vision is the most direct link to their environment that all higher animals possess. Besides being a window to the outside world, vision provides, to a very great extent, the basic organizing principal of the conscious mind. Visual images in humans often define our very conception of the world and are the currency of our most abstract thought processes.

The same is surely true of other higher animals. To understand the fundamental nature of these animals—and above all how and why they react as they do to things in their environment—we must at least make an attempt to understand the unique way each species sees and perceives the world around it.

It goes without saying that this is no easy task. A horse's eyes are obviously very different from a human's. They are huge, for one thing—the largest eyes of any land mammal. Set on the side of the head, they can together command a field of view of nearly 360 degrees, taking in the entire horizon, including almost the entire area directly to the rear.

But more important than their physical optics and placement is the way those eyes are wired to the brain, which differs in a number of significant ways in the horse. The mechanics of the horse's eye creates an optical image very different from the one produced by the human eye, and the horse's brain uses that image to construct a picture of the world even further removed from our own. Because of the paramount importance of the brain in defining visual perception, we can never truly see the world through a horse's eyes. (In fact the retina, the assemblage of nerves at the back of the eye that are stimulated by visual light and transmit signals to the brain, is really an extension of the brain itself.)

Vision is not a passive process, like light passing through a camera lens onto a piece of film; it is an active process in which the brain pieces together and processes raw visual data to assemble a completed mental image of a scene—its color, its depth, its motion, its detail. To see as a horse sees we would need a horse's brain.

Compared to other species, relatively little research has even been done on vision in horses. However, studies of the physical structure of the horse's eye, optical measurements of its focusing power, anatomical examinations of the distribution of light-sensitive cells on the retina and of the nerves that connect those cells to the brain, and psychological tests of the horse's ability to distinguish various visual objects all provide interesting clues about what a horse perceives—and what it does not—when it looks out on its world.

Standing Vigil

The panoramic view afforded by the horse's eye is an obvious evolutionary adaptation to the threat of predation. A horse holding its head level has but two narrow blind spots, which extend a few meters directly behind the rump and a few centimeters directly in front of the nose (figure 5.1). The horse's near 360-degree field of view in effect allows it to assume that it will see anything that approaches; a horse surprised in its blind spot to the rear will be all the more

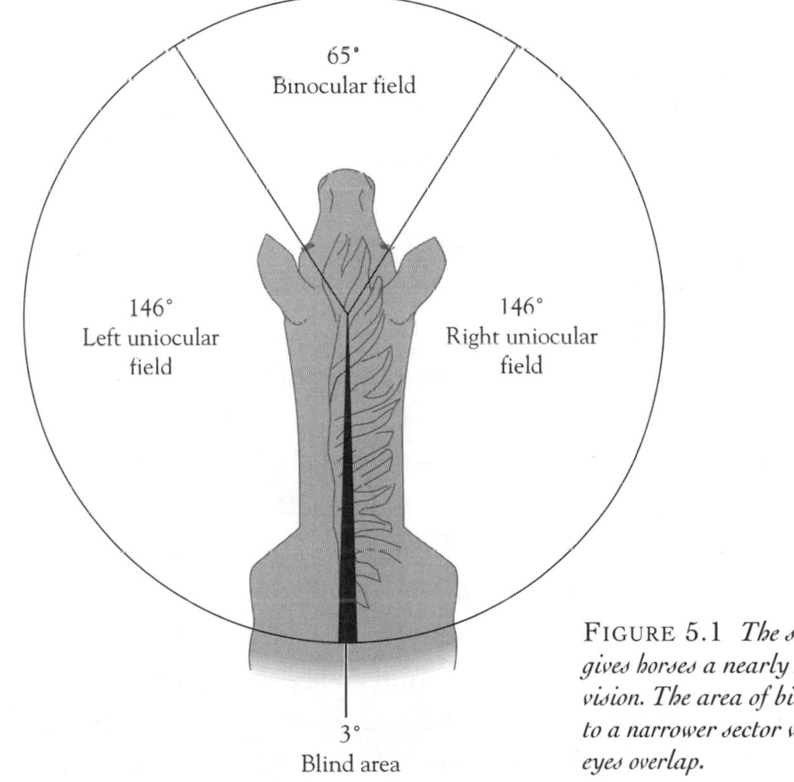

FIGURE 5.1 *The side placement of the eyes gives horses a nearly 360-degree field of vision. The area of binocular vision is limited to a narrower sector where the fields of both eyes overlap.*

startled because it is so accustomed to *not* being surprised.

A wide field of view comes at a price, however. The placement of the eyes on the side of the head allows for a panoramic view in the horizontal plane of vision, and the long muzzle that separates the eyes from the mouth allows a grazing horse to keep its eyes peeled for danger. But it creates blind spots in other situations. Although a horse looking straight ahead has only a very small blind spot directly in front of the nose in the horizontal plane of vision, it has a much greater blind spot on the ground below, where the nose gets in the way. A horse rotating its forequarters upward to take off over a jump cannot see the jump. It must rely on the image of the jump it obtained a stride or two out and negotiate the actual jump blind. (Sometimes horses will tilt their heads sideways to try to get a good look at a jump at the last second.)

The lateral placement of the eyes also limits the range of the visual field that can be commanded by both eyes simultaneously, and thus the horse's ability to perceive depth stereoscopically (more on this below).

Another mechanical limitation of the horse's eye has to do with its focusing ability. Fundamentally, the eye works to focus an image onto the light-sensitive cells of the retina at the back of the eye by means of the curved lens at the front of the eye. For a lens of a given shape and size and material, near objects are focused to a point farther back behind the lens than are distant objects (figure 5.2). To bring near objects into focus on the retina, an animal needs to change the shape of the lens, a process termed accommodation. Accommodation in humans and many other animals is accomplished with muscles that squeeze the lens, in effect making it fatter, thereby shifting the focus of near objects from a point behind the retina so that it falls squarely on the retina.

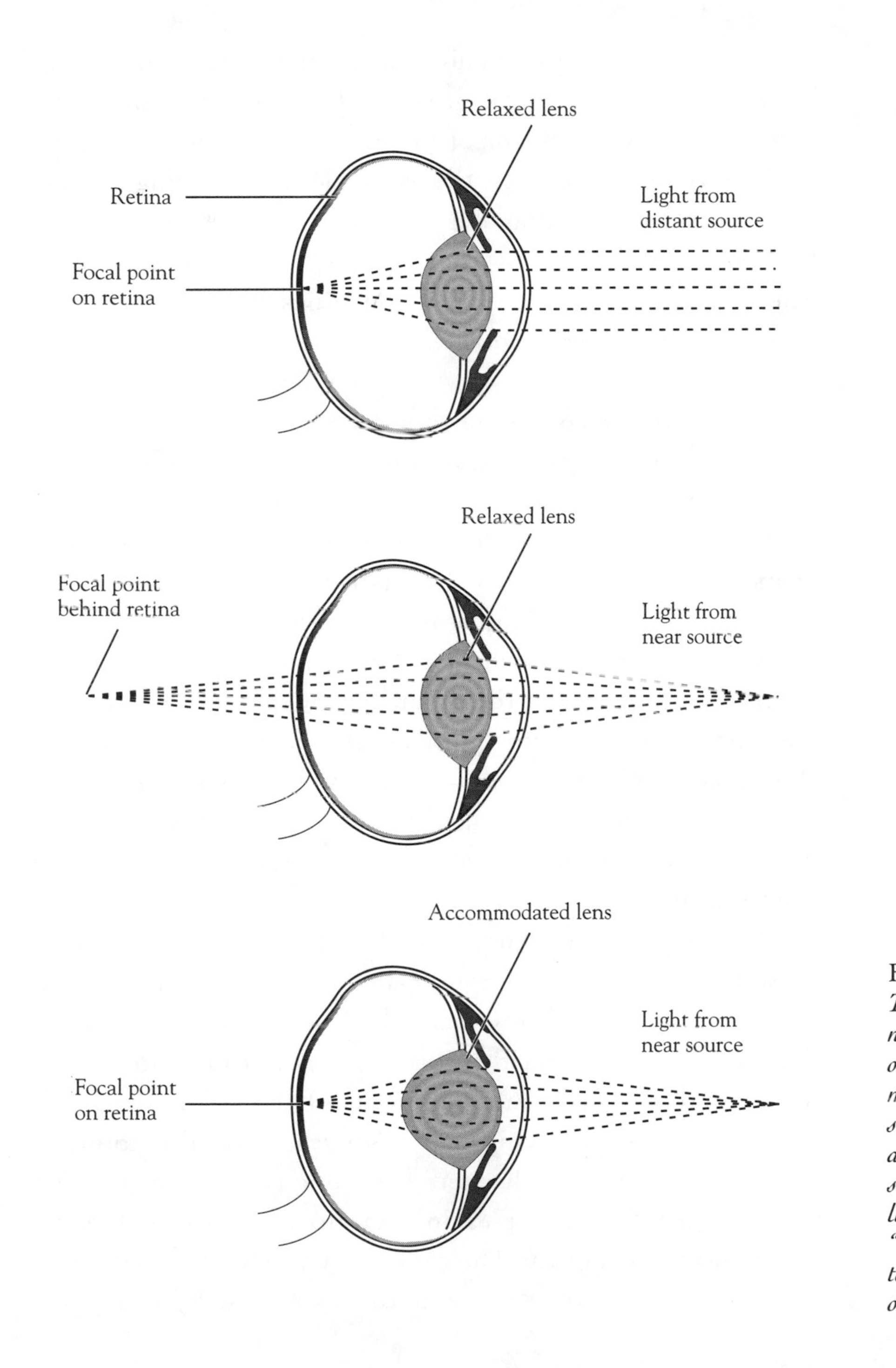

FIGURE 5.2
The horse's eye is naturally focused on distant objects; muscles that squeeze the lens and change its shape provide a limited amount of "accommodation" to bring close objects into focus.

Humans and other animals that use their hands to manipulate objects have by far the greatest ability to accommodate; in humans the optical power of the lens can change by as much as 10 diopters, which is the equivalent of putting on and taking off an exceptionally thick pair of eyeglasses indeed (normal eyeglasses rarely exceed about 4 diopters in power). Rabbits have zero accommodation, dogs have about 1 to 2 diopters, cats several diopters, and otters and beavers many more.

Horses were at one time thought to have no accommodation at all but an ability to partially overcome this limitation by virtue of a unique "ramp retina." The idea was that the shape of the horse's eye varied in such a fashion that the distance from the lens to the retina was shortest along the main horizontal visual axis, but increased above and below it. Thus close objects viewed above or below the axis of the eye would be in focus at the same time that distant objects viewed along the axis were also in focus. A horse would be able to bring close objects into focus automatically simply by tilting its head slightly; and while grazing, it could simultaneously focus on the grass in front of its face and the distant horizon to keep watch for predators.

The ramp retina theory is still frequently repeated, even in some veterinary textbooks; however, a major study of horse eyes in 1975 firmly discredited it. In fact it was found that the lens-to-retina distance is *shorter* above and below the main axis. Direct measurements of the refractive power of the lenses of a (living) horse's eyes were also found to vary by as much as 2 diopters from one reading to the next, indirect proof that horses in fact do have some dynamic accommodation ability. The same measurements have shown that the normal horse eye is naturally focused just right to bring a distant object sharply into focus on the retina.

Other studies have since found that a narrow horizontal strip of the horse retina, lying directly along the main axis, contains a very high concentration of light-sensitive cells and their associated nerve cells, or ganglia. The concentration of ganglia was found to be as high as 5,000 cells per square millimeter along this sensitive streak; above and below it the concentration was less than one-hundredth as great (figure 5.3). This means that images of objects viewed off-axis fall on insensitive regions of the retina, which are incapable of perceiving fine detail.

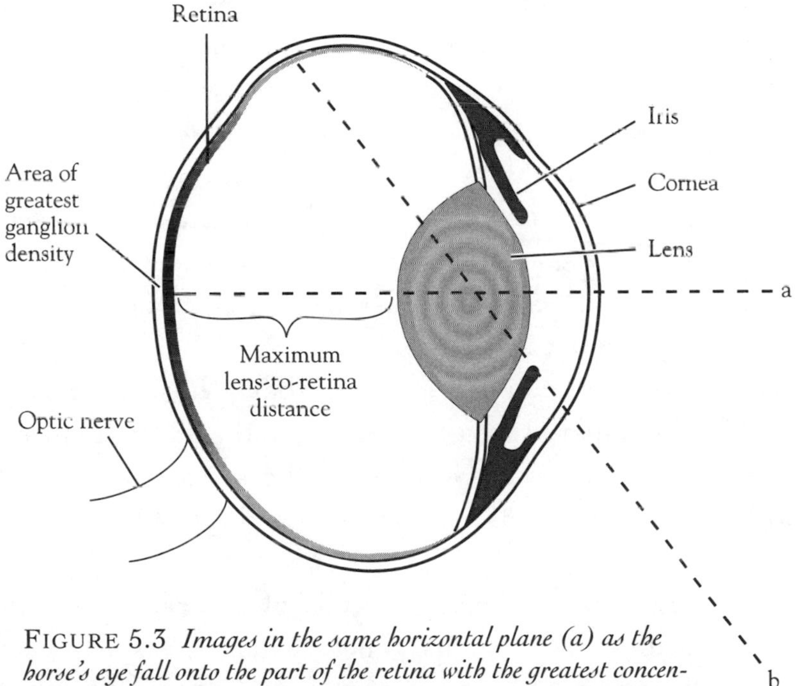

FIGURE 5.3 *Images in the same horizontal plane (a) as the horse's eye fall onto the part of the retina with the greatest concentration of ganglia, the light-sensitive nerve cells of the eye. Images above or below the plane (b) fall on less sensitive regions of the retina.*

These findings suggest that horses may indeed have to move their heads up and down to see objects in sharp detail. And they may well explain why a horse will suddenly shy at an object that has been within its field of view for some time; what is probably happening is that a poorly perceived object within the visual field suddenly sails into sharp view as the horse moves its head or body and the image falls on the visual streak.

The large size of the horse's eye and its natural state of sharp focus on distant objects combine to give the horse a high degree of visual acuity. This is the ability to distinguish details of an object at a distance. One way this can be measured is by training an animal to choose (by pecking or nosing) a card marked with alternating black and white stripes in preference to a solid gray card, and then presenting it with cards containing ever narrower stripe patterns. At the point where the stripes blur together, the animal will no longer be able to distinguish between the two cards. A blue jay can discern extremely narrow stripes, ones that fill as little as a hundredth of a degree of its visual field; humans can perceive stripes that fill more than about one-thirtieth of a degree of field; horses, about one-twentieth of a degree.

Another way of expressing this is that a horse's acuity is about 20/33 compared to a normal sighted human; that is, a detail a human can discern at 33 feet a horse can discern only if it is 20 feet away. But that is better than dogs (20/50) or cats (20/100).

A preponderance of rods, the cells of the retina that are sensitive to dim light, versus cones, which are sensitive to color, gives horses excellent night vision. This is aided by a structure called the tapetum, a layer of cells behind the retina that actually acts like a mirror to reflect light back, in effect giving the light-sensitive cells of the retina a second shot at picking up small amounts of light that enter the eye. The tapetum, which is also found in dogs and cats and many other mammals (especially nocturnal ones), is what accounts for the glowing eyes of animals caught in a headlight's beam. (A flash picture of a human tends to produce "red-eye" from the reflection of the red blood vessels behind the retina; dogs show up with orange or yellow eyes from the direct reflection by the tapetum of the light of the flash.)

But "excellent" night vision is a relative term. Day or night, vision depends upon light, and nothing can alter the fact that there is not much light around at night. It takes longer at night for the light-sensitive cells of the retina to accumulate enough light to trigger a response, and fast-moving objects can dart by unnoticed. The reflectivity of the tapetum amplifies what light is available, but also tends to smear the incoming image, triggering several receptors at a time; the effect is like increasing the pixel size on a computer screen or the graininess of film. A horse can certainly see better than we can at night, but it does so at the price of a considerable loss in acuity.

Living Color

Horses have far less need to see in color than do birds or insects that feed on fruits and flowers. But the color-sensitive cones of the eye play a role beyond simply allowing an animal to see in color. The highly sensitive rods can be overwhelmed in bright light, while cones, which require more light to trigger a signal, are better adapted to bright conditions. So at least the rudiments of color vision are a simple consequence of the need for an eye that can see during both night and day.

But it takes more than just cones to see in color: it requires having more than one kind of cone. Cones (and rods, too) are most sensitive to light of a specific wavelength. They absorb light most strongly when it matches that optimal wavelength; the absorption, and thus the strength of the nerve signal sent, drops off as the wavelength moves away from this peak. Rods, or a single type of cone, can tell how *much* light is coming in, but they cannot by themselves distinguish between a reduction in intensity and a shift in color; both cause a drop-off in response. An animal with nothing but cones most sensitive to, say, the wavelength of green light would perceive colors as various shades of gray, with green perceived as the brightest gray and blues and reds as darker shades. But it could not even tell red from blue.

Humans and other animals, including most primates, that are able to see in full color have three kinds of cones, each sensitive to a different wavelength of light; these correspond approximately to blue, green, and red. By comparing the relative response of each type of cone to an incoming light signal, the eye and brain are able to sort out both the intensity of the light and where in the wavelength spectrum it falls. The best color vision is in the parts of the spectrum where the response curves of all three cones overlap—that provides the best fix on the wavelength.

Studies in horses seem to suggest that they, like many other mammals, are what are known as dichromates—they have two kinds of cones, allowing a limited sort of color vision that is analogous to color blindness in humans.

Determining whether an animal has color vision at all is a tricky proposition. The usual method is first to train an animal by rewarding it for picking a colored panel versus a white panel, and then to find out whether it can still consistently pick the colored panel when it is presented alongside a gray panel. Part of the problem is that differences in brightness between the colored and gray panels can inadvertently give cues that even an animal with monochromatic, black-and-white vision can pick up on. The way to control for this is to match the total reflectance of the colors to the reflectance of the grays as closely as possible to start with, and then to present each color in a range of brightnesses alongside a variety of gray panels also covering a range of brightnesses. If the animal can pick the colored one in every case, it is reasonably certain that it really can see the color.

A recent study by David Pick and his colleagues found that after training in about 100 trials, a horse could learn to consistently pick red over gray; it was able to pick blue from gray after a further 243 trials; and it failed ever to consistently tell green from gray despite more than 1,400 trials.

Having only red-blue color vision does not precisely correspond to any of the most common forms of human color blindness, but it means that colors such as green, which fall between blue and red in the spectrum, and thus stimulate the two types of cones equally (and weakly), cannot be distinguished from whites or grays. Thus the failure of the horse to tell green from gray. It also means that at either end of the spectrum, where really only one cone at a time is sensitive to light to any considerable extent, it is impossible for the horse to tell the difference between changes in hue and changes in intensity. Red, orange, and possibly yellow all probably look much the same, just relatively darker or lighter (plate 5).

The adaptive value of color vision in horses is a matter of controversy, but one important consideration may be that color vision helps animals see through camouflage, something important for predators and prey alike. Hiding from an animal that can see only in black and white is much easier than hiding from one that can see in color. Blending in in black and white is just a matter of matching the overall intensity of light reflected by the surrounding background; to blend in in color is a much more demanding proposition, especially given the multiplicity of colors found in nature. Color vision provides an extra reality check that makes ambushes a lot more difficult.

Depth Perception

The need of predators to penetrate camouflage when stalking prey puts a premium on another aspect of visual ability: depth perception. A camouflaged insect clinging to a leaf is hard to see in a two-dimensional photograph (or with one eye covered); it is easier to pick out in real life because our stereoscopic vision allows us to perceive that it is sitting on the surface of the leaf and not in the same plane as the leaf.

Stereo vision is possible when the field of view of both eyes overlap to take in the same scene. The overlap is maximized in animals that have forward-mounted eyes, such as primates and predators like cats and hawks; it is restricted in animals such as horses with side-mounted eyes.

Because each eye is viewing the same object from a slightly different position in binocular vision, there is a discrepancy between the image formed by each eye that increases the closer the object gets. (You can verify this by holding a finger close in front of your eyes and alternately closing each eye; the finger appears to shift quite a bit left and right as it is viewed in turn by each eye. When you hold it at arm's length, the shift is noticeably smaller.)

In lower species, such as monotremes like the duck-billed

platypus, the visual signals relayed by each eye are nearly completely segregated when they reach the brain. The nerves from the left eye run to the right brain, those from the right eye to the left brain. But in primates, there is a nearly even split—50 percent of the information that travels on the optic nerve from each eye is sent to each half of the brain. This sharing of information allows the brain to more readily compare the discrepancy, and thus accurately judge depth. The resolving power of the human eye and brain is extraordinary; if you hold two needles, one above the other, at arm's length, you can tell if one is as little as 0.2 millimeters closer than the other.

In the horse, only about an eighth to a sixth of the information from each eye crosses over and is sent to the corresponding side of the brain. Horses also have a limited field of binocular vision: the field of view of the two eyes overlaps by about 60 degrees of arc at the front.

Although this certainly suggests that horses have at least a limited ability to see stereoscopically when looking straight ahead, it does not prove it. Simply because the fields of both eyes overlap does not mean the brain is actually making use of the information—or rather the *discrepancy* in the information—coming from both eyes to create a three-dimensional visual image.

To test stereoscopic vision in horses, psychologist Brian Timney and his co-workers at the University of Western Ontario did a series of interesting experiments. First they trained horses to always pick (by pressing it with their nose) a panel painted with a flat image of a square superimposed on a background of dots. The other panel was similar, except that the square actually protruded from the background. Then Timney tested how well the horses did with one eye covered. In general, they picked the right panel only about one-fifth as often, and they had a much harder time distinguishing the two panels as the distance the square protruded was reduced. The researchers found that horses, when using both eyes, could perceive a depth difference of about 10 centimeters when viewed at a distance of 200 centimeters. Cats and pigeons show about the same ability.

A second experiment offered even more direct proof of horses' ability to see in stereo. The researchers used what are called random-dot stereograms, pairs of two-dimensional images that on casual inspection appear to be identical patterns of random dots and blobs. But the dots in a portion of one of the two images are slightly shifted relative to the other. When one of the images is viewed by the left eye while the other is viewed by the right eye, the shifted patterns combine, in viewers that possess true stereoscopic vision, to produce a three-dimensional image. In effect, these stereograms are optical illusions that exploit the way the brain translates a discrepancy in signals coming from the left and right eye into a perception of depth.

In order to direct each image to the correct eye, one image can be printed in green and the other in red; the viewer is then fitted with glasses that have a green lens on one eye and a red lens on the other. (This was the basis of the 3-D movies that had a brief vogue in the '50s.) Timney's group accordingly fitted their horses with red and green goggles, and in place of the image of a real protruding square presented a random-dot stereogram that created an image of a protruding square when viewed through the colored lenses. The horses that had been trained to pick the image of the flat square over the one with a protruding square also showed a marked preference for the flat image in these tests.

In judging the distance or depth of an object, many animals

can use a variety of cues that do *not* rely on the ability to see in stereo. Thus, even when viewing objects that fall outside their limited field of binocular vision, horses may well have some depth perception. (One indication that a horse is viewing an object binocularly is if its ears are erect and pointing forward.)

Humans, for example, apparently derive a certain amount of depth information just from the angle at which the eyes are focused on an object. Chickens use shadows to determine whether an object is convex (a piece of corn) or concave (a small hole in the ground). And many animals, ranging from frogs to human infants, will instinctively draw away from an object that appears to rapidly increase in size, interpreting such "looming" as a cue that the object is moving toward them.

Another kind of monocular depth cue involves correctly interpreting perspective effects—the fact that similar objects look smaller the farther away they are. The very fact that we are able to interpret a two-dimensional painting or photograph as a three-dimensional scene is testimony to our strong use of perspective cues. It is also why we are susceptible to many optical illusions that play on our innate tendency to interpret flat lines in a two-dimensional scene in terms of perspective effects.

To test whether horses are able to perceive perspective, Timney's group in effect tried to see if they, too, would fall for such an optical illusion. First the horses were presented with panels that had two horizontal lines drawn on them, one on top of the other. They were trained to always pick the one in which the top line was longer than the bottom one; the other panel had two lines of equal length. Then the horses were presented with the illusion: on one panel two lines of equal length were superimposed on a background photograph showing an ordinary pastoral scene; on the other, two lines, also of equal length, were superimposed on a photo of a receding railroad track. This latter is known as the Ponzo illusion, and it has been well studied in psychological tests in humans (figure 5.4). Because humans automatically interpret the perspective cues in the image of the receding railroad track (it gets narrower the farther away it is), they misinterpret the relative length of the superimposed lines. The eye expects objects of equal size to appear larger in the foreground and smaller in the background, so the equal-length lines are judged on a different scale according to their location in the

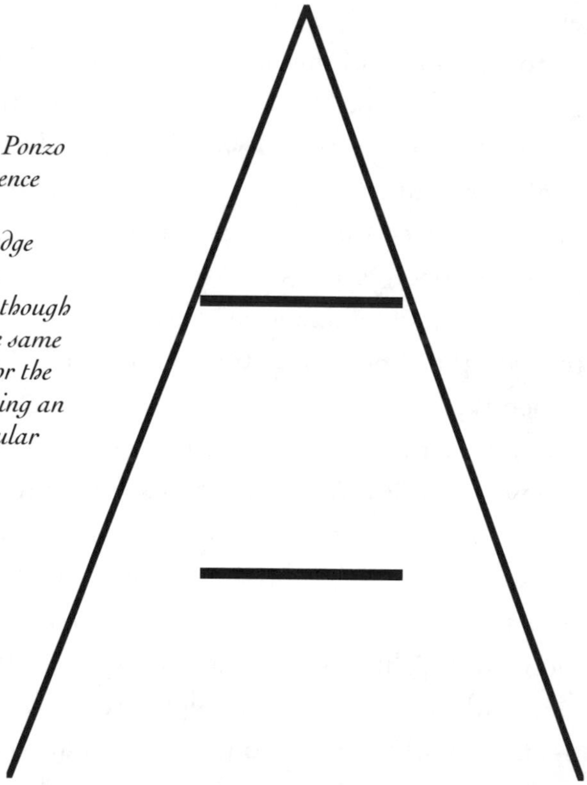

FIGURE 5.4 *The Ponzo illusion is a consequence of our ability to use perspective cues to judge distance: the top line appears longer, even though both are actually the same length. Horses fall for the illusion, too, suggesting an ability to use monocular depth cues.*

picture. The top one—the one in the "background"—gives the illusory impression of being longer.

The horses were fooled too. Having been trained to always pick the image with the longer line on top, they also picked the image in which the perspective cues made the top line *appear* to be longer (that is, the one with the railroad tracks) 90 percent of the time in 50 trials.

This certainly suggests, though it does not prove, that horses are not completely unable to judge distance, even when they are looking out of only one eye at a time. Horses are sometimes thrown off by confusing lines in front of a jump, which appears to indicate some difficulty in depth perception. On the other hand, horses are able to judge the width of a jump very accurately, especially with experience, and these monocular cues may be an essential part of the way horses make such informed, and essential, judgments about their environment in carrying out the demands we make of them.

CHAPTER 6

HORSE TALK

Compared to birds, dogs, raccoons, monkeys, and many other animals, horses have a distinctly limited vocal repertoire.

At first this seems surprising, as horses are intensely social animals, and communication is above all a means of maintaining order and cohesion in the social group. The members of any given species spend remarkably little time "talking" to other species; almost all of their vocal efforts are directed to their own kind: young calling for their mothers, males calling for mates, dominants warning off subordinates, subordinates appeasing dominants, members of the group calling the attention of others to food or danger.

As animals of the open grasslands, however, horses were able to evolve an elaborate and sophisticated system of visual communication for many of these functions. Members of a harem are rarely out of sight of one another, which makes visual signals effective and vocal signals unnecessary. There is a consistent pattern among mammals, with forest-dwelling species having more elaborate vocal signals than open-dwelling species, and social animals having more elaborate signals than solitary ones. Thus the forest-dwelling wild boar (and the domestic pig that descended from it) produces a rich array of sounds, more than a dozen different forms of grunts, squeals, and chirps; the open-dwelling cow and sheep produce comparatively few, as does the forest-dwelling but solitary deer.

Vocal signals are not only less necessary to an animal that evolved on the open grasslands; they are actually less effective, too. There is little question who the intended recipient is when a horse swings its head or raises a hoof at another; a vocal threat (such as the dog's growl) is far more ambiguous. It is interesting that pigs have a harder time learning and discriminating visual cues than they do smells and sounds. They also lack the fine structure of facial muscles that horses possess—which allow the latter to assume a much wider variety of expressive facial gestures.

Communication or Manipulation?

Attempts to assign precise semantic meanings to animal sounds have long been a preoccupation of both animal behaviorists and animal lovers. Both have been guilty of anthropomorphism. The animal lover's sentimental desire to believe that his pets are talking to him is easy enough to understand. That scientists for years should have pursued the same red herring is a symptom of a more subtle failing.

Part of the problem is that we tend to be misled by the very uniqueness of human speech. Actual language, human language, is indeed unique in both its structure and purpose. It is manifestly about *communication,* a cooperative process in which information is encoded into sounds, transferred from a sender to a receiver, and then decoded. Being only human, scientists have perhaps all too naturally looked at animal vocalizations in the same light, as a process of information transfer.

Thus animal behaviorists for many years attempted to interpret animal calls as specific signals conveying specific bits of information. An animal's vocalizations were carefully recorded and sorted into categories, and then were assigned meanings according to what the animal was doing at the time. Animals were said to have mating calls, food calls, warning calls, threat calls, and so on. Most attempts to categorize horse vocalizations have headed down this same misleading semantic path.

The objective business of looking at the various sounds of the horse as recorded on sonograms—graphs that show the pitch of a sound versus time—and then putting them into categories based on their tonal characteristics is straightforward enough, however, and there are four basic types of horse sounds that most researchers identify: the nicker, blow, squeal, and whinny.

The nicker is a quite low-pitched sound, about 100 Hz (about the same as the note G an octave and a half below middle C, or about the lowest note that a human male singer can comfortably hit in the bass range); it is a soft sound, not very tonal, and formed with the mouth shut.

The blow, made by blowing a rapid pulse of air through the nose, is much louder; a horse's blow can often be heard at a distance of 200 meters. It is a short, percussive, nontonal sound, containing a lot of different pitches blended together;

overall it tends to quickly rise and fall in both loudness and pitch.

The squeal is much louder still and contains a tonal component at around 1,000 Hz (or around C two octaves above middle C), but it still carries a lot of nontonal harshness.

The whinny, another quite loud call, often varies in pitch, starting high (up to about 2,000 Hz) and then dropping to half the starting frequency.

The problems come with the attempt to assign meanings to these various sounds. There has been no clear agreement; various authors interpret different sounds differently, or create complex subcategories or intermediate sounds (the "sigh-nicker") that are supposed to stand for different moods or messages—frustration, excitement, playfulness, or loneliness, greeting calls or mating calls.

The underlying problem with all of this, with horses or any other animal, is that the meanings assigned to specific "calls" never seem to hold up very well on closer inspection. The "food" calls researchers attributed to many birds often turned out to be used in a lot of other circumstances having nothing whatever to do with food. Calls that ought to express entirely different messages often seemed remarkably similar. A mating call of a sexually mature adult, for example, might resemble the plaintive call of a young animal begging for food from its mother—as is the case with the horse's low nicker.

A deeper problem, pointed out by evolutionary biologists, is that a complex, cooperative system of communication would often appear to defy the rules of natural selection. For a vocalization to have evolved in the first place, it has to confer some survival value on the individual animal that is actually making the sound. It is not enough to say that a certain sound "means" excitement. The real question is, why is it to an individual's advantage to make this sound under certain circumstances? How does it function to increase its chances of survival? The purely linguistic view of animal communication fails to engage this basic question of *why* certain sounds came to be used in certain contexts.

Eugene Morton, an ornithologist and authority on animal communication, argues that asking what a sound *accomplishes* rather than what it *means* is the first step toward understanding what animal communication is really about.

One of the distinguishing features of human language is that its sounds are arbitrary—there is no inherent meaning in the sounds we use to stand for particular things. (This is obviously true, since thousands of different sounds are used by human beings speaking thousands of different languages the world over to stand for the same word.) But animal communication, as Morton and others have begun to discover, falls into some consistent patterns across species. Throughout the animal kingdom the same kinds of sounds consistently seem to be used to accomplish the same ends, whether in birds or dogs or elephants. The way to begin to understand horse sounds is by looking at whines, barks, and growls. Dogs do it, of course, but so do birds and a lot of other animals that we don't usually think of in connection with these familiar sounds.

Sounding Small

It is an acoustical fact that big things make low-pitched sounds, small things make high-pitched sounds. A long cello string vibrates more slowly, and thus sounds a lower note, than a short ukulele string; the air in a tuba vibrates more slowly than the air in a penny whistle.

It is a biological fact that over millions of years of evolution, animals that learned to avoid big things tended to survive. Those that didn't got eaten. Conversely, those that ran away from every squeak of a mouse or buzz of a fly wasted a lot of energy and probably did not fare too well, either. Learning to tell who was big and who was small from the sounds they made had clear survival value.

Eugene Morton argues that these basic facts serve to explain a great deal about why animals use the sounds they do, and about what those sounds in fact "mean." Because so many species must have been preconditioned to associate low sounds with large animals and high sounds with small animals, the vocal expression of social signals would naturally evolve in a fashion that exploits this preexisting code. Threats (the dog's growl) are deep and harsh because that sound got results; it got results because birds and mammals are predisposed to avoid things that make deep, harsh sounds. Appeasing or submissive sounds (the dog's whine) are high-pitched and tonal because that sound avoids provoking an aggressive response; it does so because of the evolved predisposition to recognize anything that makes such sounds as nonthreatening.

These "motivational-structural" rules for animal sounds work exceptionally well across a vast range of bird and mammal species. We don't normally think of birds growling and whining, but if you record a barn swallow's stuttering rasp and whistle and play them back slowed down, their similarity to a dog's growl and whine is remarkable.

Barks, interestingly, are precisely halfway between a growl and a whine. They often appear as a chevron-shaped sound on a sonogram, rising and then falling; they have some of the harsh, nontonal raspiness of the growl and some of the musical tonality of a whine (figure 6.1). Morton suggests that barks (also uttered by many species—think of the short chirp of a startled bird) are deliberately ambiguous calls; they serve to summon the attention of other members of the group to something in the environment and to announce one's presence to a potential intruder in a noncommittal way. They are in effect a way of saying, "I know you're there; I'm not threatening you but I'm not backing off either—you don't know yet what I'll do. (And *I* probably don't know yet, either.)" There are many circumstances in which such a deliberately ambiguous signal is useful and adaptive. It is a waste of valuable energy to run away from every potential threat; it is also wasteful and dangerous to aggressively challenge every poten-

FIGURE 6.1 *Basic sounds common to many mammals and birds: spectrograms of a whine, bark, and growl (in this case, of a Carolina wren). Whines and growls "mean" what they do because small, nonthreatening things naturally make high-pitched sounds, while big things make low sounds. The bark is an ambiguous, intermediate sound.*

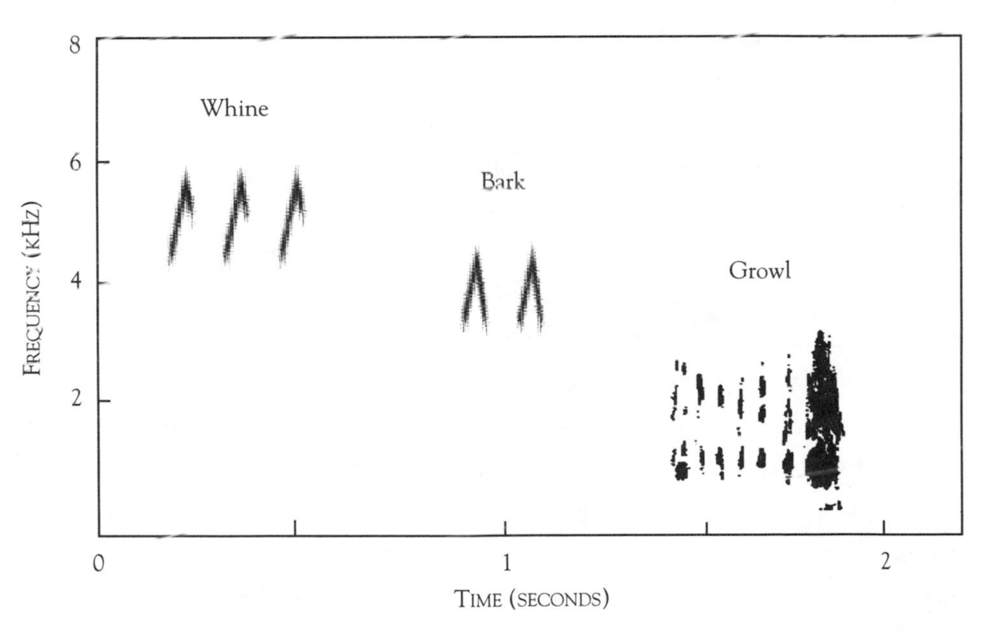

tial threat. The bark is a way for an animal to announce its presence before a fight or flight becomes inevitable, and to obtain more information before committing itself. It is also adaptive for the individual uttering the sound if it serves to summon aid (or at least mutual vigilance) from other members of the group. It is fascinating that this motivationally ambiguous signal is also structurally ambiguous according to Morton's rules.

Do Horses Bark?

How well do these rules explain horse vocalizations? Perhaps the best fit is with the horse's blow, which both acoustically and behaviorally is a classic bark.

Some researchers term the blow an "alarm" call or "danger" signal, but that is putting words into the horse's mouth (or, in this case, nose). Blows are used precisely as the motivational-structural rules would predict. A horse that is startled will turn toward the source, often freeze and stare at it for about 20 seconds, then blow and possibly make a cautious approach to investigate. In feral horses, a snort from the herd stallion will fix the attention of the other members of the group. It serves precisely the sort of temporizing function that Morton's rules suggest; it is an "interest" sound.

There is nothing in the horse's vocal repertoire that corresponds precisely to either a whine or a growl. Tapirs, a forest-dwelling relative of the equids, make a high whistle in fearful situations, and some zebras squeak and whistle in ways that might follow the general rule. But the basic expressions of threat and submission probably dropped out of the horse's vocal repertoire long ago. In the course of the horse's evolution from a forest to a grasslands animal, those functions were taken over by more effective and economical visual signals.

The horse's squeal also seems to follow the rules, but in a more complex fashion. If the bark is halfway between a whine and a growl, a squeal or shriek is a superposition of the two—a high-pitched sound with a rough, nontonal quality. Many animals utter this sort of sound in situations that combine fear and aggression. When horses squeal, typically in confrontations with other horses, the head posture is also expressive of simultaneous fear and aggression. The ears are often laid back, but the head is retracted and raised rather than extended and lowered in the usual aggressive stance. A nonreceptive mare may squeal in response to a sexual approach by a stallion, and this makes sense: it is an aggressive signal from a subordinate.

Whether the squeal is strictly speaking adaptive, or whether it simply represents the combination of two adaptive sounds and has no special adaptive value in itself, is a difficult question to answer. In some extreme situations, such as extreme pain and fright, squeals or shrieks seem to be more an uncontrollable outcry than an adaptive attempt to manipulate the environment. (Though even here there may be adaptive value on occasion; many birds and mammals will utter a "death shriek" when attacked by a predator, which once in a while may startle the predator into dropping its prey, allowing the victim to make good its escape.)

But the way stallions most often use squeals does suggest an adaptive purpose. When stallions encounter one another, four out of five times they avoid a physical fight. But they often engage in squealing "contests." Biologist Daniel Rubenstein found that the squeals of dominant stallions last about 20 seconds longer than those of low-ranking stallions. The squealing contest often seems to settle the matter, with the subordinate animal giving way. Rubenstein suggests that the duration of the squeal is a direct measure of lung capacity and the strength of a horse's chest muscles; in effect, squeals are "instantaneous indications of tenacity" in a real fight.

According to the motivational-structural rules, a squeal makes a certain amount of sense as the signal of choice for such a mock fight. It is clearly aggressive, but contains a superimposed component of defensiveness; one can imagine how an ancestral growl that expressed pure aggression and invariably led to physical confrontation was ritualized into a growl *cum* whine that conveyed the idea, "I don't like you, but I'm not going to attack you," in the context of a mock battle to be settled (not incidentally) by the use of the sound itself.

Matching the Sound to the Medium

The whinny and nicker admittedly seem to defy all the rules.

The nicker, which is clearly used to express submission, appeasement, or lack of hostile intent, is used by foals and mares greeting one another, by domestic horses begging for food, and by stallions approaching mares in courtship. According to the motivational-structural rules, submissive sounds ought to be whines—high-pitched and tonal. While the nicker *is* soft and gentle, it is also quite low-pitched, and not especially tonal.

Many mammals make similar sounds (the cat's purr); birds

do not. Morton suggests the reason is that these sounds aren't really sounds at all. They are "tactile" signals optimally designed to be felt through the body between nursing young and their mothers. Nursing young indeed do make these sounds (or maybe vibrations is a better word) as a way to make sure their mother knows where they are under her body or, in species that produce litters, to get her attention and a place at a teat. To travel through flesh rather than air, a signal *has* to vibrate at a low frequency; high-pitched sounds don't travel well through solids.

Having originally evolved for this role then, these low-pitched vibrations could naturally have become ritualized as a signal of submission or absence of threat—there is nothing less threatening than a juvenile.

Whinnies are also signals that probably evolved more for their acoustic carrying properties in the environment than for reasons involving the motivational-structural rules. Like a dog's howl, a whinny is a long-distance communication signal; like a dog's howl, too, it is acoustically optimized for carrying across long distances. In forests, signals that are tonal and relatively high-pitched, typically in the range of 1,500 to 3,500 Hz, usually travel best (the upper end of this range corresponds to about the highest note a piccolo can play). In open environments, a signal that is lower and "buzzy" is more efficient. These are indeed the characteristics of a horse's whinny, and common experience proves how far that sound can travel.

In horses the whinny allows members of the group to maintain contact when out of each other's visual range. Foals and mares will whinny if they lose sight of each other. In stabled horses, the departure of a stablemate will often evoke a whinny from the one left behind; a horse that is extremely hungry or frustrated will whinny, but generally only upon the approach of its handler. Whinnies are also sometimes used by feral horses apparently as a means of establishing their location in relation to other bands, either to make sure they stay out of one another's way, or sometimes as a prelude to an aggressive encounter.

Whinnies are, at least to some extent, individually recognizable. Mares respond more often to tape recordings of their own foals' whinnies than to the whinnies of other foals; feral horses will often reply only to the whinny of a member of their own band. Biologists James Feist and Dale McCullough, who carried out an extensive study of feral horses in Wyoming and Montana, several times observed a mare (Goldylocks) and her foal (Gold) lagging behind at a water hole after the rest of the band had moved on. When they finally left the hole, Goldylocks would often whinny; hearing this, the band's stallion (Triangle) would bring the group to a halt and wait for Goldylocks and Gold to catch up. The mare and foal were typically out of Triangle's sight and over a quarter of a mile away when they called. This degree of individuality makes good sense for a signal designed for situations where the usual form of individual recognition—physical appearance—is unavailable.

The whinny is a perfect example of what is wrong with the semantic view of animal communication. Attempts to apply a meaning to the whinny would result in many different and conflicting definitions—"I'm lost" or "Who are you?" or "Please come and help me" or "Stay out of my way" or "Wait for us to catch up." In fact a whinny is fundamentally a sound that travels well over distance; it is used whenever a horse needs to announce its presence to a horse or horses that are out of sight.

Italian Without Words

As we have already seen, horses use a wide array of visual signals for many of the important functions of social communication (figure 6.2). The evolution of these gestures is for the most part easy to explain. A head swing and an open mouth with bared teeth are a prelude to a bite; an extended foreleg is a prelude to a strike; a lifted hind leg is a prelude to a kick.

FIGURE 6.2
Aggressive visual signals are ritualized versions of bites or kicks.

These gestures have become ritualized precisely because their meaning is related in such an unambiguous way to actual aggressive actions. Similarly, as we have seen, the appeasement gesture of teeth clapping in foals is a ritualized version of grooming.

Other physical signals have undergone a further degree of ritualization that makes their origin and meaning harder for us (but of course not for horses) to immediately grasp. Laying back the ears has come to be a ritualized signal for aggression probably because that is what a horse would do to protect a vulnerable part of the body. A horse with its ears laid back is a horse prepared to fight; thus, over the course of evolution, it paid for a horse to take notice of other horses' ears if it wanted to stay out of trouble. The fact that "receivers" began to pay attention to this signal reinforced the selective advantage for "transmitters" to exaggerate the gesture as a threat even when an actual fight was not about to take place.

Tail lashing is another example of a social signal that probably evolved from such "mind reading." A horse irritated at a fly will flick its tail; in that sense tail flicking is an outward indicator of an internal, emotional state. A horse that is able to pick up on the emotional state of its fellows is likely to have an edge over less perceptive clods in the group; and so again, cause-and-effect reinforcement leads to the ritualization of the signal. If horses learn to stay out of the way of a horse that's flicking its tail (because he's in a snit over a fly that is bugging him), that sensitivity on the part of the receiver will sooner or later be exploited by the sender in other circumstances (when there are no flies involved). Physical gestures that may have originated for purely functional purposes can evolve into social signals if others in the group start using them to "mind read."

Humans, incidentally, may be even better than horses at reading horses' minds when it comes to some aspects of their body language. Although horses are clearly capable of many different facial expressions, no experiments have yet shown to what degree they actually read other's faces. Bite threats with the mouth pulled back seem clear enough, but more subtle expressions such as wrinkling the nose (irritation), drooping the lower lip (relaxation), or cocking the ear in the direction of a sound or object of interest may involve physiology more than communication. The horse's nose and mouth have many muscles and nerves, probably because grazers need sensitive muzzles to pick out their food, not because the face is important for communication. Ears obviously need to be able to point in the direction a sound is coming from. Muscles naturally tense in response to irritation and relax in response to calmness. None of which prevents us from taking note of these signs and acting accordingly. It just is not clear how much of this actually constitutes communication, in the sense of a deliberate effort to affect one's environment.

A final set of visual cues in the horse, and indeed in many animals, probably evolved from perceptions of size and from our well-established principle that big things are scarier than little things (with good reason). A dog will raise its hackles in threat, cringe in submission. Raised hackles are, in a sense, an effort to look big, as cringing is to look small.

The point is not that the dog is consciously imagining how it looks or that it is even "trying" to look big or small; the point is rather that over the course of evolution these gestures have become instinctive precisely because they work—at one time, they really did cause another animal to think it was confronting a big, scary dog or a small, unthreatening dog and to behave accordingly. In a sense these signals may not "fool" anyone these days, but that doesn't matter. It's in the interests of both sender and receiver to continue to act just as if the signal were a real measure of size—because it *is* a real measure of intentions.

Horses are less obvious about trying to look big or small, but a few postures are suggestive. A stallion showing off will stand with arched neck and raised tail; a submissive horse will tuck its tail between its legs and droop its head.

Scent Marking and Ritual

Humans are olfactory ignoramuses. Our vestigial sense of smell has left us blind to an entire world of animal communication.

Short of inventing writing, smell is the only means available to animals to communicate a message that lasts beyond the immediate moment. Smell plays a complex role in the social world of horses, primarily as a means for stallions to identify mares in heat and to keep track of the identity, degree of dominance, and location of potential rival stallions.

As with dogs and many other mammals, most of this communication takes place through urination and defecation. Feral stallions go to great pains to defecate in neat piles already used by themselves, by other members of their group, or by stallions in command of other harems (figure 6.3). Like dogs, stallions save up their eliminations, depositing only a small, controlled sample at a time on dung piles. In studies of feral horses, stallions defecated at established dung piles 90 percent of the time. They were particularly assiduous about urinating or defecating on top of eliminations from their own mares; a stallion will typically respond to a mare's elimination by sniffing the spot, then stepping over it and urinating or defecating directly on top. (Mares and geldings, by contrast, will sometimes smell the eliminations of others and then defecate without first stepping over, creating an enlarging ring of ground in the field covered with dung.)

Some researchers speculate that this may be an effort to cover up the odor given off by a mare in heat, and thus to discourage the attentions of potential rivals—a sort of jamming of the mare's signal. Stallions have a sensitive organ

FIGURE 6.3
Stallions carefully defecate on existing fecal piles in a ritual that transmits olfactory messages to other herds.

in the roof of their mouths that can detect the odor of an estrous mare; the behavior known as flehmen, in which a stallion curls the upper lip and opens the mouth, is used to draw air over this organ, and stallions will often flehmen after smelling a mare's urine or vulva (plate 4).

But other researchers point out that the acute sensitivity of stallions to these olfactory sensations makes it unlikely that they can completely mask the smell of a mare in heat simply by covering it up with their own eliminations. Indeed, the complex ritual between males at dung piles suggests that some other form of signaling is going on besides just jamming. In bachelor groups, males will compete at length for the privilege of being the last to defecate; in one instance a researcher watched two horses alternately marking the same pile eight times in succession. More often defecation occurs according to the established dominance order, with the most dominant the last to go.

Stallions from different groups not only will routinely defecate on established dung piles encountered in the course of their daily migrations, but will invariably defecate in the course of confrontations with rivals. Often, after careful sniffing of each other's eliminations and a squealing contest, the confrontation will end.

This evidence suggests that these confrontations may serve the important purpose of allowing horses to form a "catalog" associating particular stallions with the smells they will later encounter at dung piles over their range. The contests serve not only to establish which stallions are dominant, but to firmly link dominance rank with the smell of an individual horse's dung.

The habit of marking territory at specific sites is usually associated with animals that defend specific territories (such as wolves), and some researchers have suggested that the creation of dung piles is a "vestigial pattern" in horses inherited from ancestors that lived in forests and that presumably were territorial. The modern-day territorial equines, Grevy's zebra and the African wild ass, do indeed use dung piles in precisely this manner, as boundary markers.

But most students of horse behavior argue that such a complex ritual must continue to serve some adaptive purpose in horses, whatever its evolutionary origins. And indeed the face-offs in which stallions establish each other's dominance status and smell suggest that the dung piles are a way for them to establish their presence, and perhaps for subordinate stallions to avoid face-to-face encounters between their own band and those of dominant rivals. Rival bands of feral horses do in fact appear to avoid encounters much more than chance would predict, given the high degree of overlap of their ranges.

The amount of potential information contained in these piles is quite large: not only the identity of individual stallions, but also how recently they passed through the area, whether mares are in heat, whether a mare is part of a harem, even what the relative dominance order is of as yet unknown stallions. (Although the last to defecate on a pile may not eliminate the odors of those below, his odor is certainly likely to be the strongest.)

That we know so little about this potentially complex system of communication in horses is testimony to our own sensory ineptness.

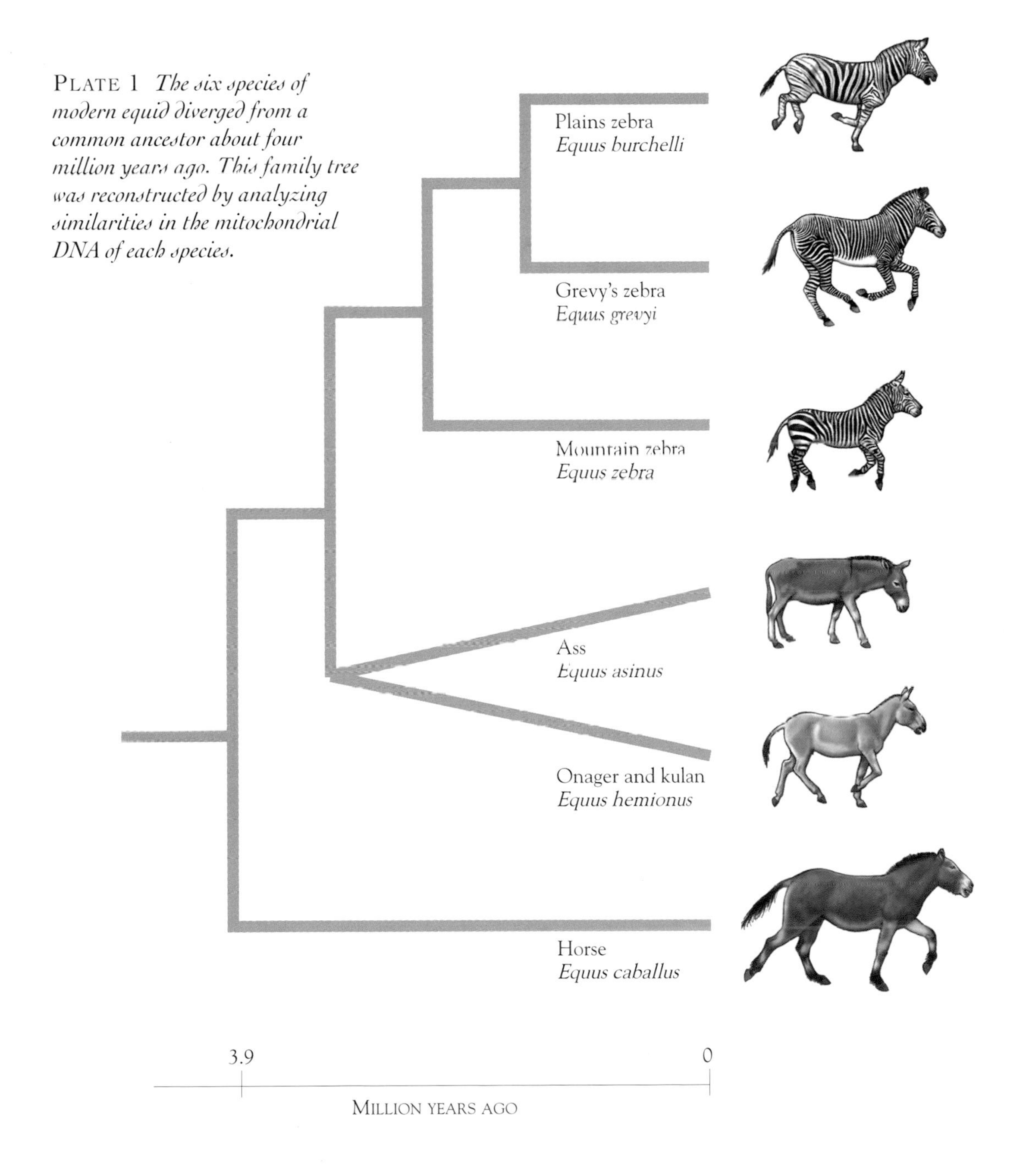

PLATE 1 *The six species of modern equid diverged from a common ancestor about four million years ago. This family tree was reconstructed by analyzing similarities in the mitochondrial DNA of each species.*

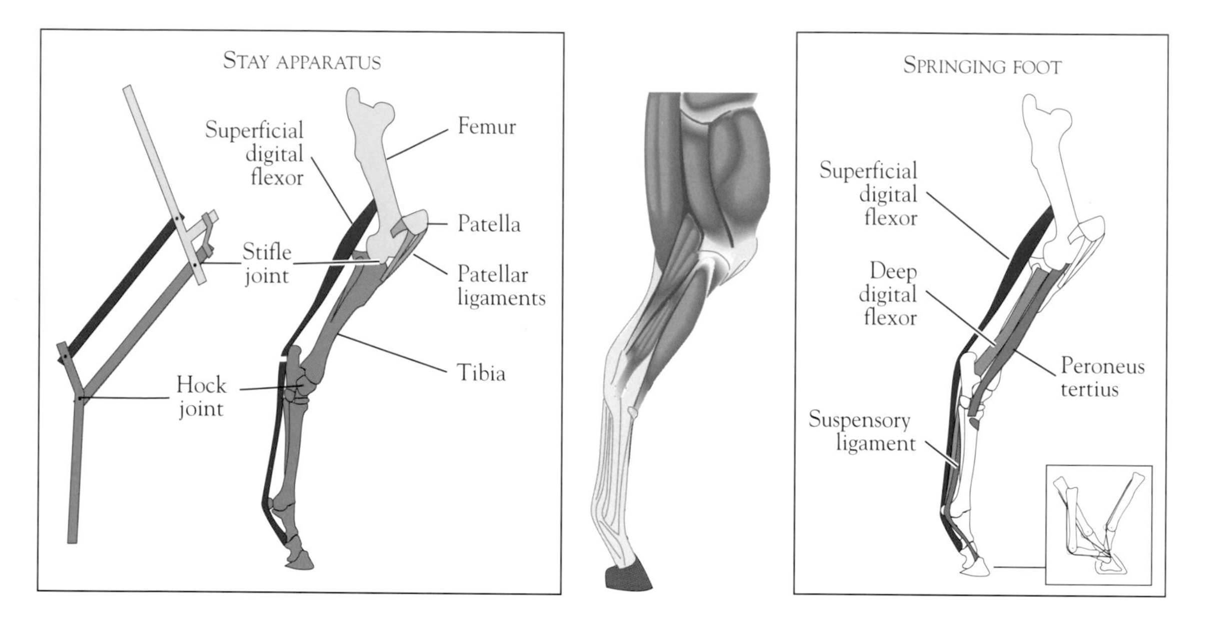

PLATE 2 *The joints, tendons, and ligaments of the horse's hind limb are optimally designed to conserve energy, whether standing or moving. The passive stay apparatus allows the leg to support weight at rest without any muscular effort. The patella normally slides in a groove in the femur, but it can be slipped over a bump in the patellar groove, locking the stifle joint open; the parallelogram formed by the tibia, superficial digital flexor tendon, and hock joint is then unable to flex. The tendons and ligaments of the "springing foot" act like elastic bands that stretch to absorb the shock of impact as the fetlock bends, storing energy that is recycled as the foot snaps back. The forelimb has similar mechanisms.*

PLATE 3 *Horses and their equipment are a constant theme in classical art. Clockwise from top left: Scythian gold plaque from Crimea, fourth century B.C.* (Werner Forman/Art Resource, NY)*; black-figured wine jug from Attica, around 500 B.C.* (The Granger Collection, New York)*; bronze horse bit from Iran, tenth- to eighth-century B.C.* (The Granger Collection, New York)*; tomb relief from Eighteenth Dynasty Egypt* (Nimatallah/Art Resource, NY).

PLATE 4 *Domestic horses retain the fundamental behaviors exhibited by their wild and feral counterparts. Top: feral Camargue horses mutually grooming* (Animals Animals © Henry Ausloos)*; bottom: a Przewalski's stallion exhibiting flehmen* (© Sygma/Bernard Bisson)*; right: play behavior in foals* (Animals Animals © Robert Maier).

Red – green – blue vision

Red – blue vision

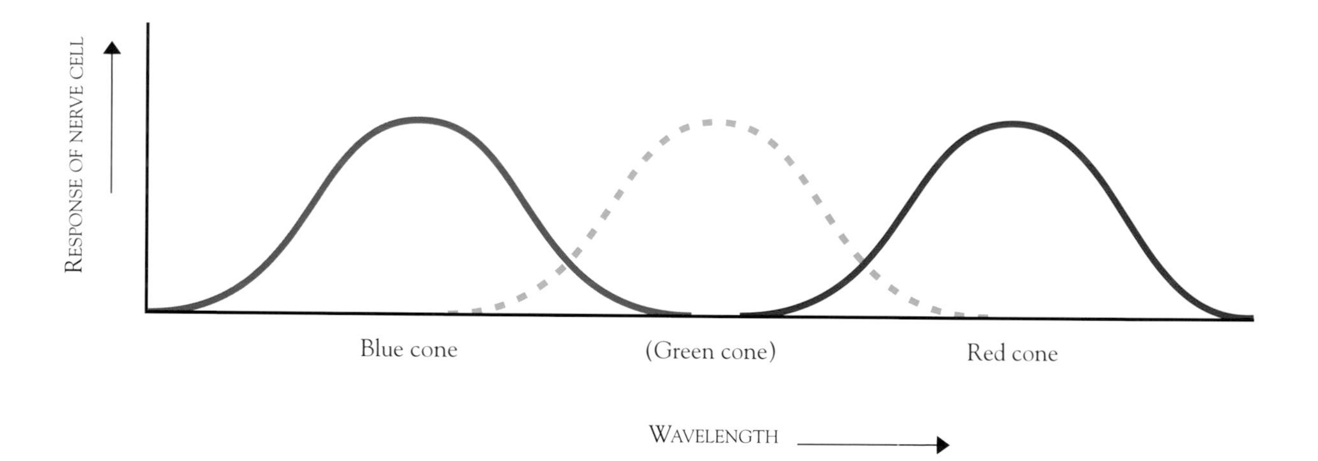

PLATE 5 *With retinas that contain three kinds of cones (red, green, and blue), humans can see the full spectrum of colors. Horses probably have red-blue vision only. They perceive reds and oranges, for example, as the same color, just relatively lighter or darker. In the center of the spectrum is a range of colors that stimulate the red and blue cones equally; to the horse, these greens (and possibly yellows, too) are indistinguishable from white light.*

PLATE 6 *Like a cracking whip, the horse's leg at the trot or gallop transfers a small angular movement of the shoulder into rapid acceleration of the much lighter lower leg.*

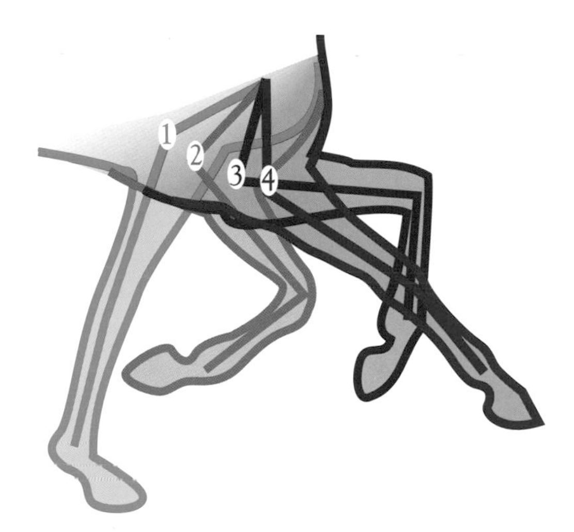

PLATE 7 *By varying the speed of a motorized treadmill, researchers can measure a horse's oxygen consumption (and thus energy consumption) at different gaits and speeds.*

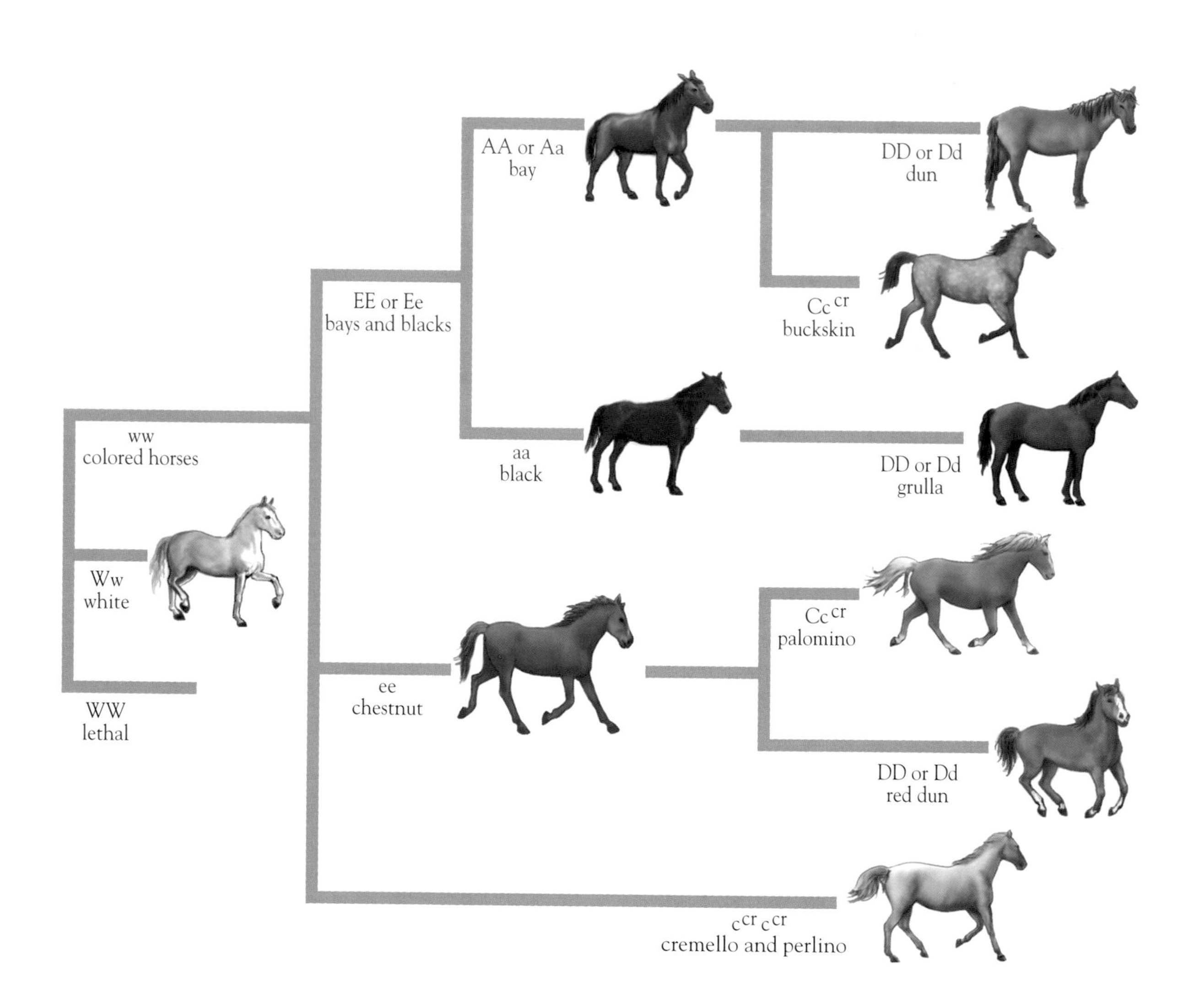

PLATE 8 *The coat color of horses is the result of a complex interaction of many genes. Dominant genes are indicated by upper case letters, recessive genes by lower case. Bay/black coloration, determined by the E gene, is dominant to chestnut; bay coloration, determined by the A gene, is dominant to black. The C and D genes act to dilute these basic coat colors. The complete genotype of a grulla would thus be written wwE_aaD_, where the blanks can be either dominant or recessive (E or e and D or d). Other genes, not shown here, are responsible for roan, dappled, gray, and spotted coloration.*

CHAPTER 7

HORSE SENSE

The good news is that horses have a relatively large brain for an animal of their size. The bad news is that they use most of it just to keep their feet in the right place.

This is something of an exaggeration, but not much. The agility, speed, and variety of gaits that the horse is capable of create a huge demand for "hardwired" controls in the central nervous system. Organizing the coordinated movement of four limbs at high speed over uneven ground, turning, dodging obstacles, changing leads—these are hardly actions suited to conscious mental control. (We do not consciously think about how to move our legs when we walk, and we have just two to worry about; if we did try to think our way through it, we'd probably fall flat on our faces.) A foal will walk, trot, and run within two hours of birth. Although play may help to increase skill and coordination as well as muscular strength for these activities, the basic wiring is clearly present from birth.

But to say that horses are therefore not very smart quickly begs the question of what we mean by intelligence. Psychologists have been wrangling for more than a century over the definition of intelligence in humans, let alone in other species, and the issue remains far from settled.

Part of the problem is that intelligence can mean many different things; it certainly does in common usage. In his *Essays,* the sixteenth-century French writer Montaigne tells of his countrymen's astonishment when he laments that he has no memory, for in the local parlance to say that a man has no memory was to say that he has no sense. Montaigne was literally talking about his inability to remember things, but at that time and place memory was taken to be the essence of intelligence, at least by common men.

In our culture, we tend to think of an ability to solve problems or to quickly make connections or to assimilate new information as more important signs of intelligence than a good memory (thus the absent-minded professor). On the other hand, we tend to dismiss innate mental skills from the equation altogether, and are perfectly willing to believe that a genius might not be able to walk half a block without tripping over his own two feet.

This is natural enough when we are thinking about human beings; after all, what we mean by intelligence in the human context is not what our brains can accomplish compared to that of an ant, but rather what sets particularly bright humans apart from other humans. We are perhaps a bit spoiled by our success as a species, and take a great deal for granted about our abilities.

When comparing the intelligence of different species, though, it behooves us to do a sort of zero-based budgeting, and to consider all the functions that an animal's brain is called upon to perform before we pass judgment on its mental ranking in the animal kingdom. Coordinating the movement of the legs in running may be a hard-wired function in the horse's brain, but it is none the less complex for being innate. Efforts to build robots with legs that walk or run—and manage to stay on their "feet" even on level ground—have pointed up what a frightfully complex information-processing problem locomotion is (figure 7.1). A legged creature on the move is not a windup toy that just goes; maintaining balance is a matter of continual feedback and adjustment. Add to that the problem of uneven ground, the need to maneuver around obstacles, and the need to compensate for the shifting weight of a not always well-coordinated or predictable rider sitting on

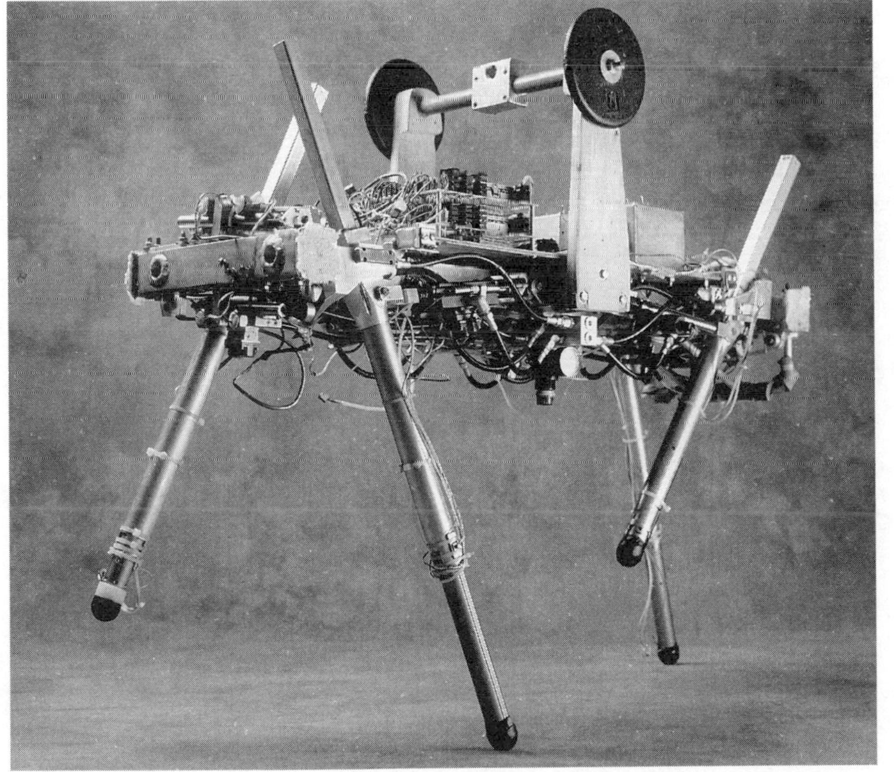

FIGURE 7.1
Designing a robot that can trot competently, even on level ground, has proved a difficult challenge—testimony to the complexity of the neural processes involved in locomotion.

its back, and the information-processing abilities of the horse seem even more impressive. All of this is surely a form of intelligence, although we rarely think of it as such.

By way of comparison, we tend to be much more impressed by certain cognitive functions in dogs that are no less innate and, in fact, far less complex. It is comparatively easy to build a computerized robot that will follow a scent plume upwind, set off an alarm when a person approaches, or find and retrieve an object—much easier than to build one that uses vision and tactile feedback to make its four legs canter smoothly over rough ground. Perhaps because what foxhounds, watchdogs, and bird dogs instinctively do resembles processes that in humans involve reasoning, we rate them so much more highly.

Is a Horse as Smart as an Octopus?

From our self-centered, human point of view, what we usually mean by intelligence in an animal is its ability to learn the tasks we set for it.

This is actually a matter of both learning and memory, but even these terms are loaded with a lot of human preconceptions. In experiments designed to test an animal's ability to learn which of two visual patterns to pick to get a food reward, monkeys learned quickly, rats very slowly or not at all. But this does not mean that rats are dense, or even bad learners; rats have a poor sense of vision but an excellent sense of smell, and when the same test was given using odors instead of visual patterns, the rats showed a very rapid ability to learn and remember the odor associated with a reward. Just as human IQ tests have been criticized for being culturally biased, so many intelligence tests for animals are "culturally" biased in their assumptions about the perceptual or manipulative abilities of a species.

Despite these caveats, formal experiments on learning in horses are still revealing. Several early experiments established that horses could learn to discriminate between an uncovered feedbox and a feedbox covered with a black cloth, and they could be taught to go consistently to one or the other to obtain a reward. The horses also "learned to learn"; that is, in the course of the experiment it took them less time to catch on when the pattern was reversed. Still, when all was said and done they were not too swift. Horses learned about as quickly in these experiments as did tropical aquarium fish, guinea pigs, and octopuses.

Horses also perform respectably, but not brilliantly, on most maze tests. These typically involve a T-maze, in which a horse is presented with a choice to go left or right; the wrong choice runs into a dead end, the correct choice to an exit out to food, water, or a field with other horses (figure 7.2).

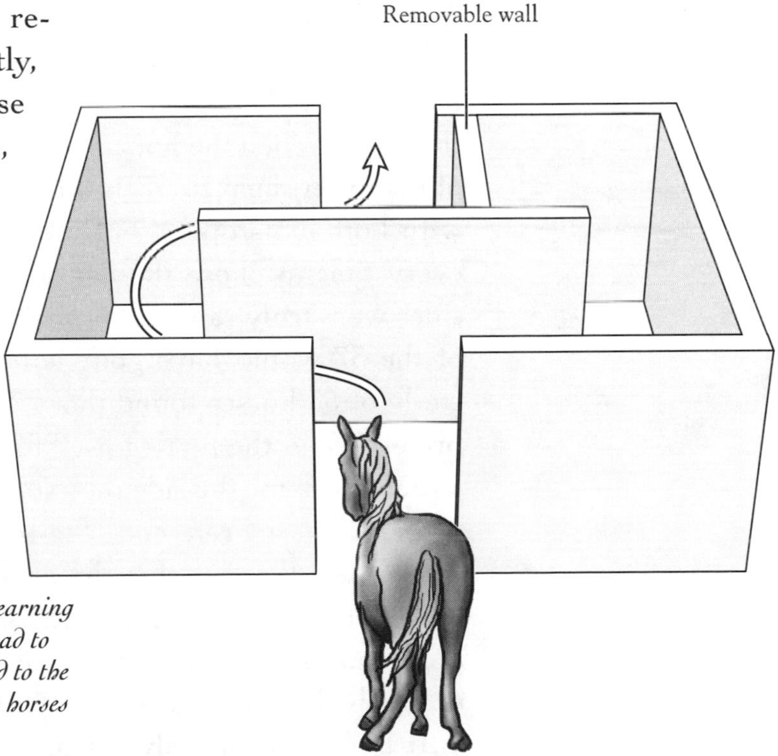

Removable wall

FIGURE 7.2 *A maze used in horse learning experiments. In this case, the horses had to learn that a left turn upon entering led to the exit. After five trials, 20 percent of the horses still turned the wrong way.*

In some of the experiments the horses are given the task of learning to turn to one side (that is, left or right) consistently; in others they must choose whichever side is marked with a brightly painted panel or other distinctive symbol. Although the horses in all of these studies clearly showed an overall improvement over time in picking the correct side, they typically still made a lot of mistakes. In a study of 37 quarter horses that were run through a T-maze every day—and allowed to wander through the maze each time for as long as it took them to find their way out (the right side was open, the left side blocked)—about 20 percent still made the wrong initial choice upon entering the maze on the fifth day of the experiment. In the course of trying to find their way out, the horses on day five also entered the wrong branch of the maze an average of 0.27 times each (down from 0.65 errors at the start of the experiment).

An interesting finding in passing from this study was that many horses began with a definite preference for one side or the other. When the horses were allowed at the very beginning of the experiment to freely walk through the T-maze five times with both exits open, 5 of the 37 horses chose the right side every time, 5 chose the left side every time. If the choice of sides were truly random, probability would predict that only 1 of the 37 would have gone left every time, 1 right. Another study of 53 horses found that 77 percent showed a consistent preference in the foreleg used for pawing, and 67 percent had a preference for the side they started off a walk with. (Only 23 percent had a preference for the gallop lead, which may in part reflect the fact that the unequal load placed on the lead and off-lead legs in a gallop encourages horses to switch leads in the course of anything but the shortest run, which in turn probably discourages any preferences from becoming set.)

If horses are not always too quick on the uptake in these

formal learning experiments, studies at least confirm what trainers and horse owners have long known—that they have excellent memories once they do manage to learn something. A horse taught to choose which visual symbol in each of 20 pairs would bring a food reward was able to remember them all on retesting; a donkey put through the same paces learned only 13 and a zebra 10. Retests at 3, 6, and 12 months showed that horses had little loss of memory as to which symbol in each pair was the right one (figure 7.3).

The ability of horses in all of these experiments to generalize, or learn to learn, is a reflection of what we might loosely

FIGURE 7.3
Horses taught to pick one of each pair of these 20 visual patterns to obtain a food reward still remembered the correct answers many months later.

call problem-solving ability, yet another aspect of intelligence as we usually understand it. In the test described above, the horses seemed to learn after the first few pairs of images what the "game" was—that one or the other would lead to a reward. Learning the correct symbol in subsequent pairs went more quickly as the test went on.

But in terms of real problem-solving ability, horses probably do not rank very high. Dogs, raccoons, monkeys, and many carnivores show a fairly high level of skill in figuring out how to get around obstacles; some of the intelligent acts of dogs that particularly amaze us really do seem to be genuine acts of generalization or extrapolation to new circumstances. A Border collie can be trained to jump over a fence on command ("over") and to circle around and cut off fleeing sheep on command ("come by"), but a dog that has had enough experience bringing sheep in to its handler is likely on its own initiative to jump a fence to cut off a sheep that slips through, even if it has never encountered that particular situation before.

Much of this probably has to do with the differences between carnivores and herbivores; problem solving is part of the survival kit of an animal that lives by anticipating the complex and highly varied actions of elusive prey. Mice move and hide, grass doesn't.

Learning Versus Training

Horses are extremely adept at making associations, however.

Behavioral psychology has freighted this whole subject of learning with concepts and terminology that have more to do with the history of laboratory experiments in this field (from Pavlov's dog on down) than with evolutionary biology, and sometimes discussions of learning tend to lose sight of the adaptive purpose behind it all. Whether it involves drawing connections between two related external events (a rustling in the bush and a tiger jumping out) or between a horse's own action and a consequence (walking too near a dominant horse and getting kicked), the purpose of learning is survival in a changing environment where the rules are not fixed. Behavioral psychologists call the first kind of learning *classical conditioning;* a reflex action (jumping away from a tiger or other fearful object) becomes associated with a new stimulus (the rustling sound) presented at the same time. The second kind of learning is *operant conditioning;* a deliberate action in response to

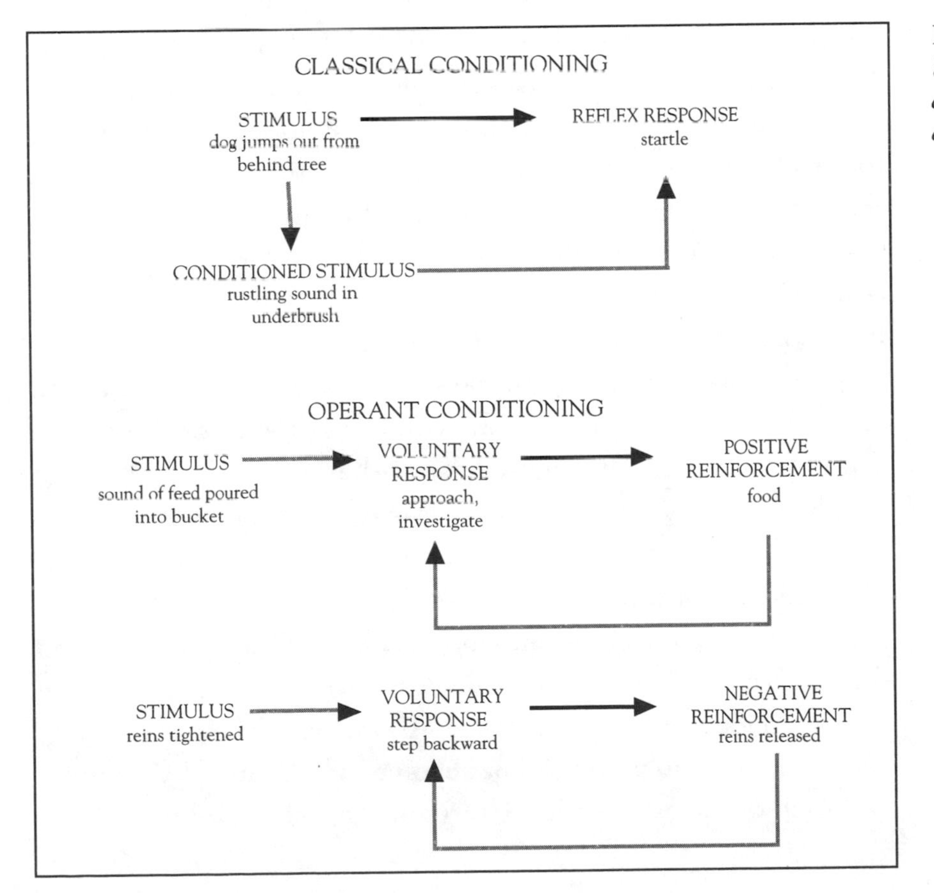

FIGURE 7.4
Paradigms of classical and operant conditioning.

a stimulus (moving away from a horse that has its ears back; putting a nose into a bucket) becomes associated with avoidance of an unpleasant consequence (a kick) or with a reward (food). (See figure 7.4.)

But whatever the terms one uses to describe this process of making associations, the purpose is survival. If all of a horse's behavior were set rigidly in its genes, it would be a poor candidate for lasting very long on this earth. Food sources vary from season to season and year to year; membership in the group changes; mares give birth to foals whom they must learn to recognize and distinguish from other foals; predators appear without warning. Learning by forming associations between actions or events and results is basic to dealing with anything but the most constant physical and social environments.

Habituation is another aspect of learning. It may be prudent to jump at a crashing noise heard in the underbrush, but it is foolish to jump every time a leaf rustles in the wind. An animal that constantly reacts to every stimulus in its environment is just as ill equipped to survive as one that never reacts. An animal needs some way to sort out which of the infinite number of things going on in its environment that it is capable of perceiving with its eyes, ears, nose, and touch are worth actually paying attention to. It would waste energy, take time away from other vital activities, and increase its chance of accidental injury to react unnecessarily. So animals exposed to repeated stimuli that are followed by no results (favorable or not) quickly learn to ignore them.

Trainers exploit both kinds of learning ability in horses, and the key word is "exploit." It is always worth remembering that it is a coincidence that horses are "trainable." They evolved to survive by learning; they did not evolve to be trained by humans.

Much of the early training of young horses involves habituation, exposing them repeatedly to stimuli that might be frightening at first, until they no longer react. Good trainers know that being as nonchalant as possible when exposing a horse to new experiences (carrying weight on its back, having a bit placed in its mouth) and making sure to avoid doing anything that might reinforce its initial fearful reaction will produce the best results.

More advanced training typically follows the model that behavioral psychologists term operant conditioning through negative reinforcement. A correct response to an aversive stimulus (relaxing the jaw and backing in response to pressure from the bit) is rewarded by removal of the stimulus (loosening the reins). A great deal can be accomplished in training simply by ignoring incorrect responses. A response to a stimulus that is neither rewarded nor punished tends to disappear of its own accord (psychologists call this extinction of the response), just as in habituation a stimulus that has no immediate consequences comes to be ignored. Trainers know, for example, that a horse that shies at imaginary objects (a surprisingly common ailment) is best dealt with simply by ignoring its misbehavior. Attempting to correct it through punishment only focuses the horse's attention on its incorrect response, and may actually reinforce it.

Studies across many species have emphasized that the abstract behavioral models of conditioning are not the whole story behind learning. Each species has individual predispositions and aversions toward learning certain kinds of associations.

Some differences in learning ability from species to species are clearly a matter of sheer brain power, of course. Primates, for example, can learn to apply multiple "rules"; they can learn to pick the box with the blue symbol on it, unless it is a square in which case they have to pick the red one, and so forth. Horses, like most other mammals that are not primates, can manage only a single rule (pick the box on the left every time, say).

But just as abstract definitions of animal intelligence are "culturally biased," so too is learning ability. Raccoons given a reward for putting coins in a coin bank (they were being trained for a TV commercial) had a very hard time—not because they apparently had any trouble grasping the concept, and not because they lacked the dexterity to pick up coins, but rather because their natural instinct of handling their food got in the way. They would pick up the coins, start to put them in the box, but then pull them out, rub them together, and so on. It is fairly easy to teach a dog to walk on its hind legs, but virtually impossible to teach it to yawn for a food reward. Cats can be taught to escape from boxes by pushing a sequence of buttons and pulling strings, but cannot learn to escape by scratching themselves.

Similarly, it is easier to teach a horse to respond to a command when the desired behavior comes naturally and instinctively, or when it involves a natural and instinctive type of association. A horse will readily learn to move forward in response to a kick; it is much harder to teach a horse to move backwards, backing being something that is not a good idea for a highly social, prey animal that cannot see directly behind itself—where a predator or a dominant member of the herd may be lurking.

Because most of the psychological experiments on learning in horses involve positive reinforcement (a food reward for a correct response), while most horse training per force involves negative reinforcement (the removal of an unpleasant stimulus for a correct response), questions have been raised about how applicable such laboratory experiments are to the real world.

A study in which horses were given tasks to learn with either positive or negative reinforcement (a food reward for choosing the right side of a maze in one case, a very mild electric shock to encourage the horse to jump from one side of a ring to another over a low rail in response to a buzzer sound in the other case) showed, however, that horses which were good at one kind of learning were equally good at the other.

Practical Consequences

Most of these results from behavioral studies of horses probably come as no surprise to trainers; indeed, Xenophon made many of the same observations 2,400 years ago. (Xenophon described both positive and negative reinforcement as "an essential accompaniment of the whole art of horsemanship. For example, the horse will take the bit more readily if, when he accepts it, some good consequence to himself follows. And he will jump over and out of ditches and do whatever else is required of him, if he expects, when he is done what he is told, to receive some relief.")

A few results, however, are not so obvious and may have some practical implications for training. In the study of maze learning in quarter horses, the researchers decided to see what would happen if they introduced a punishment for an incorrect choice. Horses that picked the wrong turn in the maze were greeted with a blast from a carbon-dioxide fire extinguisher. The horses made fewer mistakes with fewer lessons. However, they ended up spending significantly more time deciding about which way to turn. In other words, they learned faster but were more worried about getting the right answer.

Discrimination experiments also have shown how a lack of clear choices results in hesitation and confusion. When ponies were taught to tell a black feedbox from a white one, they became confused to the point of neurosis as the color of both was gradually shifted to an intermediate gray: they would hover between the two, apparently unable to decide. Consistency in training is a principle that many amateurs tend to slight—most understand the principle perfectly well, but it requires considerable self-discipline to give commands in a consistent fashion and to insist on obedience every time; every rider can think of times when he let his horse get away with something he shouldn't have (break into a canter when he should still have been trotting, cut across the ring, take a few steps after being brought to a halt). These experiments underscore the paramount importance of making sure that the horse has an opportunity to pick the right answer and that the distinction between acceptable and unacceptable responses is clear. Horse researcher C. A. McCall notes that horses can start to worry so much about getting the right answer that they become intent on watching and trying to understand the trainer rather than doing what the trainer wants them to.

A whack from a crop is surely a more forceful reinforcement than a sharp word, but studies have shown that in learning to *discriminate* between stimuli—which in the context of training means discriminating between various commands—horses learn equally well whether the stimuli are visual, auditory, or tactile. This ability to use many cues explains the horse's remarkable ability to learn bad habits through our sometimes unconscious use of cues (for example, a horse that always shies when its rider glances to the side or slightly tenses may do so because such actions have come to be associated with some actual startling experience that occurred in the past). But it also means that having trained a horse to respond to an obvious stimulus (moving forward in response to a whack on the rump), it is fairly easy to introduce a new, more subtle, and different kind of stimulus to replace it (the voice command "walk"). This replacement of an old stimulus with a new one is called trace conditioning; the new cue is given first, followed by the old familiar cue, until the horse responds. This is, in effect, a kind of reinforcement in which a new stimulus is associated with an already learned association between a stimulus and a response. Significantly, presenting the old and new cues simultaneously or in reverse order (old first and then new) invariably fails to teach the new cue. (Many of our everyday experiences with pets have the effect of unconsciously teaching them new cues. Benjamin Hart, in his book *The Behavior of Domestic Animals,* cites the newspaper lost-and-found ad that read: "Lost: Female calico cat that answers to the sound of an electric can opener.")

The tradition of making clucking noises to encourage horses is probably an example of this sort of learning. There is probably nothing intrinsically appealing or rewarding to horses about that noise; it is just a sound that, through association with other cues, horses quickly learn the "meaning" of. But people have been doing it since antiquity; in fact, Xenophon observed that "it is merely conventional" to excite a horse by "clicking the tongue," and that a horse would be equally ready to associate with excitement other sounds that were used routinely in the same fashion.

Studies in which horses received lessons according to various schedules have emphasized the importance of breaking up training into shorter sessions with longer intervals in between. When ponies were taught to avoid a mild electric shock in two-day, seven-day, or one-day-a-week training sessions, the one-day-a-week group learned in fewer lessons—though of course the total elapsed time was much greater. Again, this is a phenomenon that is probably well known in experience but much ignored in practice, either justifiably because of the time demands placed on professional trainers or less justifiably because of the overenthusiasm of amateurs. Shorter sessions in effect keep a horse from getting bored, and also seem to give the animal time for the lesson to sink in.

Studies that have attempted to correlate learning ability with other traits, such as dominance status, age, body condition, and feeding, have come up mostly dry. Researchers have found no evidence that dominant horses in the social hierarchy are any smarter. There is some evidence that horses which are less emotional and calmer are faster learners, which suggests that learning may have more to do with temperament than with intelligence per se. Indeed, some intelligent horses are notoriously difficult to train (as are dominant horses); they become adept at training their trainers, for example by discovering that unmanageable behavior will cause a lesson to stop. Horses from somewhere in the middle of the pecking order may be the most trainable, having the best balance between self-confidence and subordination to authority.

Very few studies have been done that attempt to rank the relative intelligence of different breeds of horse. Quarter horses and thoroughbreds that were taught to push open the one door of three that was marked with a checkerboard pattern in order to obtain a food reward showed some breed difference. The quarter horses reached the point where they would choose the right door 80 percent of the time significantly more quickly (5.4 days versus 8.4 days in the first test). However, the quarter horses were also rated (by experienced observers on an admittedly subjective scale) as less emotional than the thoroughbreds, so the results do not necessarily mean that quarter horses are "smarter." The one thing that can be said with certainty is that, at least in this experiment, they were better learners.

Finally, experiments have consistently failed to support the belief, firmly held by many, that horses can learn directly from watching other horses (or from watching people). Horses that were allowed to watch a "demonstrator" horse perform a task did not learn the task any more quickly than horses lacking such an advantage. Interestingly, horses were also remarkably bad at figuring out where food was located even after watching a person hide it inside one of three or four boxes. Most did well only if they were permitted to pick a box within a few seconds of seeing the food placed inside; one mare performed no better than chance would predict if the delay was as little as 15 seconds. None of the horses studied in this way were able to make the connection if more than a minute passed. Again, horses retain an excellent memory of an association once learned, but they have difficulty forming the association in the first place if there is a long gap between cause and effect. Seeing another animal demonstrate the cause-and-effect association is apparently no substitute for discovering it oneself.

This does not necessarily refute the folk belief that horses pick up bad habits such as cribbing and weaving from one another, but it does seem to support a simpler explanation for such apparent contagion—that horses in the same environments will tend to react the same way. Rather than being picked up from horses, such stable vices may be picked up from the stable itself.

Mind Reading

Horses do, however, have a remarkable ability to acquire bad habits by making inopportune associations. They also are frequently credited with an ability to mind read or anticipate our desires or plans. A horse that comes in calmly every morning will be excited on the day he is to go fox-hunting. A horse will canter before his rider tells him to; will become alert when his rider merely *thinks* about a jump ahead in the field that is still out of view; or will whinny to an approaching horse that (to us at least) seems to be out of sight, smell, or hearing.

Some of this, as we saw in chapter 4, is merely a matter of acute perception—a horse's keen sense of smell may pick up the far-off scent of a fellow horse that is not discernible to our inferior, human senses.

But most of these feats of mind reading and anticipation are generally explainable as conditioned responses to cues from us or from the environment that we are ourselves unconscious of. It makes for an interesting experiment to try to discover how a horse knows it is going hunting. Some of my hunting friends have found through trial and error (and strong self-control) what it is they do differently on a hunting day that is providing cues to their horse: wearing different clothes or subtly altering their morning routine or perhaps simply displaying a nervousness themselves that the horse picks up on. The nervous excitement that is a reflexive response to the stimulus of galloping and jumping has become, through classical conditioning, associated with a new stimulus that is consistently presented along with (or just before) the activity of hunting.

I realized that my horse was consistently anticipating my commands to move to a faster gait because of a bad habit I had unconsciously acquired. I would usually ride on loose reins at a walk, but when I was about to shift to a trot I would pick up my reins. Since picking up the reins (the new cue) was always followed by the familiar squeeze of my legs (the old cue to trot), my horse quickly assimilated this unconscious bit of trace conditioning and learned to associate my picking up of the reins as the signal to trot.

Even a subtle tensing of the rider's muscles is a cue that horses have repeatedly been shown to pick up on. The most famous example is the case of Clever Hans, who has become a classic cautionary tale in the annals of animal behaviorism. Clever Hans was a horse that made headlines in Berlin in the early years of the twentieth century for his ability to solve mathematical problems, tell time, identify various coins and musical scores, and answer questions about geography and politics (figure 7.5). He would count out the answers to math problems by pawing with his right forefoot and would shake or nod his head to answer other kinds of questions. His owner, an elderly Berlin schoolmaster named Wilhelm von Osten, firmly believed in Hans's mastery of the subjects he had tutored him in, and indeed he had a reputation as an honest man who would hardly stoop to perpetrating a deliberate hoax.

A commission sent by the Prussian Academy of Sciences finally was able to explain what was going on. Hans turned out to be unable to answer questions when no one in the room knew the answer—for example, when two people separately whispered to Hans numbers to be added together, but did not tell them to each other.

In fact, Hans had simply learned to respond to consistent, if barely perceptible, cues in a fashion that was consistently rewarded. (When Hans got the right answer he got a sugar

FIGURE 7.5 *Clever Hans showed an amazing ability to solve arithmetic problems and to answer questions about world politics. In fact he was just picking up on subtle and unconscious cues provided by his questioners.*

cube.) Unconsciously, von Osten was cueing Hans by tensing up as the horse started to count and then relaxing when he got to the right number. With enough trial and error, Hans learned that if he stopped pawing at that point he would get a sugar cube; if he kept on going, he didn't. Hans was occasionally able to get the right answer even without von Osten present, but that was only because even the skeptical commission members were unconsciously providing exactly the same cues. When they knew the answer they were naturally anxious to see if Hans would get it right, and were betraying some sign of acknowledgment when he did.

More dramatic claims of mind reading in horses have

turned out to be deliberate hoaxes. In Virginia in the 1920s, a horse named Lady Wonder was proclaimed to be not only clever but clairvoyant, able to answer questions that people had whispered not to her but to her owner. After the secret question was posed, Lady Wonder would move wooden blocks with her nose to spell out words. Her owner would be standing well out of the way during these feats, which was apparently enough to impress one prominent academic believer in parapsychology; he published a scholarly article swallowing all of the owner's claims.

A subsequent investigation by the professional magician John Scarne revealed that Lady Wonder's owner was in fact deliberately signaling the horse (by moving a whip held in his hand) when she had her nose over the right block; the gullible parapsychologist apparently did not realize that a horse's peripheral vision was much greater than his own.

The ability of horses to become conditioned to subtle cues sometimes extends to cues they themselves manufacture. Just as stable vices involve a feedback loop of self-stimulation, so some horses seem to almost enjoy scaring themselves. They will snort, or tense up and stumble, and then react with fright to the snort or the stumble. Such self-stimulation is reinforced through association of the self-generated stimulus with the response; the horse then begins to anticipate the fright it is preparing to give itself. It is interesting that this fits the pattern of self-stimulation disorders, which reflect the more basic instincts of a particular species. A Border collie, whose most basic motor behavior is the predator's chase of prey, will, if frustrated by a lack of things to chase, paw at the ground until a pebble or something else moves and chase that. A horse whose most basic motor behavior is flight from predators chooses instead to create situations that activate that response.

Direction Finding

The well-known ability of horses to find their way home, sometimes even in unfamiliar terrain, has inspired all sorts of speculation about a sixth sense. Little research has been done on navigation and homing in horses, but what has been done may be a bit disappointing to those who want to believe that something magical is going on.

Horses undeniably have a strong homing ability. It is more than myth that they can often find their way back to their stable if given their head. The natural adaptation of the horse to open grasslands and a migratory way of life implies a strong need to find one's way around across many square miles of territory, to know and be able to return to water sources, shelter, and areas of good grazing. Many animals that have been studied more intensively show a definite ability to construct "mental maps" of their range, learning landmarks and remembering what turn leads where. This is technically known as type I orientation, or "pilotage." Steering by landmarks requires a good memory, but there is nothing mysterious or extrasensory about it. It involves remembering the sequence of landmarks that lead to a particular goal and then following them in the right order. The landmarks may be visual or they may be smells, but they are cues acquired through learning the terrain.

The second kind of navigation, type II orientation, is "compass orientation," the ability to steer in a fixed compass direction. Many long-distance migratory birds appear to use this method; they simply steer north or south and hold a fixed course until they reach the vicinity of their goal. There is no evidence to suggest this ability in horses.

Type III orientation is the sort that has made homing pigeons famous; only this type is true navigation, the ability to orient toward a goal from any location, including ones that are completely unfamiliar.

Some of the most remarkable feats of true navigation actually involve a fairly simple mechanism, though one requiring extraordinarily acute senses. To spawn, salmon navigate to the place where they themselves hatched, running hundreds of miles up long rivers and correctly negotiating many forks along the way. Studies have shown that the salmon are cueing in on the particular smells unique to their home tributary, which were imprinted on their memory at the time they hatched out. At each branch of the river, they choose the right fork by "sniffing" for the odor they are homing in on.

Other species, such as pigeons, may use a more complex system analogous to a human with a map and compass, but the jury is still out on this; pigeons appear to be able to use the sun as a compass, but the nature of the "map" remains uncertain. Claims that pigeons use the strength of the earth's magnetic field as a cue to their location relative to home remain controversial; they unquestionably have a magnetic sense but may just use this as backup to the sun compass. Of course it is not enough simply to know which way north is; equally important is knowing in which compass direction home lies. Some recent studies suggest that pigeons may construct a map of olfactory landmarks by learning which smells are associated with particular wind directions when at home.

Horses are quite good at finding their way back over familiar ground, and this ability is the basis for most stories about horses' feats of homing. It probably involves a combination of learning (landmarks familiar from a previous ride out form a mental map) and just following their own tracks: horses trying to find their way back or to catch up with other horses will often sniff the ground at a trail junction. The biologist Daniel Janzen, while working in Costa Rica, observed a packhorse following the trail of a stablemate "casting" for scent much like a dog. Traveling along a beach that the stablemate had crossed an hour earlier heading for home, the horse repeatedly encountered spots where the tide had swept away the tracks of the preceding horse; at intervals, the horse would drop its nose to within a centimeter of the sand and begin angling across the beach, sometimes casting back and forth. When it encountered a place where the retreating tide had left the earlier horse's tracks uncovered, it would lift up its head and then follow exactly in the stablemate's footprints.

I have had much the same experience with my horse several times when I was left behind the rest of the field while out hunting; galloping along a wooded path that the other horses had traversed several minutes earlier, my horse would suddenly come to a stop where the trail forked, drop his nose to the ground, and then unerringly take off down the correct fork. In some cases it seemed possible that he was seeing the tracks of the preceding horses, but in at least one instance that I can remember both paths were heavily trodden, and he still had no difficulty choosing the right branch—most likely by smell.

Smell may also be the key in the occasional feat of homing over unfamiliar ground. In some brief experiments conducted by the psychologist Moyra Williams, horses let loose in unfamiliar territory a few miles from home tended to travel upwind rather than homeward; even when quite near home they could not find their way if the right direction was downwind. Feats of homing in unknown terrain may be dependent on the wind coming from the right direction to carry a familiar smell within range. (Note that salmon don't have such problems in homing in on their tributary: water always flows downstream.) Of course it may also simply mean that horses tend to move upwind, period, when lost, and are not using any senses to guide them at all; if it happens that once in a while the wind is blowing from home, then home they go. More exacting studies would be needed to sort out what the actual homing abilities of horses are and what senses they rely upon. And there is no evidence that horses can orient to compass directions, much less perform "true navigation" of the map-and-compass type.

Imprinting

Most animals that are precocial—that is, whose young are able to be up and moving on their own shortly after birth—have evolved a special kind of learning known as imprinting. The term was coined by the behaviorist Konrad Lorenz, who conducted some now famous experiments in which goslings and other precocial birds that he had hand-reared bonded to him in precisely the way normally reared goslings bond to their mothers. The goslings readily followed him, and would continue to do so even after seeing real geese. Lorenz found that in fact goslings will bond to the first moving object they see upon hatching. Such bonding only occurs during a relatively brief period, however, when the young seem to be "programmed" to accept imprinting.

The adaptive value of this form of learning would seem to be especially important in precocial species precisely because newborns don't have the time to learn who their mother is through the normal channels of associative learning. Animals that stay in the nest for some time after birth appear to form bonds with their parents gradually over the course of days and weeks, learning by simple association. But in animals that may need to move suddenly (to flee from predators, for example), the danger of being left behind or of not identifying one's parents correctly is too great for such learning to be left to normal channels.

Foals readily imprint on their mothers within the first few days of birth; foals hand-reared by humans will readily imprint on them. Imprinting involves more than simply learning who to follow. Many species of birds reared by foster parents will, as adults, show a sexual preference for birds of their foster parents' species or color instead of their own. Foals hand-reared by humans will similarly show inappropriate sexual behavior toward people on occasion. Imprinting seems to create a mental template that a foal carries for the rest of its life—a mental template of what a horse is "supposed" to look like. This may conceivably explain why some stallions show such a singular preference for mares of a specific color.

Recent research suggests that foals may also be imprinted with food preferences during their first few weeks. Foals show a sudden onset of "adult" grazing behavior at about six weeks. Up until about three weeks of age, they engage in a sort of play or exploratory grazing, frequently mouthing weeds and poisonous plants as well as grasses. But almost as soon as real grazing begins, foals show a distinct, learned ability to discriminate between good plants and bad. (One possible avenue for this imprinting in foals is the smell or taste of various plants in the feces of their dams. Foals regularly eat small amounts of their mother's feces, a behavior that had been explained in the past as a means to acquire the gut bacteria needed to digest cellulose. Although this idea of imprinting through coprophagy is speculative, observations of mares and foals do suggest that foals are *not* acquiring their food preferences by watching what their mothers eat; many foals were observed never to graze close enough to their mothers to see which plants they were choosing.)

Because foals are so susceptible to imprinting in their first few days and weeks of life, and because the lessons learned through imprinting are so durable, some trainers try to expose newborn foals to a wide range of new experiences very early on. "Imprint training" of a foal involves thorough handling of all parts of its body, placing a bit in its mouth, picking up its feet, and exposing it to loud noises, electric clippers, horse trailers, and many other potentially frightening stimuli. The idea is to habituate the foal by repeatedly exposing it to these experiences, while holding it so that it cannot flee, until the foal relaxes and becomes resigned to them.

Trainers report very good success in easing subsequent training. It is not clear that all of this is true imprinting, however, as opposed to simple habituation. A foal may be habituated to new experiences more easily than an older horse simply because it has had less time to acquire inopportune associations that must be unlearned. The fact that a handler can easily restrain a foal, preventing it from fleeing in response to potentially frightening stimuli, also makes it easier to repeat the stimuli to the point of habituation, without permitting any initial fearful response to be reinforced by flight.

Some skeptics have gone so far as to deny that imprinting exists at all as a special form of learning different from normal associative learning. And recent research tends to suggest that Lorenz and other behaviorists were too absolute in their claims that imprinting created permanent and irreversible associations and that it occurred only during a precisely limited "critical period." But neurological studies have identified distinct physiological changes in one specific part of the brain (the intermediate medial hyperstriatum ventrale, a part of the top of the forebrain) following imprinting. Moreover, lesions in this region of the brain tended to decrease imprintability but had no effect on the animal's ability to learn in other ways.

How much of early learning is truly imprinting is a question still unanswered. Puppies that are not exposed to humans even briefly at six to ten weeks, when they are most sensitive to imprinting, never learn to accept humans properly; even though puppies have already imprinted on their mother by then, exposure to humans during this period seems to exploit the imprinting "channel," allowing some extra and long-lasting learning to be wedged in. It seems likely that the exposure of foals to humans during their sensitive period likewise results in some extra imprinting that facilitates their later acceptance of people as suitable companions.

CHAPTER 8

THE MECHANICS OF MOVEMENT

Being big is a small advantage in terms of speed but a big mechanical disadvantage in many other ways. In chapter 1 we encountered the interesting paradox that, to a first approximation, large animals actually run no faster than smaller animals. An animal's speed equals the length of its stride times the number of strides it takes in a minute. Large animals have longer legs, and so have a proportionately longer stride, but they have a harder time making their bigger legs move back and forth as fast.

In fact, the advantage of longer legs is almost perfectly canceled out by their increased cumbersomeness as an animal's size increases. The force a muscle can bring to bear on a limb to make it accelerate is proportional to the cross-sectional area of the muscle fibers—a thick rope can pull harder than a thin one. So big animals can exert more force on their legs than small ones can. But that advantage is more than offset by a disadvantage that accrues much faster with increasing size: limbs get heavier. Cross-sectional area increases only with the length squared, while the mass of an animal, and of all its separate moving parts, increases with volume, or length cubed. Thus as an animal gets bigger, the weight of its legs increases faster than the muscle power available to make those legs move quickly. It would be like trying to make a car go faster by putting in a bigger engine, only to find that all of the extra weight of that bigger engine and the beefed-up framing needed to support it actually made the car run slower.

So while stride length *increases* in proportion to the length of an animal's leg, stride frequency *decreases* in much the same proportion; so speed stays much the same regardless of size.

This calculation only holds for animals that are geometrically similar—that is, whose limbs and muscles are all built to the same proportions. But horses have evolved some ways to get around the cookie-cutter plan, and so beat the odds. Their legs are disproportionately long for an animal of their size, and their muscles are arranged in special ways to increase stride frequency. These adaptations allow horses to hit top speeds greater than those of any other land animal of equal size.

Yet the more remarkable thing about the mechanics of the horse is not so much how it attains the speeds it does, but rather how it deals with the accompanying problems of being fast and big.

It is in the realm of endurance that the horse truly excels. Despite its considerable weight, a horse can maintain speed over huge distances. Horses have clocked 80 kilometers in a little over four hours. Such performance demands extraordinary efficiency in mechanical design.

At the same time, being big, heavy, and fast places enormous structural loads on the limbs. They must be lightweight to attain high accelerations, yet strong enough to sustain the impact of galloping over uneven terrain.

Designing something that is at once light and strong is a classic mechanical engineering problem. Engineers not too long ago began to realize that the same methods developed to analyze how materials bear up under load in buildings or airplanes could be applied to animals and plants to understand why they take on the forms they do. These "biomechanical" studies have on occasion even pointed to engineering solutions to difficult aerodynamic or robotic design problems—solutions that nature had already hit upon through the long trial and error of evolution. The story of how the horse's legs evolved to strike a complex balance among speed, efficiency, and strength is likewise a story of engineering.

Designing for Speed

As we have seen, there are two basic ways an animal can run faster. It can take longer strides, or it can take more strides per minute. Both tend to be dictated by an animal's size, the former increasing, the latter decreasing in proportion to size. Thus the first question an engineer would ask is whether there are ways to modify the design to get around these basic constraints that size imposes.

Clearly one way to get a longer stride is to grow proportionately longer and skinnier legs—increasing length without having to pay the usual exponential penalty of increased mass that accrues when all dimensions are increased by the same proportion. Horses have done exactly this in the course of their evolution. Compared to many other mammals, their legs are disproportionately long and light. The horse's hock is the anatomical equal to the human ankle, the front "knee" is the equivalent of the wrist (figure 8.1). The horse's legs are unusually long for an animal of its size because it is standing on its toes—and because those toes have also become so elongated that they make up a good third of the total length of the leg.

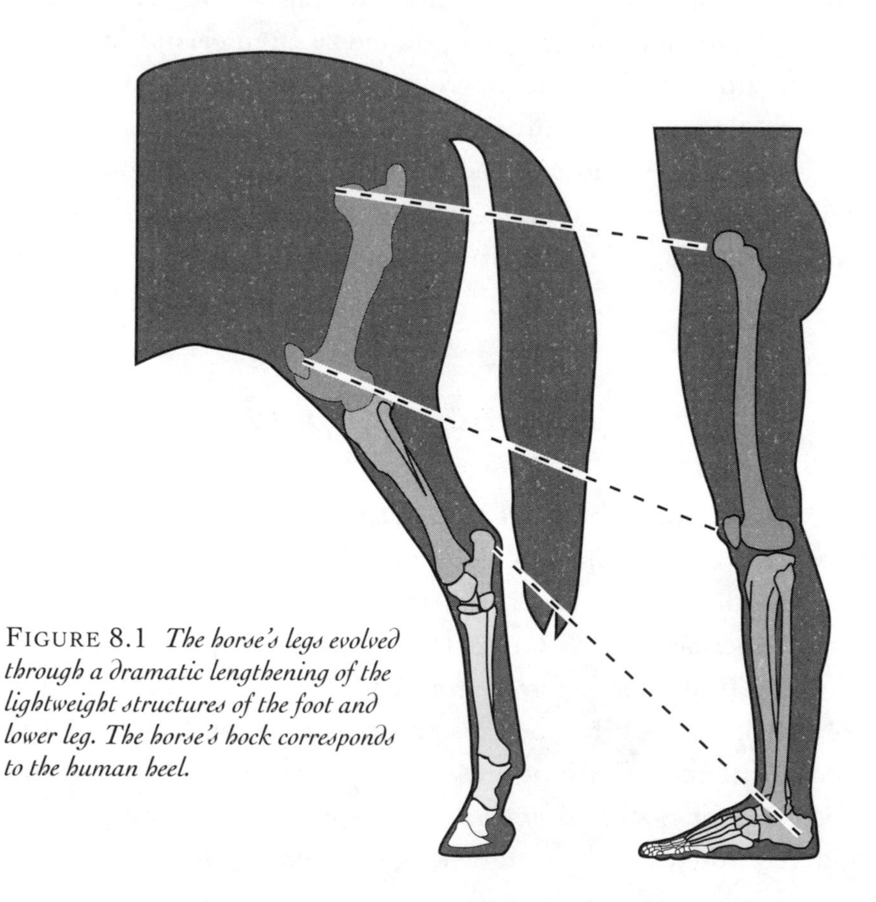

FIGURE 8.1 *The horse's legs evolved through a dramatic lengthening of the lightweight structures of the foot and lower leg. The horse's hock corresponds to the human heel.*

This evolutionary change has made the horse's legs not only disproportionately long, but also disproportionately light. If the lengthening had occurred at the other end, close to the body, it would have come at the cost of a lot of extra fleshy weight. But the toes are lightweight structures, carrying minimal bone and tendon, and no muscle at all.

Compared to its close relations the rhinoceros and tapir, the horse's legs make up a greater proportion of its body length; they are even longer, proportionately, than the speedy cheetah's. But, as the zoologist and pioneering student of animal locomotion Milton Hildebrand has pointed out, there is only so far you can push this design approach. If a horse's legs were any longer, its back legs would constantly be striking its forelegs (as indeed they do on occasion at a fast trot). An animal as long-legged as a giraffe is in fact unable to trot at all for this very reason. So while horses clearly have gained something in speed by stretching their legs, the gain is a relatively modest one and is fairly sharply constrained.

Making the legs swing back and forth faster is an even tougher design proposition. Again, the stride frequency is, in the first instance, fixed by an animal's size (figure 8.2). A galloping horse may take two strides a second, a galloping rabbit four per second, a galloping mouse nearly eight per second. Hildebrand noted that many seemingly promising ideas for getting around this basic constraint don't pan out on closer inspection. For example, it might seem that attaching muscles closer to the joints, so as to increase their mechanical advantage, would cause the limbs to whip around quicker. This would be like moving a doorknob closer to the hinge side of the door; the closer the knob is to the hinge, the wider the arc through which the door will swing for a given amount of pull. The trouble is that placing the doorknob closer to the

FIGURE 8.2
Animals with longer legs take longer strides, but as legs get longer they also get heavier, slowing the rate they can swing back and forth. At the gallop, horses increase their speed mainly by lengthening the stride rather than by increasing the number of strides per minute.

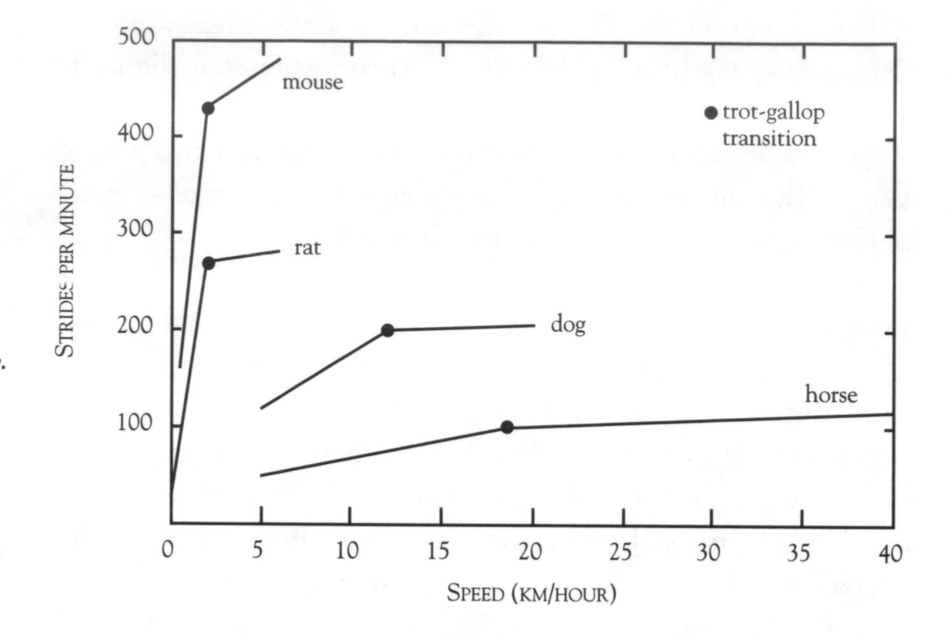

hinge also increases the force that has to be applied to achieve this result. And loading down muscles tends to *slow* the rate at which they can contract. So while it takes less muscle contraction to achieve the same effect, it probably winds up gaining nothing in speed.

A better bet to make the legs swing back and forth faster is to use two muscles to do the job of one. Obviously, simply connecting two muscles at the same spot does nothing to speed things up. (Hildebrand says this would be like expecting two athletes to run faster than one!) But if one muscle turns the upper leg while another turns a lower segment simultaneously, the velocity at the end of the leg will be the sum of the two. Because horses can swing their shoulder blades in a forward and backward arc (our shoulder blades lie flat on our backs and are fastened to the collar bone; those of the horse lie vertically and are free to turn), they are able to achieve some of this additive effect (figure 8.3). But again, the gain is fairly small.

The challenge in making legs longer was to avoid solutions that at the same time increase their weight by the usual exponential proportions, which would exact a penalty in stride frequency offsetting any gain in stride length. By the same token, changes that reduce weight for a leg of a given length will increase stride frequency. The speed at which an animal can accelerate its leg forward as its foot leaves the ground and then accelerate it backwards to begin another stride is a function not just of how much mass it has to move but of how that mass is distributed. Concentrating the heavy stuff near the pivot means the heavy stuff does not have to move as far. (You can swing a bat faster holding the fat end than holding the normal skinny end: in the former case the mass is more concentrated near the axis of rotation, giving it what a physicist would call a low moment of inertia.) The fact that the horse's lower leg is a stretch version of inherently light structures (toes versus hips) helps considerably to reduce the moment of inertia.

FIGURE 8.3 *A shoulder blade that can swing forward and back allows the horse's legs to swing faster and stretch farther.*

Some special design features of the horse's legs make them even lighter where it counts. Bone is light, muscle is heavy; in the horse many muscles have simply been stripped out of the design altogether. Humans have joints and corresponding muscles that allow the hips to rotate, the wrists and ankles to bend up and down and from left to right, and the fingers to flex from side to side and up and down where they meet the palm. The corresponding joints in horses restrict motion to a single plane only: forward and back. The hip joint, instead of being a ball and socket that can rotate freely in any plane, is more of a crosswise cylinder that allows the thigh bone to swing only forward and back. (This is why a horse cannot easily kick you if you stand next to its hip.) The stifle, hock, and fetlock, corresponding to the knee, ankle, and the palm-finger joints in humans, have grooves and flanges in the bones that prevent any twisting or side-to-side flexing; they have become simple hinges. The two bones of the human forearm that allow it to rotate, the radius and the ulna, are in the horse fused.

All of these adaptations serve to replace active stabilizers in the form of heavy muscle with passive stabilizers in the form of lightweight bone. At the sacrifice of some flexibility and agility, the horse sheds a lot of weight in the lower leg.

Additional weight is saved by virtue of a design that orients the long cannon bone of the leg in line with the forces it must withstand. Because nearly all of the force that impacts the cannon bone runs along its length and takes the form of compression (impact against the ground below and weight of the horse from above, both of which tend to press the bone lengthwise), its interior structure can be much lighter than it would be if the bone had to resist twisting or pulling forces. The filaments that form the structure of the cannon bone run mostly lengthwise, forming an open, porous structure that is strong and lightweight, like the honeycomb structure used in some packaging and building materials.

This light structure and absence of heavy muscle in the lower leg are of course not without problems. Part of the reason the cannon bone is so susceptible to injury is that it has nothing but skin, ligaments, and tendons to protect it; the heavy musculature of the upper leg offers relatively much greater protection. Because the bone is designed to resist longitudinal forces only, it is also dangerously vulnerable to transverse forces—for example if the leg strikes an object.

Under the considerable tyranny imposed by the laws of size, horses do the best they can to maximize speed.

Designing for Endurance

The real genius of the horse's mechanical design is its efficiency. The passive support mechanisms in the leg joints that boost speed also boost the horse's "fuel economy." Most of the work performed by an animal in locomotion consists of the energy consumed to move the legs relative to the body. Lighter legs mean less work.

The concentration of weight near the pivot point allows for high speed, as we have seen, but it also functions as part of an energy-saving device. Milton Hildebrand found that, like a cracking bullwhip in which a small flick at the heavy handle turns into a supersonic whiplash at the light tip, the horse's leg motions are optimized to turn a small effort from the upper leg into a large motion at the bottom.

As a horse lifts a leg off the ground, it accelerates it forward at the shoulder but then almost immediately slows the swing of the shoulder, allowing the momentum generated by the heavy upper leg to transfer itself to the lighter lower leg. At a slow trot, the horse will sometimes actually halt the forward swing of the shoulder altogether momentarily while the lower leg snaps forward. The shoulder again begins to accelerate forward once the knee reaches its furthest extension forward and then starts to return to bring the hoof in contact with the ground. By conserving angular momentum in this way, the horse avoids expending more energy than is necessary to generate each stride (plate 6).

Like humans on pogo sticks, bounding kangaroos, and many other mammals while running, horses also have a mechanism for recycling energy by storing it up in a spring with each stride. The suspensory ligament—the so-called "springing foot" we encountered in the discussion of horse evolution in chapter 1—acts, along with several other tendons and ligaments, as a spring, or perhaps a rubber band would be a more vivid description. These tendons and ligaments are stretched taut around and behind the fetlock joint as the hoof strikes the ground and the joint bends way back under the horse's full weight; they then snap back, straightening the joint with considerable force and propelling the hoof back and off the ground. As in the mechanism which conserves angular momentum, energy is saved here because the horse does not have to expend the full energy that would otherwise be required to accelerate, decelerate, and reverse the movement of the limbs at each end of the stride; some of the energy invested in accelerating the limb forward is stored in the spring and recycled, helping to slow it down at the end of the cycle and propel it backwards.

Animals such as cheetahs and rabbits that can achieve very high speeds in short bursts were shown by Hildebrand to perform this feat by bringing their backs into play. With the back dramatically flexed and all of the limb joints flexed and extended through a much greater range (a cheetah will actually lift its hind feet higher than its knees when traveling at full tilt), the gallop stride can be considerably lengthened. Relative to its height the cheetah's stride is twice that of the horse. But this extra athletic effort comes at a price: it is much more exhausting, and the cheetah cannot maintain its top speed for more than about 15 seconds.

Most of the energy an animal expends in locomotion is spent moving its limbs in relation to its body; what makes the cheetah's stride so energy-expensive is the work the animal must perform simply to move the mass of its legs up and down so much in each stride. The horse, by contrast, maintains a remarkably level plane to its movements. The horse's relatively rigid spine does not permit bursts of speed like the cheetah's, but it does conserve energy by minimizing the animal's up-and-down movements (figure 8.4).

FIGURE 8.4 *By dramatically flexing its back and raising its hind feet above the knees, the cheetah can achieve a huge stride. But the extra muscular effort required is quickly exhausting. The horse maintains a much more even, and energy-conserving, trajectory. Broken lines show the trajectory of the right hind foot.*

When any animal walks or runs, it raises and lowers its center of mass with each stride. This is easy to envisage if you think of each leg as an upside-down pendulum, with the pivot at the foot and the animal's center of mass poised at the top (see figure 8.11, p. 199). As the foot touches the ground at the start of a stride, the center of mass describes an arc through the air, rising and then falling. Some of the energy expended in lifting the mass through the first half of the arc is of course recovered during the free-fall of the second half of the arc—but not all. Horses avoid some of this heavy lifting thanks to the flexing of the fetlock joint. Because it is most flexed, and thus closest to the ground, at the midpoint of the stride—just when the center of mass is at the top of the arc—the joint's action works to flatten the trajectory and to minimize the up-and-down movement required with each stride.

The commonplace that the horse is perfectly adapted for running should probably be modified: the horse is in fact perfectly adapted to saving energy. Its need to cover vast distances in search of food and water was most likely the crucial factor in its biomechanical evolution.

The Great Gait Debate

It is a striking fact that despite the 6,000 years that man has ridden and driven and raised horses in captivity, and the many tens of thousands of years more that he hunted and followed wild horses, it is only in the last 100 years that we have been able to describe the correct sequence and timing by which a horse's limbs strike the ground at the various gaits. Thousands of hunting prints are testimony to the once common belief, or at least the artistic convention unchecked by better knowledge, that a horse's fore and hind legs are fully extended fore and aft during the airborne phase of the gallop. Equestrian statues from ancient times to the nineteenth century betray an ignorance of how a horse's feet move in sequence at the walk. And a major dispute raged until the late nineteenth century over whether all four feet ever leave the ground simultaneously at the trot.

It is indeed remarkably hard for the unaided human eye to follow the sequence, much less the overlap, of four moving feet; seventeenth-century efforts to precisely describe and define gaits by observing the legs and listening to the sounds made by the hooves striking the ground all produced inaccurate conclusions. Some later studies attempted to sort things out by fastening bells that sounded different tones to each of a horse's four legs, or by fashioning shoes that left a distinctive track from each foot. These did a better job, but still were unable to answer the important question of when each foot was raised off the ground, and thus by how much each leg's stride overlapped with the others. A similar failing bedeviled the otherwise ingenious measuring apparatus devised by the French scientist E. J. Marey in the late nineteenth century. Marey attached india rubber balls under the hooves of a horse; as a hoof touched the ground the ball would be squeezed, which would in turn expel air through a rubber tube leading from the ball to the lever on a paper recorder carried by the rider. A similar device could be attached just above the fetlock to measure and record movements of the leg. Marey also devised a set of recorders to track the vertical movements of the withers and croup as the horse moved at various gaits. His measurements successfully established the sequence of footfalls at each gait, but he was unable to get accurate data on how long each foot remained in contact with the ground. As a result, he concluded incorrectly that horses never have three or four feet in contact with the ground simultaneously when moving at normal gaits.

It was not until 1877 that the breakthrough came. The eccentric American photographer Eadweard Muybridge invented a remarkable system for taking sequence photos of animals (and people) in motion (figure 8.5). He lined up a battery of as many as 24 still cameras that would be triggered sequentially as the subject passed by. A motorized timer, or wires embedded in the track, or threads stretched across it, would trip each camera in turn. From these photographs he was able to prove for the first time that a trotting horse moving at racing speed does indeed lift all four feet off the ground during the suspension phase of the gait.

Muybridge was also, incidentally, the apparent inventor of the photofinish; in 1882 he wrote a letter to the British scientific journal *Nature* suggesting that his device could be used to determine the winner of horse races, an idea first put into practice in 1888. In 1880 he invented a revolving disk (the "zoographiscope," among other names) that could project his stop-action photos in sequence onto a screen to produce a sort

FIGURE 8.5 *Eadweard Muybridge's stop-action photographs of horses (and many other animals) revolutionized the study of animal locomotion.* Culver Pictures.

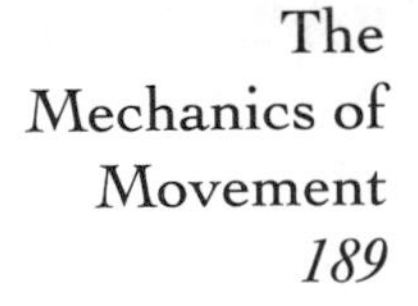

of primitive motion picture. He photographed not just horses but cats, ostriches, camels, bison, and other mammals at various gaits (including scantily clad hopping humans). Muybridge's extensive documentation of the motion of so many different animals under standardized conditions proved enormously important to the subsequent scientific study of animal locomotion, and is still being used 100 years later. A 1977 study by R. McNeill Alexander used Muybridge's photos to show that horses increase their gallop speed by increasing both stride length and stride frequency; Alexander also was able to derive some basic theories about why animals change gaits from Muybridge's photos (we will return to this later).

Yet Muybridge was less well recognized during his lifetime. His interest in photographing moving animals had been sparked when Leland Stanford, the governor of California, invited him to photograph his trotter—and so settle the issue of whether all four feet leave the ground. Stanford subsequently published under his own auspices *The Horse in Motion,* a book that included drawings based on Muybridge's photos but which failed to give him credit; Muybridge's subsequent lawsuit against Stanford was unsuccessful.

Classifying Gaits

The use of high-speed cinematography and a variety of electronic transducers that can precisely measure the forces and motion of moving limbs has at last allowed the various gaits of animals to be fully defined (figure 8.6). Their variety and complexity turn out to fully justify the thousands of years of confusion surrounding the issue. The ways in which four feet can be used in sequence produce dozens of possible combinations; walk, trot, and gallop are only a start.

Most animals, however, limit their choice of gaits, and the monumental work of Milton Hildebrand in cataloging and classifying the gaits of more than 1,000 different animals has produced some simple and powerful rules to explain why this should be so, as well as some simple and elegant concepts to use in defining gaits. To those used to thinking only in terms of walk, trot, and canter, Hildebrand's concepts for classifying gaits will seem unfamiliar and a bit obscure at first, but mastering them will more than repay the effort: they clarify not only exactly what horses (and other animals) do with their feet at each gait, but also how the various gaits relate to one another.

To begin with, gaits fall into two broad categories, symmetrical and asymmetrical. Symmetrical gaits include the walk and trot; in these gaits the left and right feet of each front and back pair strike the ground at evenly spaced intervals, with each foot remaining in contact with the ground for the same length of time. Although each foot starts its cycle at a different time, the left forefoot and the right forefoot go through exactly the same cycle; a movie of one would be an exact mirror image of the other. In most of the symmetrical gaits, the hind feet do

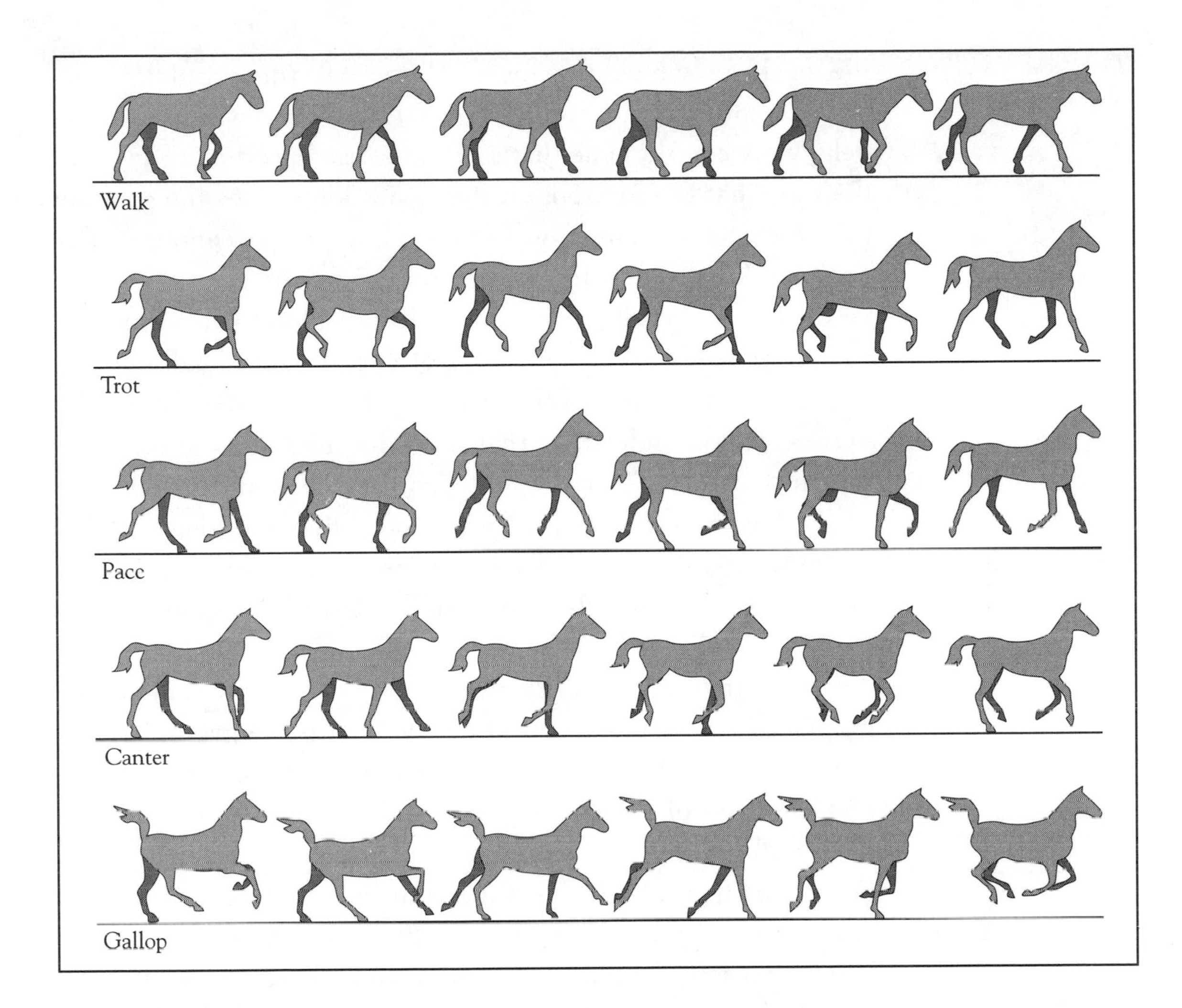

FIGURE 8.6
Limb placements and sequences at the various gaits. W. E. Jones, ed., *Equine Sports Medicine*, © 1989.

the same: the cycle of the left hind is the same as that of the left fore, and the ground contact time is the same, too.

Hildebrand's classification scheme is based on the powerful observation that there are really only two variables that completely define a symmetrical gait. One is the percentage of time that each foot remains in contact with the ground during the entire cycle of its stride. (The ground-contact portion of the stride is usually called the "stance phase"; the portion of the cycle in which the foot is lifted off the ground is the "suspension phase." See figure 8.7.) The other variable is the delay between the time that a hind foot strikes the ground and the time that the forefoot on the same side strikes the ground; this too is conveniently expressed as a percentage of a complete stride cycle for a single foot.

The symmetrical gaits of a horse are plotted in figure 8.8 according to this scheme. Walks of various speeds all fall in a broad band that crosses the graph horizontally at about the 25 percent mark, indicating that each forefoot falls about one-fourth of a cycle after the hind foot on the same side. This is easily demonstrated by the fact that, at the walk, the four feet strike the ground at evenly spaced intervals; this can only be possible if each one is staggered by exactly a quarter of a stride from the next. When each foot remains on the ground for more than 50 percent of its cycle (the right half of the graph), two or three feet will always be on the ground at the same time, which accounts for the stability of the walk.

The pace falls at the zero percent line, indicating that the fore- and hindlegs on each side strike the ground simultaneously. The trot falls at the 50 percent line, with fore- and hind limbs on each side striking exactly half a stride out of phase.

The reason the gait diagram forms these three discrete "fingers" is clear: with four legs you can divide each stride evenly into two halves or four quarters, but nothing else in between.

Increases of speed within each gait are effected by moving to the left side of the graph—that is, by reducing the fraction of stride during which each foot remains on the ground and increasing the suspension phase correspondingly. The running walk of horses such as the paso fino and the Tennessee walker are, as the graph shows, literally just that—fast walks. The

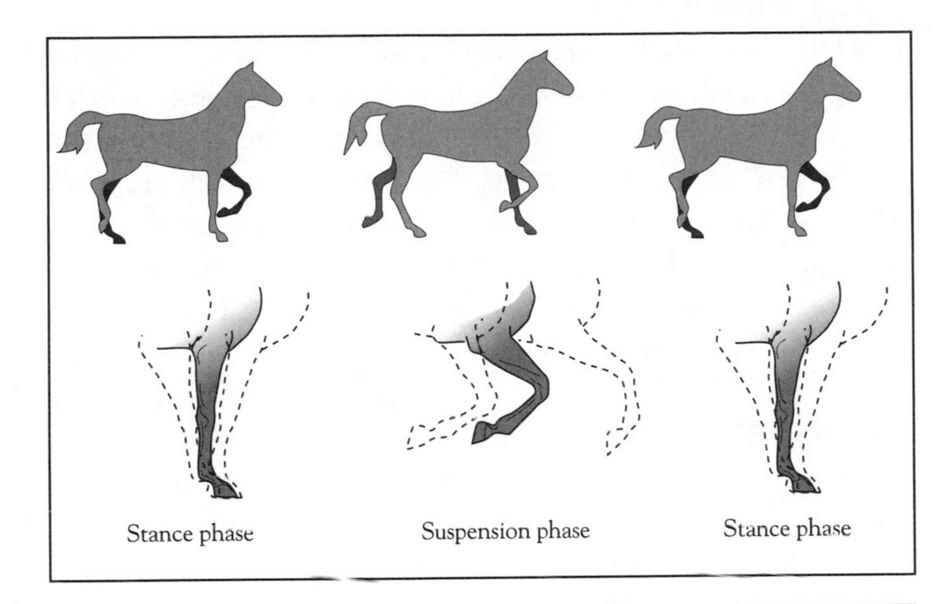

FIGURE 8.7 *Each foot's stride is a cycle made up of a stance phase and a suspension phase. In the symmetrical gaits — walk, trot, and pace — the left and right limbs of each front and rear pair follow the same cycle but are out of phase with one another.* W. E. Jones, ed., *Equine Sports Medicine,* © 1989.

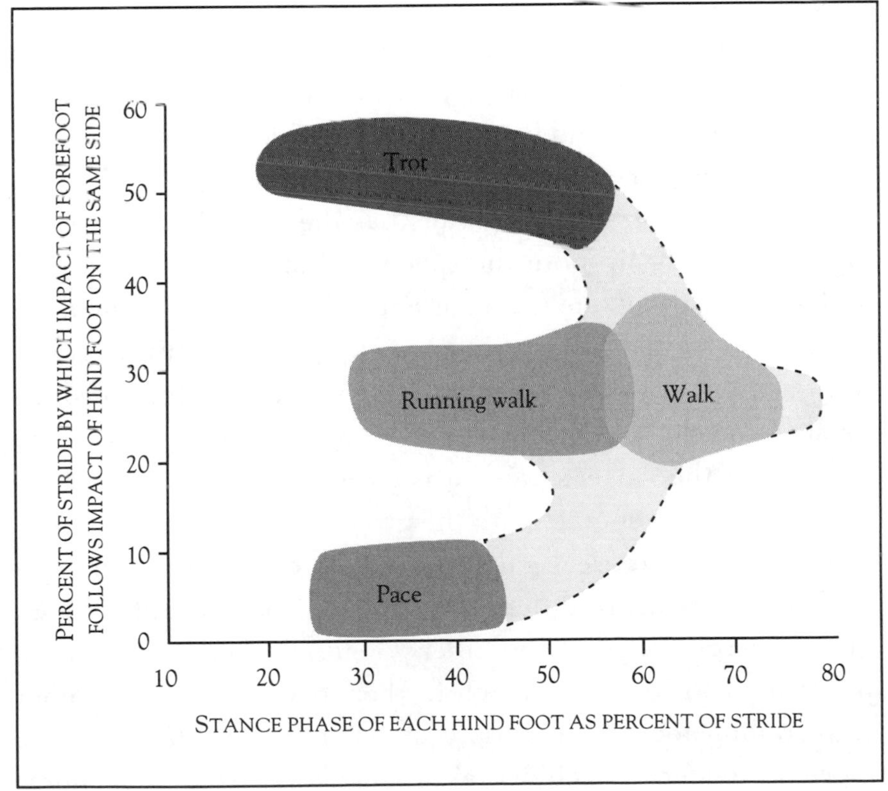

FIGURE 8.8 *The interrelationship of the symmetrical gaits of the horse. See text for further explanation.*

feet fall in exactly the same sequence as they do at the regular walk, but each foot remains on the ground for less than 50 percent of its cycle. This means that at no time are three feet on the ground simultaneously. The walk, slow gait, and rack of these "gaited horses" are really just variations of the same basic gait; they differ only in the percentage of time that each foot remains on the ground during each stride. But note that none of these running walks reaches farther left on the graph than about the 30 percent stance phase: if each foot at a running walk were on the ground for only 25 percent of the stride or less, the horse would be momentarily airborne as each foot left the ground.

By the same token, in all but a slow jog, horses moving at a pace or trot have a stance phase of less than 50 percent, which means there is a point during the stride when no feet are on the ground at these gaits, which have a half-cycle shift between fore- and hind legs on the same side (trot) or between left and right pairs (pace).

This system of describing gaits has the considerable advantage of pointing up both the speed and stability of each gait, and even without any further analysis it can explain a lot about why animals select the gaits they do. The gait diagrams in figure 8.9, which plot the movements of each foot through its stride cycle, are another useful way to quickly assess the stability of the various gaits; it is easy to see at a glance how many feet are in contact with the ground at one time.

In the asymmetrical gaits, the cycles of the left and right feet of each pair are different; a movie of one would *not* look like a mirror image of the other. Generally, one foot in each pair (the lead foot) will reach farther forward than the other (the trailing foot). The variety of possible gaits here is even more bewildering; Hildebrand calculated that the horse should in theory be able to perform 21 different asymmetrical gaits. The two major variations, however, are the transverse gallop and the rotary gallop (figure 8.10). Horses will occasionally use a rotary gallop when changing leads, but like all large, fast-moving animals, they tend to use the transverse gallop as a rule.

Detailed analysis of these gaits becomes extremely complex, so we will content ourselves with the results. Again, stability and speed are the major considerations that seem to determine the selection of gaits by various animals, with maneuverability being an additional factor in the gallop. The transverse gallop is both more stable and more energy efficient than the rotary gallop. When three feet are on the ground at the same time in the transverse gallop, they form a larger triangle of support than do the three feet that touch the ground simultaneously in the rotary gallop (the feet are extended fore and aft in the transverse gallop, contracted in the rotary gallop); and when only two feet are in ground contact, they are more often a diagonal pair, which is more stable than a lateral pair. The limbs are less likely to collide in a transverse gallop, too. Finally, when all four feet are off the ground in a transverse gallop, they are usually collected rather than extended, which requires less muscular effort and keeps the animal closer to the ground and on a more even forward trajectory.

The rotary gallop, however, has one major advantage: maneuverability. A galloping animal can turn stably only toward the side of its lead forefoot. A fast rotary gallop has two suspensions—points in the gait when all four legs are off the ground—as opposed to the one suspension of the transverse gallop, providing an additional opportunity to change leads. Rotary gallops tend to be used by fast sprinters such as

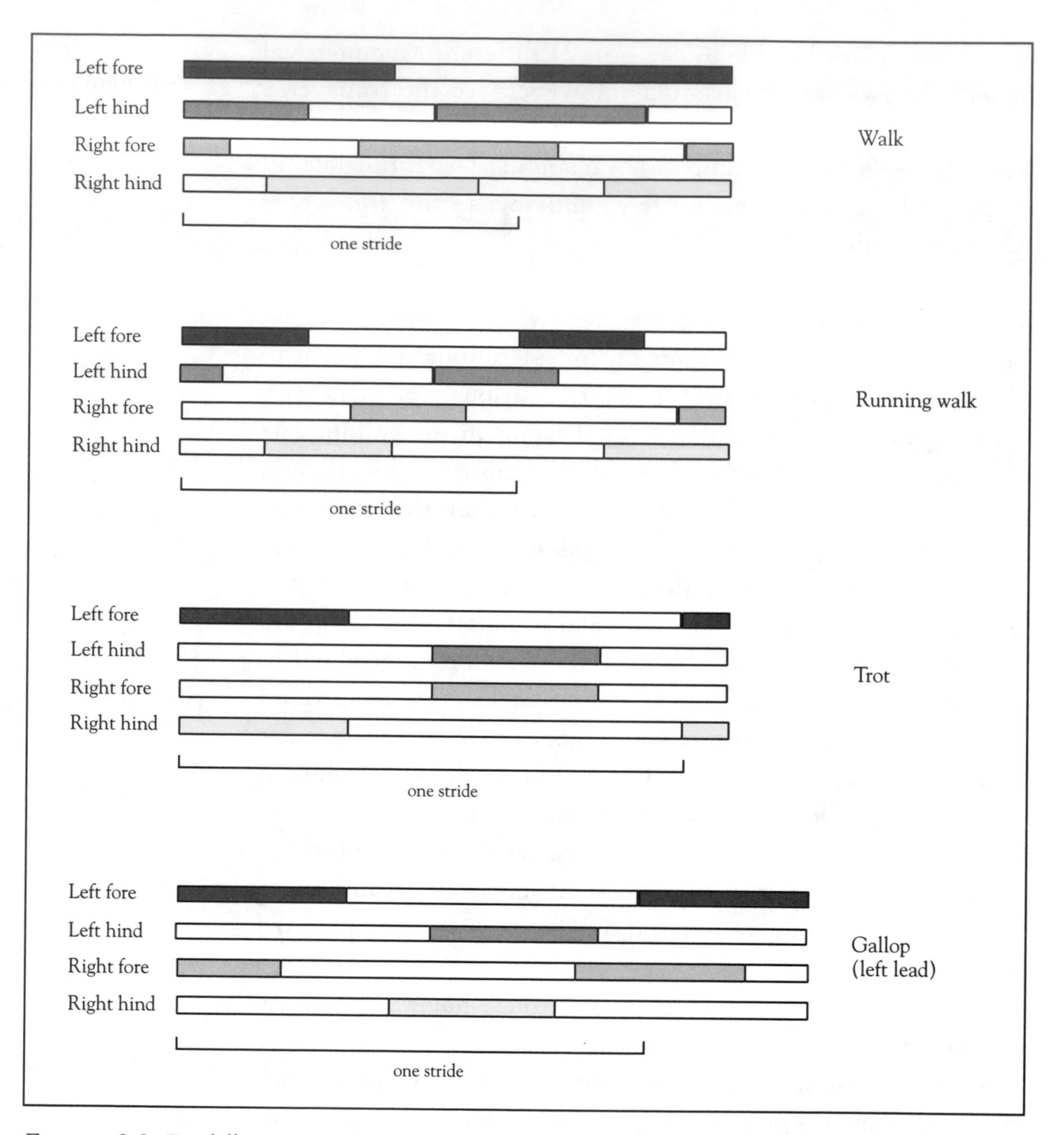

FIGURE 8.9 *Footfall sequences at the walk, running walk, trot, and gallop. The shaded bars indicate when each foot is touching the ground. In a normal walk, two or three feet are always in contact with the ground at any given time; at the running walk, one or two feet simultaneously touch the ground; at the trot and gallop all four feet leave the ground for part of the stride.*

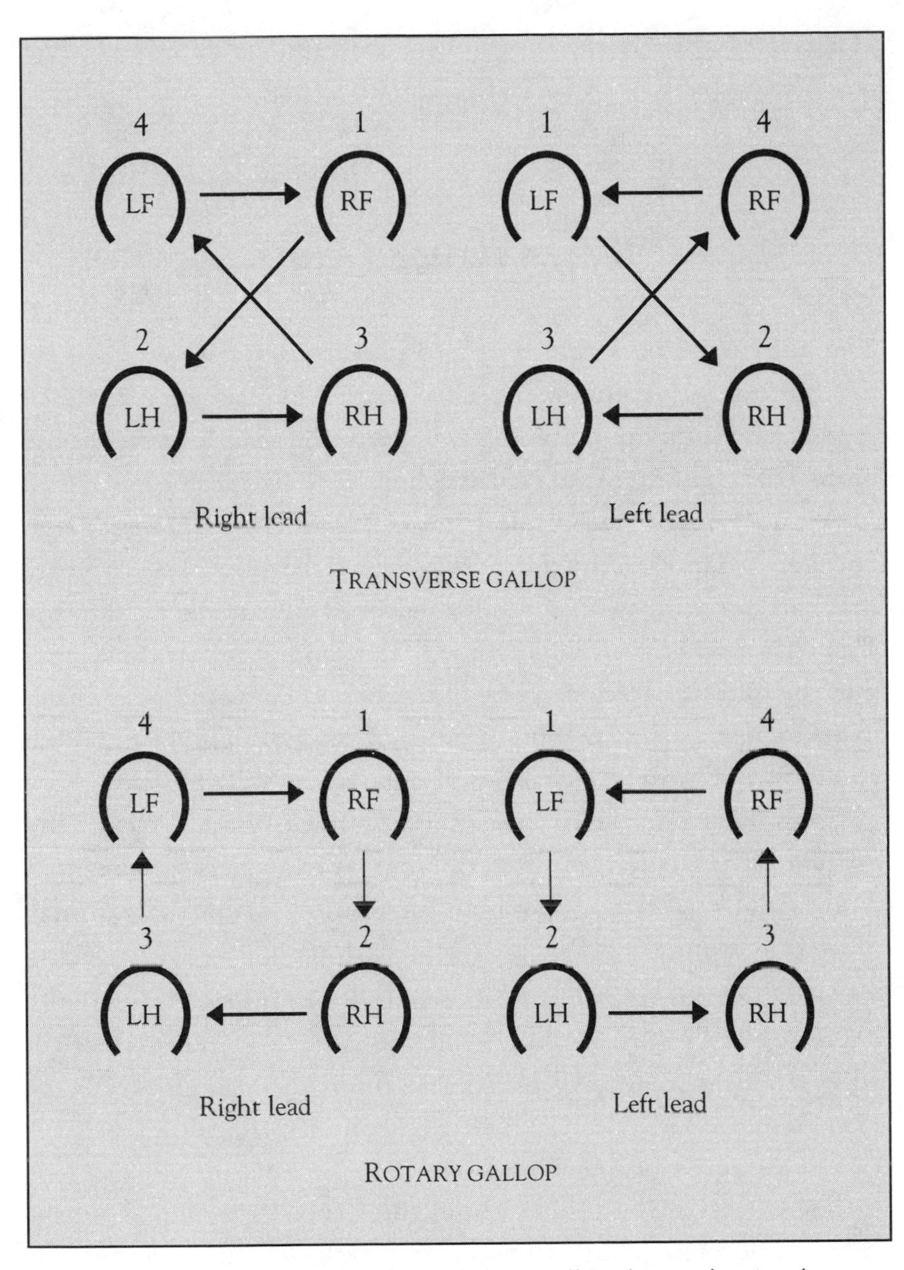

FIGURE 8.10 *Horses occasionally use a rotary gallop when accelerating, but generally rely on the more stable transverse gallop.* W. E. Jones, ed., *Equine Sports Medicine,* © 1989.

cheetahs and small antelopes, precisely the same animals that use flexing back muscles to boost their speed.

Why Change Gears

The gaits that the horse is *able* to use are determined both by the bounds of geometric possibility and by considerations of speed, stability, maneuverability, and the need to keep the limbs from banging into one another.

A somewhat different question is *why* a horse changes from one gait to another in the first place. It is only very recently that this question has been fully answered. We are so used to the idea that a walk is slow, a trot is faster, and a gallop faster still that the question is indeed one that few people would even think to ask. But there is nothing obvious about why animals change gaits: why couldn't a horse simply walk faster and faster?

Something must limit how fast a walk can be. A part of the answer is provided by R. McNeill Alexander's analysis of Muybridge's photos of animals in motion. When Alexander plotted an animal's stride length at various gaits (expressed as a percentage of its leg length) against a parameter called the Froude number, he found that regardless of the animal's size, all of the data points fell pretty much on a straight line. Moreover, almost all animals changed from a walk to a trot at a Froude number of 1.0 (figure 8.11).

The easiest way to think about the Froude number is that it is the ratio of inertial forces to gravitational forces acting on the animal's leg. Going back to the model of the walk as an inverted pendulum, the Froude number is the ratio of the centrifugal force pulling the body's center of mass upward as it swings over the arc described by the leg, to the force of gravity acting to pull that mass down. As the walk gets faster and faster, the animal's center of mass of course moves forward faster. The centrifugal force acting on it increases as well—just as a rock tied to the end of a string pulls harder and harder the faster it is twirled around. Meanwhile, the gravitational force remains the same regardless of speed. As the speed keeps increasing it will eventually reach a point where the upward centrifugal force exceeds the downward gravitational force—the ratio of the two, and thus the Froude number, will be greater than 1.0—and the pendulum will fly off the ground.

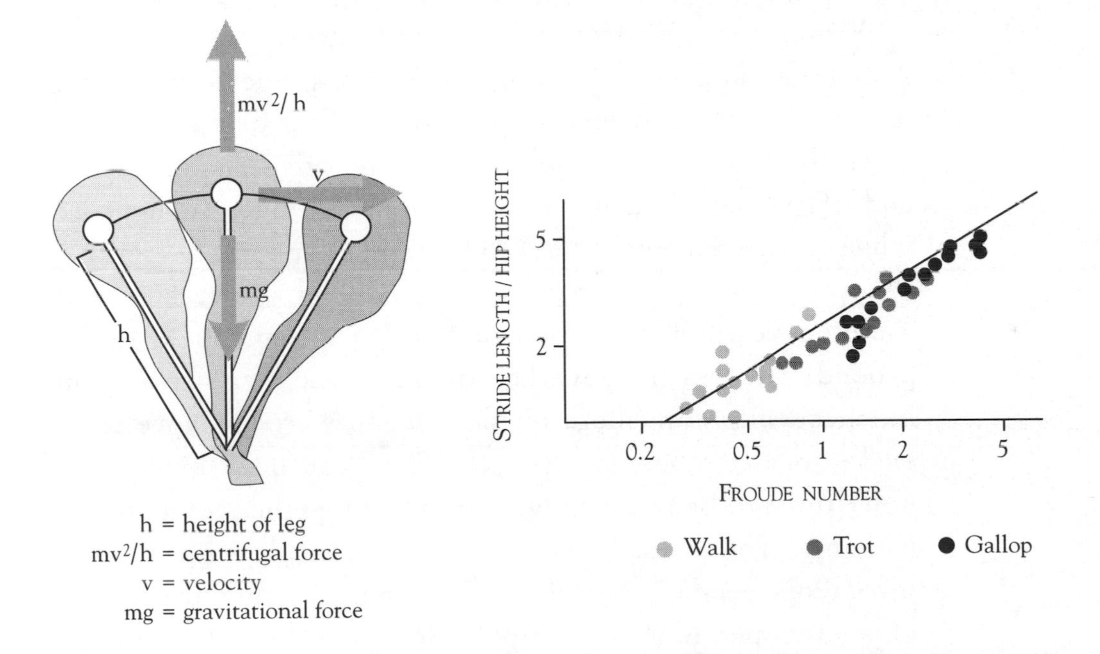

FIGURE 8.11 *At the walk, an animal's leg moves as an inverted pendulum, swinging the center of mass* (m) *through an arc of radius* (h). *In many different animals, the transition from the walk to the trot or the run occurs at a forward velocity* (v) *that corresponds to a "Froude number" of about 1.0. This is exactly the point at which the upward centrifugal force acting on the inverted pendulum* (mv^2/h) *exceeds the downward gravitational force* (mg), *causing it to fly off the ground.*

This appears to be why a walk can only be so fast and no faster. Humans shift from a walk to a run at about 9 kilometers per hour, which corresponds to a Froude number of 0.8; horses shift from a walk to a trot at about 5 kilometers per hour, which equals a Froude number of 0.7 to 0.9.

Because it is impossible to stay on the ground at a Froude number greater than 1.0, to go faster requires a gait that does not stay on the ground—thus, the trot or run, each of which contains an airborne jump. Another way of thinking about this goes back to the earlier observation that speed equals stride length times stride frequency. Jumping is in effect a way to increase speed by stretching the stride length beyond the limits imposed by the length of one's legs.

Although both stride length and stride frequency do increase as the speed of a gallop increases, studies suggest that it is the ability to stretch every last inch out of a stride that gives the fastest racehorses the winning edge. At the upper end of the speed range, stride length continues to increase while stride frequency starts to level off. The total length of a gallop stride is a function of how much each foot overlaps with the others during the period that each is in contact with the ground. The less they overlap, the more each leg's stride can independently contribute to the total forward distance traveled in one complete gallop cycle. (Think of how far you can move forward by hopping with both feet together compared to running.) The average overlap declines sharply with increasing gallop speed, from nearly 50 percent at a slow canter (20 kilometers per hour) to 20 percent or even less at a racing gallop (60 kilometers per hour). Cinematographic analysis of the famous 1973 Belmont Stakes face-off between Secretariat and Riva Ridge showed that Secretariat's homestretch gallop had an overlap of only 18.6 percent versus 24 percent for Riva Ridge. It was his longer stride that brought him home.

Saving Energy—and Limbs

The transition from trot to gallop is driven by somewhat different forces from those that determine the walk–trot transition. Racing trotters are capable of extending the trot to remarkably high speeds; the record speed for a standardbred trotting a mile (54 kilometers per hour) is indeed not much less than that of a thoroughbred galloping the same distance (63 kilometers per hour). Moreover, at the point of transition from the trot to the gallop the stride frequency increases only very slightly (about 10 percent or less), and only slightly beyond that as the gallop speeds up. The gallop actually has a shorter airborne phase than does the trot (20 to 30 percent of the stride for the gallop versus 35 to 43 percent for the trot).

What is the advantage of galloping at higher speeds, then? A partial answer is energy efficiency. The zoologist C. Richard Taylor made an extensive study of energy consumption in animals traveling at various gaits. He trained animals to run on a treadmill whose speed could be varied, and he calculated energy consumption by fitting the animals with face masks that measured how much oxygen they consumed as they worked (plate 7).

When he studied horses (actually Shetland ponies, as his treadmill was not big enough to accommodate horses), he found a striking pattern. At each gait—walk, trot, and gallop—there was one narrow range of speed where energy consumption was lowest. These optimum speeds were almost precisely the same as the speeds the animals themselves naturally chose at each gait (figure 8.12).

When the ponies were forced to move at an unusually slow or fast walk, the energy they spent to move a given distance shot up; the same thing happened at the trot and canter.

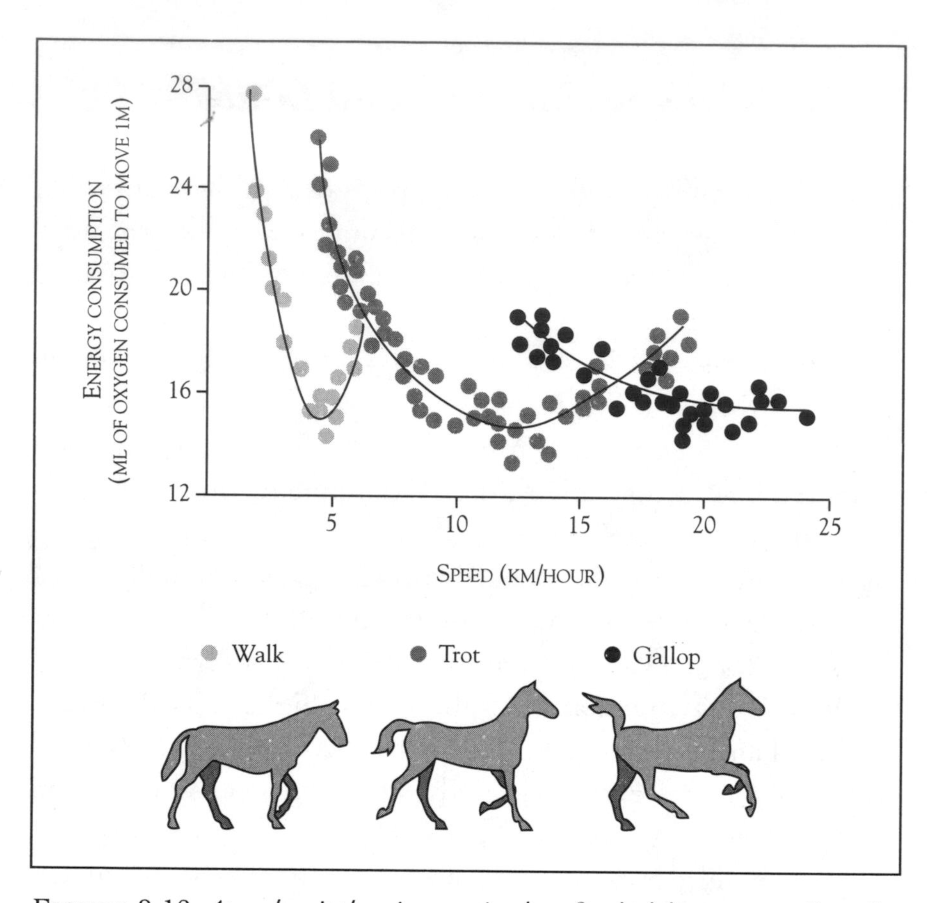

FIGURE 8.12 *At each gait there is an optimal speed, which horses naturally tend to favor, at which energy consumption is minimized. When traveling at these optimal speeds, the energy required to move a given distance is the same whether at the walk, trot, or gallop.*

Another remarkable finding—and one that has been shown again and again in other animals—was that the total energy expended in traveling a kilometer at a walk, a trot, or a canter was exactly the same, so long as the ponies were allowed to move at the optimal speed for each gait.

What this means is that a medium trot is more energy efficient than a fast walk, and a medium canter is more energy efficient than a fast trot. There is still no consensus on why there exists an optimal speed at each gait, but some very intriguing evidence suggests that it is very much analogous to the resonant frequency of a pendulum or a mass on a spring. If you swing a pendulum, it will move back and forth at a fixed rate that depends only on its length. Similarly, a mass on a spring will vibrate back and forth at a frequency that depends on the strength of the spring. As we have seen, the horse in motion is almost literally a combination of pendulums and springs. At the walk, the horse's legs act as inverted pendulums. Moving at the natural frequency of its pendulums is a way to save energy—it takes advantage of the natural acceleration and deceleration of the pendulum at each end of its arc. Pushing a swing is easy when you push in time with its natural rhythm; forcing it to go faster or slower than its natural frequency is a struggle. One is having to continually force the swing to speed up and slow down at the end of its arc. Not surprisingly, the natural walking strides of most mammals are very close to the natural frequency of the pendulums described by their legs.

The springing action of the suspensory ligaments creates another resonant frequency that comes more into play at the trot and gallop, which may explain why energy consumption is lowest when the horse moves within a narrow range of speeds at those gaits. The gallop may have a different resonant frequency in part because the muscles of the torso come into play more than they do at the trot.

Corroboration of this point was obtained by Taylor when he recruited an expert on the pogo stick to hop on his treadmill. The pogo-stick hopper, like all the other animals Taylor studied, had an optimal resonant frequency. Taylor expected that changing the tension of the pogo stick's spring would change that frequency; it did not. Further research finally clarified what was going on. As he hopped the pogo-stock hopper flexed his body, much as a kangaroo does, and it was his body *plus* the pogo-stick spring that together formed the total resonant spring that determined the optimal stride frequency and thus the optimal speed. Galloping horses likewise probably have an optimal, resonant frequency determined by the interplay of all of the various "springs" that are brought to bear at that gait.

The other half of the explanation for the trot–gallop transition was discovered by Taylor's group in studies of the forces that bear on a horse's legs at various gaits. A scale mounted on the treadmill was used to record the force with which each leg struck the ground. As the speed of the trot increased, so did the force. But the studies showed that rather than shifting from a trot to a gallop at a fixed speed, the horses shifted when the peak forces on their legs reached a certain critical level, which was remarkably consistent. When the horses were fitted with saddle packs containing lead weights that increased the force on the ground, they shifted gaits at lower speeds, but again at precisely the same ground force.

Significantly, the actual point of transition was not the best one from an energy point of view. The horses shifted gaits not where the energy consumption curves of the trot and gallop crossed, but earlier, at a speed where galloping was still more costly than trotting.

Shifting gaits did decrease the impact on the legs, however. The gallop is a more "compliant" gait; the legs touch the ground sequentially, which makes it smoother, and the peak up-and-down accelerations of the body are lower than at the trot, reducing the force of impact.

Measurements of the force required to break the cannon bone

indicate that the critical force for the gait transition corresponds to a safety factor of about three. Thus shifting from a trot to a gallop is really a way to minimize the risk of injury. With respect to the question of how a horse "knows" to shift gaits, it may not be able to sense directly how much energy it is using, but it can very directly feel the force of impact on its legs.

Jumping

Muybridge was able to accurately describe the mechanical sequence of a horse as it jumps, but the ballistics of equine jumping have proved surprisingly impervious to scientific scrutiny.

One obstacle is that plotting the flight of the horse's center of mass over a jump—a prerequisite for ballistic analysis—is extremely difficult. The center of mass of a standing horse has been calculated, but the centers of mass of the limbs and segments of the body, especially as they alter in the course of galloping and jumping, are unknown.

Cinematographic studies of Grand Prix jumpers and measurements of leg forces on takeoff and landing, however, have established the basic principles that a horse applies in negotiating a jump (figure 8.13). As the horse approaches the jump at a canter on its final stride, the nonlead foreleg acts as a prop to change the forward motion into an upward rotation. The lead foreleg, which is in contact with the ground for a shorter period, adds a smaller amount of upward angular momentum. In converting forward thrust to upward thrust, the forelegs in effect slow the front of the horse, so that as the hind legs come forward to contact the ground for the last time before the jump they actually reach farther forward than the forelegs did. In other words, the hind legs leave the ground closer to the jump than do the forelegs. The horse's front is already rotated upward by the time the hind legs strike the ground. The hind legs then push off to propel the horse into a ballistic trajectory whose takeoff angle has been determined by the degree of rotation established by the action of the forelegs.

Upon landing, the nonlead forelimb is the first to touch the ground. It generates a largely propulsory thrust; that is, it continues the forward motion of the horse. The lead forelimb touches down next and acts as the major brake of the landing, generating a considerable backward thrust. The trailing hind limb that is next to make contact then brings the horse back into a normal canter with a powerful forward thrust; by the time the lead hind limb touches ground things are back to normal, and that leg shows a pattern of vertical and forward forces comparable to those of an ordinary canter stride.

Experienced horses are apparently able to adjust the take-off angle over a fairly wide range to adjust to different fence

FIGURE 8.13
Jumping sequence, based on high-speed cinematography.

heights. Equitation manuals sometimes suggest that the ideal takeoff point for jumping a simple vertical fence is a distance equal to its height, which would make for a consistent 45-degree takeoff angle whatever the height of the fence and an arc that peaks just over it. That is also the angle that theoretically maximizes the distance traveled in a ballistic trajectory for a given amount of propulsive effort.

But in fact, Grand Prix jumpers filmed negotiating both vertical and spread fences from 1.1 to 1.4 meters high were observed to choose the same takeoff distance fairly consistently, regardless of the height of the fence or whether it was a spread or a vertical. Takeoff distances from verticals were generally much greater than the height of the fence. Another study found that younger horses tended to jump from farther out (2.4 times the fence height) than more experienced horses (1.5 times). In all cases, rather than choosing a takeoff point that would maintain an optimal parabolic arc, the horses seemed to choose a much flatter trajectory and to adjust the shape of that trajectory to suit the fence.

Force studies have shown that when horses jump small fences, the vertical impact on the legs upon landing is almost indistinguishable from that in an ordinary canter, so perhaps the flatter trajectory is in part a way to keep these vertical forces low even when jumping high fences. But jumping is a complex combination of perception, experience, and riding style, and there may be many other explanations. For example, the horse's inability to see the fence at the moment of takeoff may predispose it to err on the safe side by jumping from farther out, rather than run the risk of crashing into it. Or maybe the action of the forelegs in establishing the takeoff trajectory has something to do with it; perhaps for reasons of relative muscle strength or the timing of the takeoff sequence, it is easier to supply the extra propulsive effort required from the hind legs to power a flat trajectory than it is to supply the extra angular momentum required from the front legs to attain a higher takeoff angle.

Shoes and Tracks

Horseshoes fitted with miniature force sensors have furnished some interesting data suggesting that at least some conventional notions about what shoes and feet do are wrong.

We saw earlier that models of locomotion were based on the assumption that almost all of the work done by an animal involves accelerating and decelerating its limbs relative to its body. The actual work done by the limbs against the environment is small. The studies with instrumented horseshoes confirm this. Though it may seem obvious that the feet "push off" against the ground, in fact they are merely acting as pivots. The actual horizontal (forward and backward) force exerted by the hoof against the ground is extremely small. In a horse trotting at about 30 kilometers per hour, the measured maximum acceleration forces on the hoof are only a small percentage of the horse's body weight. (Vertical forces exerted against the ground, by contrast, are much greater, reaching a peak of about 60 percent of body weight at the walk, 90 percent at the trot, 170 percent at the gallop, and as much as 200 percent on the landing side of a jump.)

Some trainers use shoes with a "toe grab," a raised bar under the front of the shoe that is supposed to increase the horse's propulsion by enhancing the push off as the hoof is raised off the ground. In fact, force transducer measurements show that horizontal forces, never very large, actually hit precisely zero at the moment of toe off, which suggests that toe grabs add little or nothing to the horse's effort (figure 8.14).

One idea that has been little explored is the relationship between track surfaces and speed in horses. Studies of human runners by the biomechanician Thomas McMahon led to the discovery that a track whose natural springiness is "tuned" to match a runner's stride frequency can markedly improve performance. The ideal surface should "give" as the foot first comes in contact with the ground, then begin to rebound halfway through the stance phase, and reach full rebound just as the foot lifts off. That way the track's springiness works in concert with the leg's motions; it allows the runner to regain some of the energy he loses to the environment as his foot strikes the ground.

By the same token a surface that is too stiff rebounds too quickly, which merely adds to the shock of impact; a surface that is too mushy rebounds too late to be of any help. A properly tuned track for runners feels unusually springy to those unaccustomed to it, but runners report markedly fewer injuries and find running on such a surface to be unusually comfortable. When McMahon helped to build such a track at Harvard, average running speeds increased by about 2 percent.

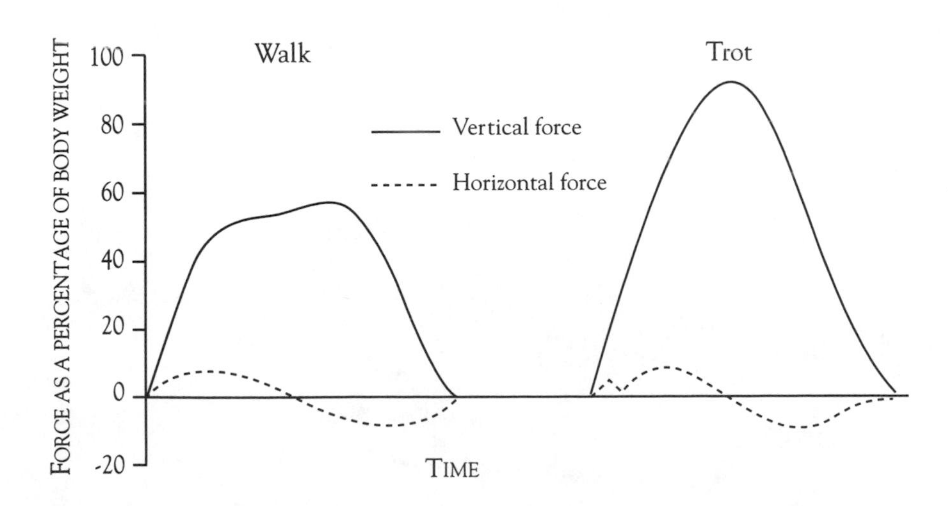

FIGURE 8.14
During the first half of the stance phase the foot exerts a forward (decelerating) force against the ground; during the second half it pushes back to accelerate. Note that at the instant of takeoff, the horizontal force exerted by the foot is zero.

A similarly tuned track for horses would be about four times stiffer than the track for humans, and in fact would feel unusually firm to human athletes; calculations suggest that a properly tuned equine track would be one firm enough that the hoofprints of a galloping horse would make an impression about half a centimeter deep.

Some studies suggest, however, that the most important factor in whether horses suffer injuries in races is not the hardness of the track per se but the conditions that affect fatigue. A retrospective study of injuries at three racetracks in the United States found that breakdowns occurred most often on fast tracks and sloppy tracks and least often on good tracks and muddy tracks; in other words, there was no obvious correlation at all with track firmness. Rather, the factors that most closely correlated with injuries were high temperatures and humidity, which are in turn closely tied to muscular fatigue. As we shall see in the next chapter, clinical studies agree that breakdowns may be related more to strain and overuse than to track conditions or the frequently blamed "bad step."

CHAPTER 9

ASSUME A SPHERICAL HORSE

Olympic athletes of the human kind continue to break records. The winning time in the 800-meter run has dropped in the last hundred years from 2 minutes 11 seconds to 1 minute 43 seconds; marathon runners have shaved nearly a full hour off their time, dropping the record time from about 3 hours to an incredible 2 hours 9 minutes; the record long jump has gone from 5 feet 11 inches to over 7 feet 9 inches. Virtually every track and field record currently on the books was set since 1980, many since 1990.

The advent of sports medicine in the late 1970s and 1980s played no small part in the continuing improvements in human athletic performance. Biomechanical analyses of athletic techniques, studies of how training affects aerobic fitness, research into the effect of diet on performance—all contributed dramatically to measurable gains on the athletic fields. And that success set off a wave of quite natural enthusiasm for the idea that equine sports medicine would do much the same for racing and competition horses.

It did not. Thoroughbred speed records, for example, have remained virtually unchanged for the last 50 years (figure 9.1). And while the winning times in harness races have dropped significantly in recent decades, standardbreds still have shown nowhere near the improvement of human athletes.

FIGURE 9.1 *The winning times in human athletic events in Olympic competition have dropped substantially over the last century. Thoroughbred speeds have dropped only slightly, and in some events have actually increased during the last 50 years.*

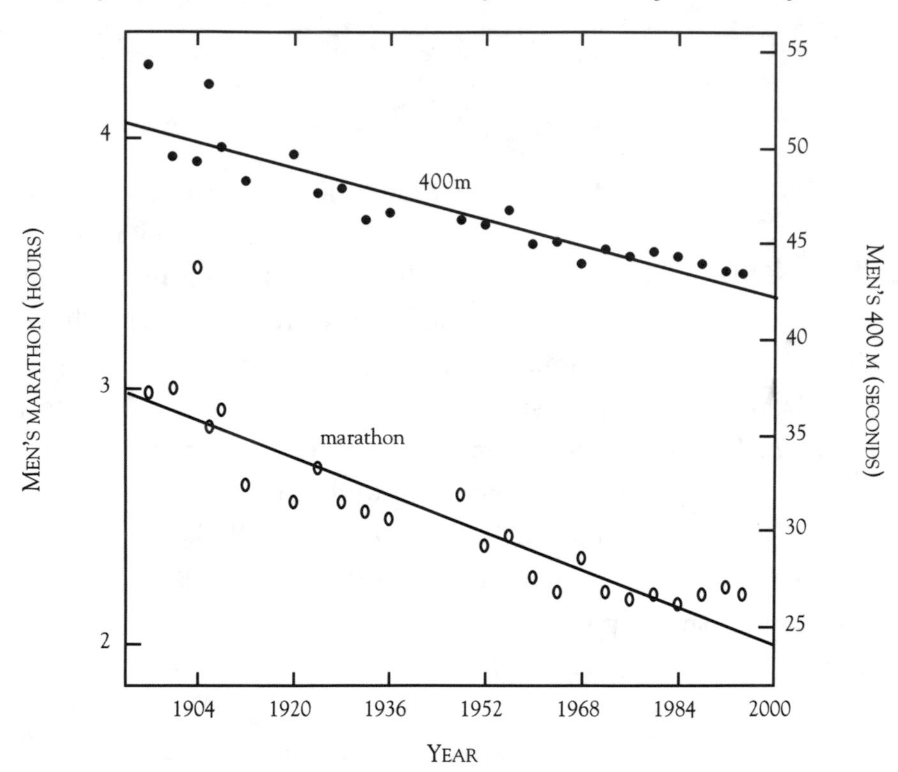

Overconfident assertions by scientists new to the field of equine sports hardly helped matters. Scientists (many of whom "didn't know one end of a racehorse from the other," says one veterinary researcher) glibly told trainers that if they would simply follow their instructions and exercise their horses with long slow workouts, or repeated short fast workouts, or some other such scheme, they would vastly improve their fitness and speed. In the end the backlash against the whole field of equine sports medicine was inevitable.

The title of this chapter comes from an old joke, one that actually predates this fiasco, but which has proved prescient: A group of bookies decides to give an M.I.T. scientist a grant to carry out a state-of-the-art computer simulation of race-

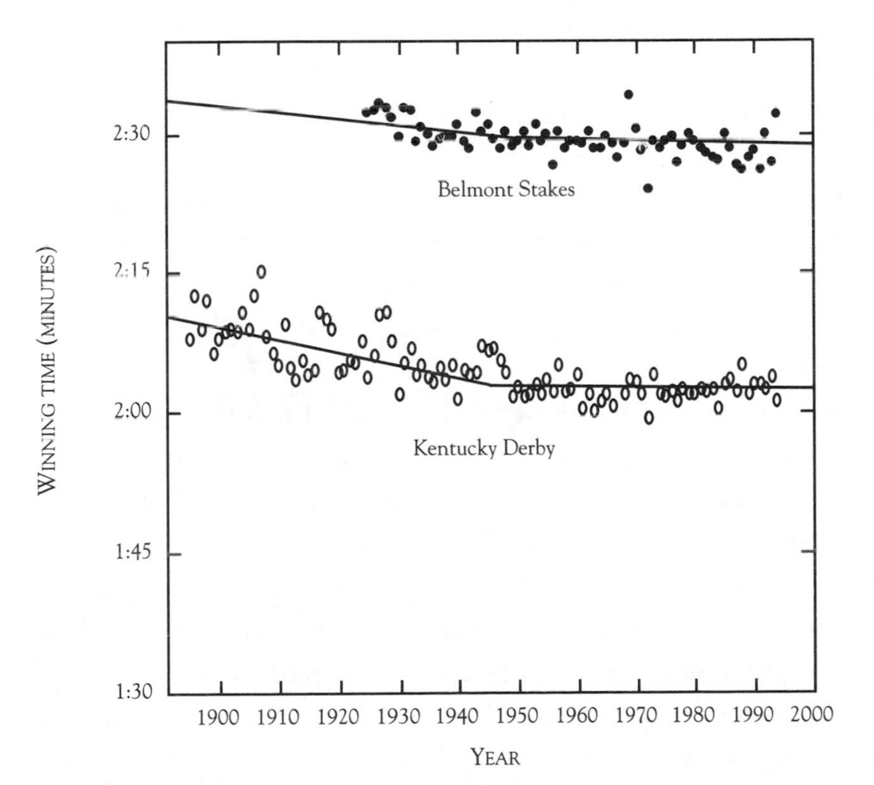

horses, which they will use to help pick winners in future races. At the end of the year the bookies arrive on campus for a briefing. The researcher starts by explaining that in all computer models, of course, certain simplifying assumptions have to be made. "What do you mean simplifying?" asks one of the bookies. "Well," the researcher replies, "in this case we've assumed a spherical horse."

Actually, the assumptions of the equine sports-medicine enthusiasts were not all that bad. The studies of human athletes that inspired them showed that the limiting factor for many athletes was peak metabolic output. That is a combination of many factors often lumped under the term "fitness." It includes the ability of the lungs to supply oxygen to the blood, the ability of the heart to move that blood rapidly and efficiently to the muscles, and the ability of the muscles to put the delivered oxygen to use converting into useful work the energy stored in various molecules (all of which is sometimes called "aerobic fitness"); it also includes the ability of the muscles to generate work from energy stores without the need for oxygen at all ("anaerobic fitness").

The studies in human athletes also found that training regimens could significantly increase many of these limiting factors.

So why didn't this work for horses? The simple answer is that it is hard to make horses better because they are naturally built to operate at the very limits of what hearts, lungs, and muscles can do. On a plot of the maximum metabolic output of various mammals versus their size, the horse soars above the curve: when exercising at peak capacity, a horse generates nearly four times as much energy as expected for a mammal of its size. Once trained, a thoroughbred racehorse is able to maintain its aerobic fitness with remarkably little exercise.

Actively competing thoroughbreds typically race only once every two weeks. Between races they will often see racing speeds only once or twice, and that only over a short distance, perhaps half a mile. Most days they will be exercised at only a slow gallop, for two miles and no more; in the days immediately following a race they will be taken out at no more than a walk.

The very ability of thoroughbreds to generate the flood of energy required for a race with so little intervening work—and the failure of more intensive training regimens to improve this performance—points to a number of fundamental limiting factors that an exercising horse pushes up against when moving at speed.

Dumping Heat

Several of these limiting factors have to do with the basic metabolic mechanisms that power muscles. An exercising horse can increase its metabolic rate by as much as 90 times over its resting rate. One inescapable fact is that work makes heat. An exercising horse is capable of sustaining a much higher level of output, in terms of work produced per kilogram of body weight, than a human can. But as a larger animal, it also has proportionately less surface area. (Mass increases with the linear dimension cubed, much faster than surface area, which increases only with linear dimension squared; a human has a skin surface of about 1 square meter for every 35 to 40 kilograms of body weight, versus 1 square meter for every 90 to 100 kilograms for a horse.) This smaller surface area means that keeping cool is a much harder job for a horse, for it has less skin through which to transport the heat that exercising muscles accumulate. Horses also lack one basic mechanism for lowering blood temperature: because horses cannot breathe through the mouth, they are unable to pant like dogs (or people), and thus cannot use the respiratory system for cooling.

Horses are famous for their ability to sweat, though. An exercising horse can produce five times the volume of sweat per area of skin that a human can. Sweating cools the body through evaporative cooling; as water evaporates it absorbs large amounts of heat. But that only works if the sweat *can* evaporate. Extra sweating that does not evaporate does no good. Horses exercised for about 10 minutes at 90 percent of their peak capacity were found to lose almost 10 liters of water. The actual cooling achieved was equivalent to the evaporation of just 4 liters, and that was less than the total amount of heat produced by the exercising muscles. By the end of the work period the temperatures of the muscles had shot up 6 degrees Celsius. In other words, the horses were already producing heat beyond their capacity to get rid of it, a capacity determined by the laws of geometry (surface to volume ratio) and physics (the heat of evaporation of water).

Researcher David Hodgson and his colleagues thus concluded that despite the horse's great sweating capacity, there is no getting around the limitations it faces by virtue of its size. When muscles reach about 45 degrees Celsius, which is about 7 degrees above the normal resting temperature, the muscle enzymes that play a crucial part in transforming stored energy into muscular work begin to denature, or break down. The brain is even more susceptible to overheating; in experiments with goats, the animals rapidly became fatigued when their brain temperatures were artificially elevated to 42 degrees Celsius, even when their body temperatures remained relatively low. A small number of experiments in horses suggests that horses have a similar threshold, which may be related specifically to overheating of the hypothalamus—the portion of the brain responsible for regulating body temperature.

Getting rid of heat is not a limiting factor in most races, which last two minutes or less. But even moderately intense exercise that lasts much longer cannot be sustained without taxing a horse's thermoregulatory mechanisms to their very limit. The laws of physics that govern how quickly horses can get rid of the heat generated by their muscles impose an impenetrable ceiling on the upper limit of their performance in endurance races or other extended events. This is all the more so in hot and humid conditions, which undercut the effectiveness of the evaporative cooling mechanisms.

Mobilizing Energy

Making muscles work is at heart a matter of converting stored chemical energy into mechanical energy. And it is here that other basic facts of equine life conspire to resist improvement.

The chemical energy that drives a muscle comes most directly from a molecule called ATP, or adenosine triphosphate. This molecule contains a series of high-energy phosphate bonds; when a chemical reaction within the muscle cell breaks one of these bonds, its considerable energy is released to power the biochemical reactions that make the proteins of the muscle contract.

Muscle cells at rest contain a small stock of ATP waiting to set the muscle in motion. But ATP is not so much like the stored fuel that powers an engine as it is like the steam that directly causes the turbine to turn. A muscle at rest maintains a small head of steam in reserve, but it is other chemicals, mainly sugars and fats, that act as the stockpiles of fuel that must be burned to bring the pressure up to meet the demands of real work.

Muscles use three principal methods to generate ATP (figure 9.2), and each contributes in a slightly different way to the horse's ability to variously accelerate to a fast start, sprint at peak speed, and maintain a steady pace over a long course. It is this combination of different energy-generation schemes that allows the horse to match its energy output to widely varying demands; it is their complex interplay that also

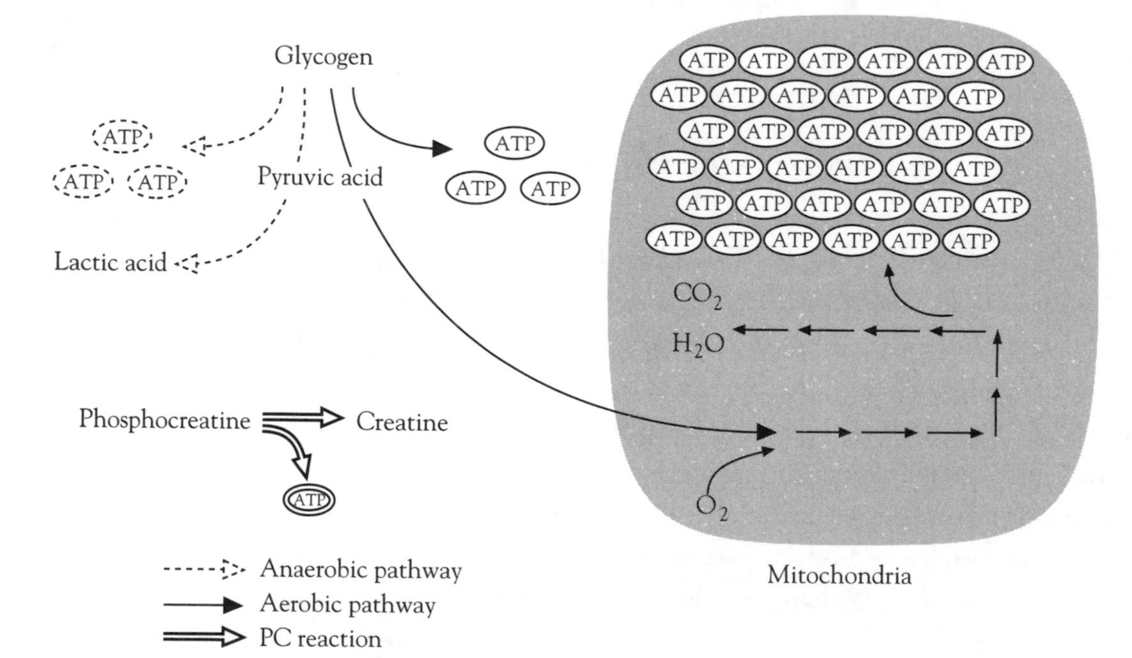

FIGURE 9.2
ATP, the molecule that powers muscles, is produced through three different metabolic pathways.

explains why a horse's performance may be only minimally affected by efforts to enhance aerobic fitness.

When a sudden demand is placed on a muscle for a burst of energy, its first recourse is to throw on fuel that is nearby and that ignites with a bang. Muscles keep a small load of just such a fuel on hand in the form of a molecule called phosphocreatine (PC). A single, quick chemical reaction turns PC into ATP. Together with the very small reserve of ATP stored in the muscle, the PC reaction provides enough fuel for about 10 to 15 seconds of peak muscular activity. A thoroughbred accelerating out of the starting gate, a jumper or hunter pushing off over a fence, a roping horse or barrel racer or any other horse engaging in a very short but very high-intensity event is drawing almost entirely on these rapidly deployable—and rapidly depletable—reserves.

Within about 10 to 20 seconds, or at just about the same time that the muscles are running out of their ready-made ATP and their on-hand stocks of PC, a second mechanism begins to take over. This one is slower to get going because it involves many more chemical steps; it is analogous to throwing on a fuel like coal, which burns hot once it starts but requires a lot of kindling before it will ignite. In this mechanism, called anaerobic glycolysis, energy stored in the muscles in the form of a fat molecule called glycogen is converted to ATP to keep the muscles going. Its advantage is that, like the PC pathway, it does not require oxygen—and there is an inevitable delay between the moment the heart and lungs start stepping up their output and the moment the increased flow of oxygenated blood actually arrives at muscle cells in distant reaches of the body.

The disadvantage of anaerobic glycolysis is its inefficiency—it liberates only about one-thirteenth of the energy that can be milked out of a glycogen molecule. A more serious disadvantage is its deadly by-products. The quick and dirty combustion of glycogen produces as an immediate by-product pyruvic acid, which must be disposed of as quickly as possible to prevent the glycolytic pathway from being clogged and immediately coming to a halt. The stopgap solution is to convert pyruvic acid into lactic acid, but under these circumstances lactic acid can rapidly build up in the muscle cells; the increased acidity throws critical enzymes out of whack and leads to rapid muscular fatigue—the aching sensation in a tiring muscle. If a horse had to rely solely on anaerobic glycolysis, it would come to a screeching halt after just 60 seconds of maximum muscular effort, having exhausted its stores of glycogen and having accumulated too much lactic acid for the muscles to continue to function even if further glycogen stores were available.

While anaerobic glycolysis is slower to get going than the PC reaction, it is still quicker than the oxygen-burning pathway that is the third principal mechanism cells use to generate ATP, and which involves a lengthy chain of a dozen or more reactions.

This mechanism, known as aerobic metabolism, is usually thought of as the "normal" energy-producing pathway in the body. It generates the largest amount of ATP and the minimal amount of by-products; the pyruvic acid generated in the course of aerobic metabolism is completely broken down by further reactions, leaving only carbon dioxide and water.

But in fact aerobic metabolism may not come into play at all in sprints such as quarter-horse races or in thoroughbred races under 6 furlongs. The delay involved in pumping extra oxygen to the cells, plus the time it takes to get the multiple biochemical reactions of this pathway cranked up to their maximum rate, means that it takes 45 to 60 seconds after the body first senses an extra energy demand before the aerobic pathway reaches full ATP production.

Once aerobic metabolism is up and running, however, it is capable of powering a long, sustained effort. Not only is it far more efficient at converting stored energy to ATP, it is also able to make use of glucose pumped to the cells through the bloodstream—glucose derived from the vast stores of glycogen stockpiled in the liver and fatty tissues of the body.

In a thoroughbred race at longer distances, the PC reaction and anaerobic glycolysis supply most of the energy at the start. Aerobic metabolism takes over by the second half of the race, allowing the costly (and lactic acid forming) anaerobic pathway to back off some. But calculations show that the total power requirements of galloping at racing speed cannot be met by aerobic metabolism alone, even at its maximum output, so some anaerobic glycolysis continues. Depending on how quickly the horse is able to bring the aerobic pathway on line early in the race, it will have more or less lactic acid buildup and more or less ability to pour on additional anaerobic glycolysis in the final sprint to boost its already maxed-out aerobic metabolism.

In standardbred racing, the metabolic pathways contribute rather differently in the course of the race. Because standardbreds accelerate only slowly at the start (the actual start occurs with the horses already in motion, abreast behind a pace car), they don't call upon their PC reserves at the beginning of a race. The burst of speed that is typical of the final quarter of a standardbred race is the result of ATP generation from the untapped PC reserves being summoned into action at the very end.

But in both cases, total speed is dependent upon the contribution of all three metabolic pathways. With exercise, a horse's heart capacity, blood volume, blood circulation, and overall aerobic potential all are known to improve. Yet such aerobic factors are only part of what it takes for a horse to perform, and not necessarily the most important part; indeed, for a sprinter these factors may be almost irrelevant. A horse with a great heart and lungs may not be the fastest horse over a short distance, for the simple reason that heart and lungs don't come into play.

Muscle Types

More evidence that the horse's athletic capabilities are a matter of nature rather than training comes from studies of muscle fiber. Like other mammals, horses possess a mixture of "slow-twitch," or type I, muscle fibers and "fast-twitch," or type II, fibers. The particular mix of the two fiber types varies considerably from individual to individual. And to some extent the mix may determine a horse's natural athletic abilities.

Slow-twitch fibers, as their name implies, contract and relax relatively slowly. But they are also more efficient and have greater staying power because they contain a larger complement of the enzymes needed for aerobic metabolism.

Fast-twitch fibers are capable of quick action and can perform readily in the absence of oxygen because they possess an extra helping of the anaerobic glycolysis enzymes. But by the same token their poorer capacity for aerobic metabolism means that they cannot as readily switch over to that more efficient and sustainable pathway, even after the lungs and heart gear up to deliver oxygen in abundant quantities. They more quickly accumulate lactic acid and tire.

The best human athletes appear to possess a mix of fiber types that closely matches the demands of the sport in which they excel. The leg muscles of a champion sprinter may have as much as 85 percent type II fibers; champion marathoners or bicyclists can have a like proportion of type I fibers. (The average person has around 50 percent of each.)

The same trend appears in horses that have been studied. Successful endurance-raced horses, those that consistently attained average speeds of nearly 15 kilometers per hour in races up to 180 kilometers long, had a significantly greater proportion of type I fibers (51 percent) in the deep muscles of the hindquarters than did unsuccessful horses (37 percent). Moreover, the type II fibers they did have were disproportionately of the type called IIa, which have a higher aerobic capacity; they had almost no type IIb fibers (3 percent, versus 19 percent in the unsuccessful horses), which have a very high anaerobic capacity but reduced aerobic capacity.

Similarly, studies of sprinting horses show that the best sprinters have the highest proportion of type IIb fibers and the lowest proportion of type I. Some quarter horses have been found to have nearly 100 percent type II fibers in the large muscles that propel the hindquarters.

A certain amount of shuffling between the two types (and between type IIa and IIb) can occur in response to exercise in horses. The proportion of slow-twitch, type I fibers declined in thoroughbreds given 12 weeks of high-intensity training, and a number of studies have shown substantial increases in the ratio of type IIa to type IIb fibers in response to exercise. Some increase in aerobic capacity in all three muscle types occurs with exercise as well. The marked breed differences in muscle fiber types, however, seem to suggest that these are endowments that a horse is fundamentally born with.

But perhaps the most striking finding of metabolic studies of racehorses is that there is an almost perfect match between the ability of the lungs to supply oxygen to the blood, the ability of the heart and circulation to deliver that oxygen to the cells, and the ability of the muscle cells to utilize that oxygen when the horse is exercising at peak performance. There is, in other words, no limiting factor; everything is in balance to get the most out of the entire system at maximum output.

Some recent attempts to stack the metabolic deck by altering a racehorse's feed have attracted considerable attention from both trainers looking for an extra edge and race officials worrying about where to draw the line between legitimate nutrition and the illegitimate use of drugs. Some studies have suggested that adding extra fat to the diet can increase the anaerobic potential of horses, possibly by increasing the stocks of glycogen that the muscle cells can tap during anaerobic glycolysis. Overall the data appear to be inconclusive, however, and high amounts of dietary fat may actually have the reverse effect. Feeding horses creatine has been tried as a way to enhance the PC reaction and improve sprinting and acceleration, but again the data are profoundly inconclusive.

Another popular (and rather horrifying) practice is feeding huge amounts of bicarbonate of soda—as much as half a kilogram, via a feeding tube inserted into the stomach through the nose—before a race. The idea is that, as an acid buffer, bicarbonate can neutralize the acid buildup in muscle cells as lactic acid accumulates during anaerobic glycolysis, reducing the fatigue associated with it. Although studies have failed to show any improvement in performance when horses are fed sodium bicarbonate, the practice does appear to improve the rate of anaerobic glycolysis in muscle cells, as indicated by a higher concentration of lactate in the blood. The practice has been banned in Australia and is the subject of considerable controversy elsewhere.

The fascination with dietary gimmicks is nothing new among horsemen, of course, and to a certain extent reflects a basic human hunger for magic shortcuts. But it also serves as indirect confirmation of just how difficult it is to improve, by more legitimate means, the performance of horses that already are operating at or near the limits of their potential.

Breathing and Moving

Exercise does appear to improve overall aerobic fitness in horses, just as it does in humans. Blood volume actually increases, circulation improves, the heart is able to pump more blood with less effort; overall, the amount of oxygen that the heart and lungs can deliver to the muscle cells per minute increases.

The lungs of a racehorse are able to respond to an enormous, and enormous range, of demand for oxygen from the muscle cells as the work load increases. A horse at a walk consumes just a liter of oxygen a minute; at a racing gallop, oxygen consumption can approach 60 liters a minute.

Yet researchers have found that the mechanics of the equine respiratory system impose a fundamental limit on how fast a galloping horse can breathe, which all the training in the world cannot alter. Horses are different from humans in this regard primarily because of the role the forelimbs play: Because horses have no collar bone, the motion of the forelimbs is tied directly to the ribs and spine by the horse's powerful muscles. As the forelimbs strike the ground at the canter or gallop, the compressive loading transmitted through the legs forces the ribs upward, which acts to squeeze air out of the lungs like a bellows. At the same time, the horse is lowering its head and neck, which acts to press the rib cage backward, adding to the compressive effect. And, finally, the front of the body is decelerating at this instant in the gallop cycle as the forelimbs touch the ground; this causes the internal organs, which are attached to the diaphragm by springy ligaments, to slosh forward, giving the lungs a further squeeze.

As the head and neck are raised and the load is lifted off the

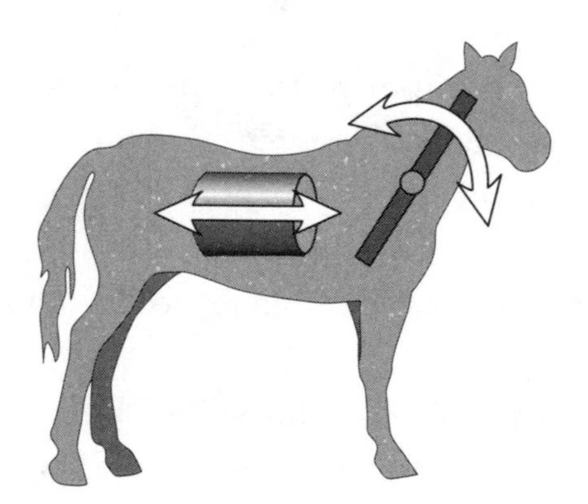

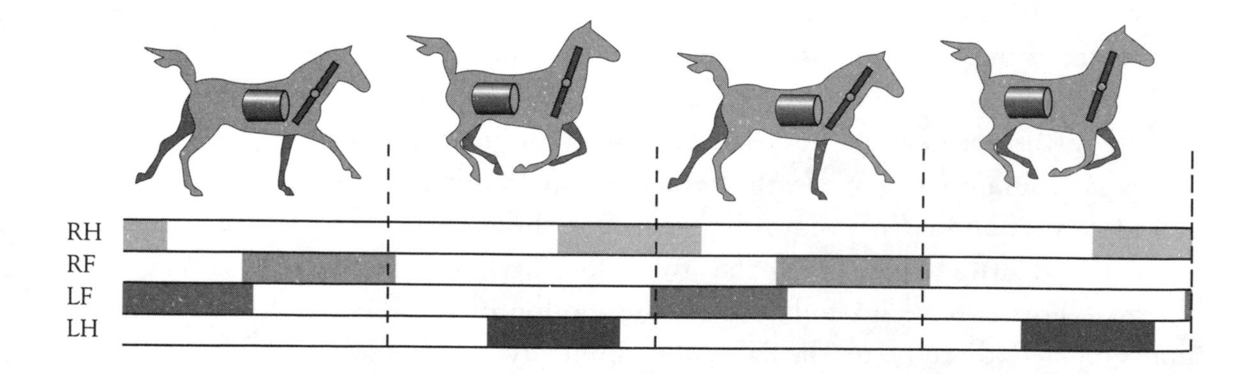

FIGURE 9.3 *The head and neck act like a pendulum, and the internal organs like a piston, that alternately squeeze and expand the lungs in rhythm with each stride at the canter or gallop. Below, the shaded bars indicate the portion of each leg's stride during which the foot is in contact with the ground.*

forelimbs, the rib cage and sternum are pulled forward and down; the front of the body accelerates and the "piston" formed by the internal organs slides backwards. Both actions cause the lungs to expand, drawing air in (figure 9.3).

Because both the piston and the head–neck pendulum are mechanically tied to the gallop stride, the horse's breathing is normally synchronized to its pace. It takes exactly one breath per stride. Inspiration occurs during the suspension phase as the forelimbs lift off the ground, expiration during the stance phase as the forelimbs strike the ground.

This linkage between stride and breathing occurs in four-legged mammals ranging from gerbils to rhinoceroses. All take one breath per stride at the gallop. (The wallaby takes one breath per hop.) Studies of diaphragm muscles in mice, rats, and rabbits suggest that the diaphragm itself may play an active part in keeping the rhythm going; the diaphragm muscles appear to expand and contract with the greatest power at a natural resonant frequency that closely matches the animal's preferred galloping frequency.

At the canter there is still a 1:1 coupling between respiration and stride, but the cycles of the two are shifted slightly out of phase compared to the gallop: the horse continues to breathe in for a bit after the nonlead forelimb strikes the ground, and there is a slight delay before expiration begins. This is probably because, by striking the ground simultaneously at the canter, the diagonal pair (nonlead forelimb and lead hind limb) absorbs some of the initial force exerted by the nonlead forelimb, and the force is transmitted to the rib cage more slowly.

Up to a point, this remarkable mechanism works to keep oxygen supply perfectly matched to oxygen demand over a huge range. Just as speed equals stride length times stride frequency, so lung output per minute equals the depth of each breath times the number of breaths per minute. The 1:1 coupling between stride frequency and breath frequency allows the two to keep pace with one another automatically.

But as we have seen, there are limits to how much a horse can increase its speed by increasing the number of strides per minute. At their fastest, horses appear to increase speed primarily by taking longer strides. Although there is some evidence that longer strides mechanically force the lungs to take deeper breaths, the fundamental coupling of breathing to stride means that a limit has to be reached eventually. At the highest speeds, the forced breathing cycle begins to lose efficiency as the time available for each breath is shortened. A horse that minimizes the overlap of its feet as they contact the ground will have a longer stride but will also minimize its suspension time, and it is during suspension that a horse inhales. At high speeds the ratio of inhalation time to exhalation time in fact begins to drop. The horse simply does not have enough time to take in a full breath.

A horse that is beginning to tire for lack of sufficient oxygen is stuck. Although horses do take intermittent deep breaths when running at high speeds (as do humans), the basic coupling of the respiratory and stride cycles makes it difficult to change one substantially without changing the other. Tired horses often appear to alter their gait in an attempt to force more air through their lungs. They will prolong the suspension phase of the gallop; they will also make exaggerated up-and-down motions of the head and neck, in effect trying to pump the pendulum harder to force deeper breaths. Both tactics may be effective in maintaining high lung output per stride, but they inescapably alter the gait and take their toll on speed.

There is no comparable coupling of breathing and gait at the trot, pace, or walk, which makes sense—the muscles that tie the forelimbs to the rib cage act alternately on the left and right sides at these gaits, in effect canceling each other out. The level carriage of the head and neck at the trot and pace also stills the pendulum.

Some coupling between breathing and stride does appear for brief periods at these gaits, however; horses at a trot will at times take precisely one breath per stride or one breath every two strides. And X-rays of trotting dogs show a more subtle form of forced coupling at the trot in which different parts of the lungs fill and empty independently. The front left and front right lobes of the lungs seem to fill and empty alternately, each in time with the movements of the forelimb on its side, while the back left and back right lobes are driven together by action of the visceral "piston." It seems likely that the same mechanism may operate in horses and other quadrupeds. And it would again suggest that to the extent breathing even is a limiting factor in the performance of horses, it is a limiting factor that is indelibly set by the dynamics of gaits.

Fitness Versus Toughness

We began this chapter by posing the question of why thoroughbred racehorses are not getting any faster (and why standardbreds, though improving, are not improving nearly so rapidly as human athletes). The answer in brief is that the best horses are already performing at their maximum potential. The scientific understanding that has led human athletes to improve their metabolic capabilities is simply not relevant to most top equine athletes, whose training programs are more than sufficient to bring those capabilities up to their highest levels. (Whether further breeding can lead to genetic improvements in the potential of the best horses is a slightly different question, one we will take up in chapter 10.) "The reason people got better is because they weren't very good to start with," notes researcher Howard Seeherman. "But horses are able to maintain a very high level of fitness."

The failure of much-heralded techniques such as interval training to produce breakthroughs in equine performance is of a piece with Seeherman's observation. The idea behind interval training—exercising a horse with a series of concentrated, intense workouts—is to stress various components of the metabolic pathways. But as we have seen there are many, many factors that limit a horse's fundamental metabolic performance. The problem is not that trainers have not yet hit on the magic formula for realizing the horse's potential; the problem is that *any* reasonably strenuous program of exercise already does so, and moving beyond that point would require a horse that can run without breathing or somehow circumvent the physical realities imposed by its surface to volume ratio or the biochemical facts of metabolism and muscle type. It is not so much that interval training does not work, but rather that it does not do much more than any other, more conventional training procedures can do.

Clinical experience in recent years supports this view. When a horse fails to live up to its apparent potential the problem is rarely a lack of fitness. Instead, the cause usually lies in limitations that fall into the categories of disease and pathology. Subtle defects in the bones of the leg or in the airways of the respiratory system appear to be surprisingly common sources of limitation in top horses. Researchers using new bone-scanning technologies have shown that many sound, apparently normal horses are in fact not normal; they have suffered from very subtle stress fractures or weakening of the bone that predispose them to further injury and even catastrophic breakdowns.

Breakdowns have generally been chalked up to the failure of normal bone under abnormal circumstances (the "bad step" on the track); in fact, bone scans make it clear that these are mostly failures of abnormal bone under normal circumstances. The most frequent sites of breakdown—the humerus, cannon bones, sesamoids, and fetlocks—are precisely the same places where stress fractures or weakening is observed in bone scans of lame, and even many sound, racehorses.

Bone is usually thought of as inert. In fact it is a living structure that is continually undergoing change. The body "remodels" bone by adding it to places that are subject to extra stress and removing it elsewhere. If the process gets out of balance, however, the stressed sites can accumulate damage and grow weak or brittle.

Although some horses are genetically immune to these problems, young thoroughbreds and standardbreds have an incidence of abnormal remodeling that may run as high as 50 percent. Decreased exercise for two to three months is usually adequate to correct the problem; Seeherman is also investigating the possible benefits of beginning exercise training of thoroughbreds in preadolescence, rather than waiting until the usual 1½ years, which corresponds to a human age of 18. (There is an interesting analogy between 2-year-old racehorses and Army recruits. In basic training as many as 20 percent of new recruits suffer stress fractures. Seeherman speculates that in both cases the problem is caused by putting relatively physically inactive subjects through a regimen of intensive exercise. Exercise programs that begin earlier, to build up muscle and bone strength more gradually before the start of intensive training, probably could prevent injuries in both cases.)

Defects (probably genetic in origin) involving restrictions of the airways or bleeding in the lungs are other performance-limiting problems seen in many racehorses. Fitness problems associated with insufficient exercise are way down on the list of the clinical problems encountered by veterinarians in horses being examined for failure to perform.

Everything else being equal, what ultimately determines the difference between the fastest horses and the also-rans may not be a matter of physiology at all. It is interesting to note that standardbreds, which face a much more demanding race schedule than do thoroughbreds—races are generally once a week, over a distance of a mile, at the much more tiring gait of the trot or pace—are also trained on a much more rigorous program. They work out almost every day between races, and at full race speeds on three of those days. Yet studies make it absolutely clear that these horses are no more fit for their extra efforts (figure 9.4). "This suggests," writes Seeherman, "that the increased training required for successful standardbred racehorses is beneficial for reasons other than cardiopulmonary or metabolic fitness."

In fact, the benefit may be largely psychological—an acquired ability to withstand the pain of the more demanding trotting or pacing race. By the same token, trainers have long recognized that horses can become bored, or "sour" or "stale," from too much training and fail to perform well, even though there is nothing wrong with them physically. A fascinating study of overtraining in horses recently confirmed this. Horses were put through strenuous, and increasingly demanding, daily exercise for nine months; on alternating days they were given either a 20-minute endurance run or interval training consisting of a series of fast 3-minute workouts. By the end of the period the horses became sluggish and irritable, refused to eat their food, and lost weight. Yet biochemical data from the horses' muscle cells showed no change that could explain this dropoff in performance. The amount of glycogen stores in the muscle cells, for example, and the ability of the muscle cells to

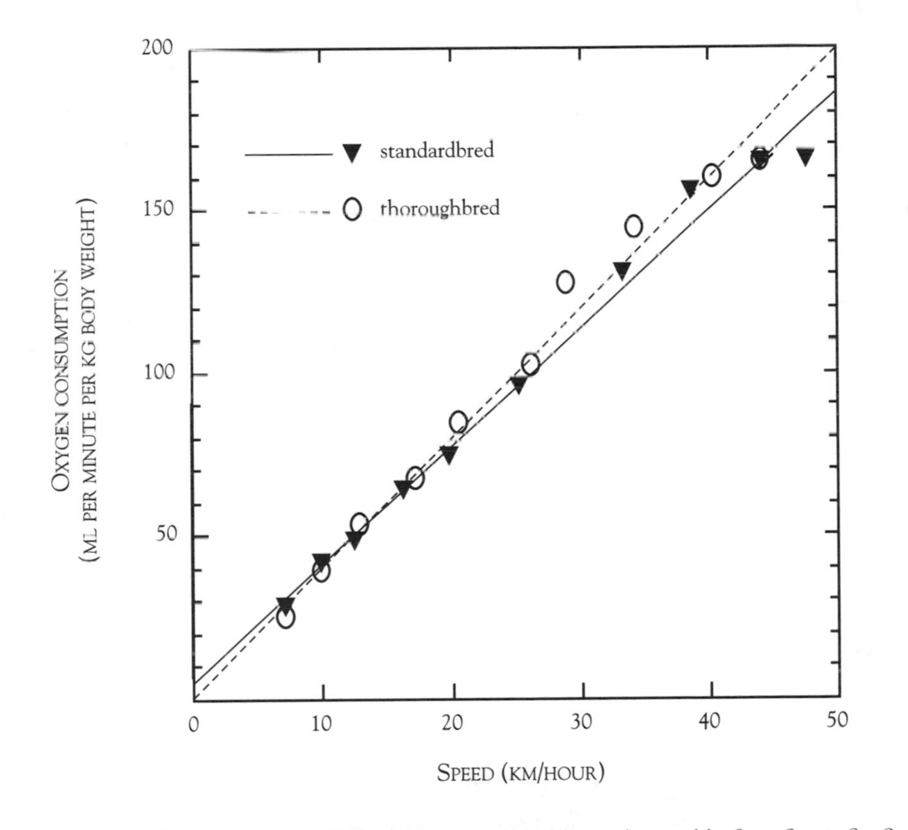

FIGURE 9.4 *Despite very different training regimens, thoroughbreds and standardbreds show very little difference in overall fitness on a variety of measures, including oxygen consumption as a function of speed, shown here.*

utilize that glycogen during exercise, did not change throughout the study.

As with human athletes, the ultimate edge of the equine athlete may lie not so much in the physical ability to avoid exhaustion as in the mental ability to ignore it.

CHAPTER 10

NATURE OR NURTURE?

In the preceding chapters we encountered repeated evidence that much of the horse's behavior and performance is "hard wired"—that is, genetic.

Yet despite the long history of selective breeding of the horse by man, despite the huge financial stakes involved, and despite an attention to pedigree that borders on the obsessive, surprisingly little has been determined about the actual genetic basis of the traits that are of economic importance in horses. There is nothing for the horse that even approaches the human genome project, which seeks to map and identify every human gene. Almost nothing has been done to identify and understand the rules governing the inheritance of genes that determine important traits in the horse (the one notable exception being coat color), and even the state of our knowledge of hereditary diseases in horses is extremely primitive, at about the same level as our knowledge of dog breeding in 1950.

Meticulous records have been kept for centuries of the breeding of thoroughbreds. Since the establishment of the Stud Book in 1791, the breeding population of thoroughbreds has been closed; that is, all registered thoroughbreds today are required, by the rules of the registering organizations, to trace their ancestry to horses registered in the Stud Book. Several hundred other breed organizations have established their own stud books in the last century to similarly define and conserve specific breeds of horses.

Breeders have long pored over such records hoping to find the key to producing the next Secretariat, and they have found that certain family lines do seem to give rise to a higher than usual number of horses with outstanding characteristics—speed, in the case of thoroughbreds, or cutting ability in the case of quarter horses.

But this traditional approach to breeding is terribly hit-or-miss. For one thing, there are plenty of offspring of great horses that are duds; Secretariat's foals were no Secretariats. For another, there has until recently been little systematic effort to isolate or even quantify objective performance characteristics—let alone the genes that determine those characteristics—before deciding which animals to use for breeding. There remains considerable scientific controversy over just how heritable many important traits such as speed, jumping ability, and intelligence are in horses.

The traditions of the business tend to work to keep things in this blissful state of relative ignorance—blissful, that is, from the point of view of the breeders. Thoroughbreds are traditionally sold as yearlings, long before their actual performance potential can be known; by default, pedigree and reputation are what carry weight with buyers. Alan Robertson of the Institute of Animal Genetics in Edinburgh points out that exactly the same situation held sway in dairy-cattle breeding until fairly recently. Bulls that won blue ribbons at agricultural shows fetched the highest prices—even though the only thing that really should have mattered was how much milk their offspring produced. It was the advent of artificial insemination that finally, and completely, changed the situation, sweeping away much of the mystique of the prize bull. The widespread availability of AI services enormously increased competition among potential breeding stock; in effect the market was swamped. In the past, a farmer might buy a prize bull knowing that its limited number of offspring would be much in demand as breeding stock, but with AI the offspring of any given bull were now available to anyone. The cachet of pedigree was undermined, and in its place came hard-headed demands to see the bottom line on performance. Bulls are now routinely rated by the milk-producing abilities of their progeny, which are continually tested and carefully recorded. Not surprisingly, this change has led to a rapid improvement in the average milk output of dairy cattle.

For an animal that can breed only once a year, and whose genetic potential often remains an unknown quantity until it is almost past breeding age (this is especially true for dressage horses and jumpers, which may be in their teens before their true potential is known), embryo transfer could be another important tool in a systematic program of genetic improvement. In this procedure, a valuable mare is bred; the embryo develops in its uterus for about a week and then is surgically removed and implanted in a foster mare who carries the foal to term. Meanwhile, the valuable mare can return to competition or be bred again. The value of the horse as a domestic species makes this an economically feasible procedure, even though the overall success rate is only about 10 percent. An even more promising high-tech approach to breeding multiple foals from a single valuable mare is oocyte transfer: immature egg cells are aspirated from the mare's uterus, allowed to mature in a test tube, then implanted in a carrier mare who is then bred. This procedure may prove especially important for mares that, because of age or previous uterine infection, are unable to conceive. Embryo development rates as high as 92 percent have recently been reported, and even old mares attained a 30 percent success rate.

Yet many of the key breed associations, including the Jockey Club in the United States, which registers thoroughbreds, refuse to register horses that have been bred through AI or embryo transfer. The result is that horses that win races generally make their owners lots of money as breeding stock, but there are few incentives for breeders to systematically analyze the heritability of specific performance traits. "You may think that what you want in breeding thoroughbreds is horses that can run fast," Robinson said at a symposium of horse breeders in Ireland, but "this is not true at all." In fact, he went on, "what you are really wanting to do is to breed animals which will sell for high prices at the Yearling Sales. And these two are not necessarily the same thing." What is in the best interests of the breed is not always in the best economic interests of the breeders.

Economics and tradition have similarly conspired to place a disproportionate emphasis on the stallion in breeding, despite the elementary genetic fact that both parents contribute equally to the genetic makeup of their offspring. (In fact the dam may if anything contribute more, at least to one important genetic characteristic that involves the utilization of energy in muscle cells—more on this below.) In terms of the entire breeding population of horses, it is of course true that the sires contribute disproportionately, because one male is used to breed many females. But for any given mating it is simply quaint to believe that the stallion has a disproportionate effect on the offspring.

Heritability

Absent a map that correlates specific genes with specific behaviors or performance traits, and absent an easy testing method for identifying potential sires and dams that carry those desirable genes, there is still much that can be gleaned empirically about the genetics of performance.

By systematically studying how traits run in families, it is possible to estimate to what degree heredity influences such traits as speed or endurance—and how much further progress can be expected through better breeding. The basic yardstick is a quantity known as heritability. Within any population that has not been extremely inbred, there is considerable variation in most characteristics. A certain amount of the variation will be due to environmental factors; for example, the variation in adult size in humans depends at least in part on nutrition and health during childhood. Whatever degree of variation is left over after the environmental factors are factored out is presumed to be the result of genetic differences from individual to individual. The fraction of the total variation that is genetic is defined as heritability; it is a number from 0 to 1, with 1 meaning that the trait in question is determined solely by the genes inherited from one's parents (a horse's coat color, for instance), and 0 meaning that the trait is determined completely by environmental factors (a person's favorite horse color, for instance).

Heritability is a useful way of seeing at a glance what selective breeding can and cannot accomplish. But it is a funny sort of a concept, one that has an operational definition only; it says nothing about the actual genetic mechanisms that underlie the traits in question. For example, calculations are often made of the heritability of earnings in racehorses. Obviously there is no such thing as a money gene in horses; there are most likely a great many genes that work together to influence how much a racehorse will earn. These include body size, muscle type, lung capacity, temperament, ability to withstand pain, and so on. Moreover, heritability really is not, strictly speaking, a measure of how much a given trait is genetic; it is only a measure of how much a given population can be improved by breeding using the best individuals. It is a measure that combines information about the degree to which a trait is genetically determined with information about how much room for genetic improvement is left in the population in question. In a pure, inbred population where every individual carries exactly the same genes and unfailingly passes on a carbon copy to the next generation, the heritability of every trait is *zero,* as there is no genetic variation at all.

Estimating heritability is usually a matter of indirect, statistical calculations. One method is to assess the amount of variation in a trait among close relatives, whose percentage of shared genes can be calculated (for example, one's son or daughter has 50 percent of one's own genes, a brother or sister on average has 25 percent, a half-sibling 12.5 percent); the variation between relatives is then compared with the variation among unrelated members of the population. The smaller the variation among near relatives compared with the variation in the population as a whole, the greater the genetic component. On the other hand, if the variation is practically the same in a population of relatives and one of nonrelatives, that suggests that most of the variation is not influenced by genes.

In practice, a high heritability means that breeding using the top performers can be expected to result in a rapid improvement in the population as a whole; the exceptional abilities of the parents will be strongly passed on to their offspring. With modestly heritable traits, selective breeding can still be quite effective, but it becomes more important to examine not only the performance of the potential sire or dam but that of its relatives as well—to make sure, in effect, that his or her exceptional performance really is due to superior genes and not to environmental factors.

Studies of performance records have yielded a wide range of heritability estimates for many key measures of performance. But all, somewhat surprisingly, are relatively modest. While a trait like weight or height has a heritability estimated at anywhere from 0.5 to as high as 0.9, a trait such as average racing time in thoroughbreds has a relatively low observed heritability (the average from a large number of studies is about 0.15). Pulling ability in draft horses has an average heritability of 0.25; score in the National Cutting Horse Association Futurity contest for three-year-olds has a heritability of 0.19; jumping ability (usually as measured by earnings in Grand Prix jumping events), 0.18; best winning times in races for trotters, 0.25; for pacers, 0.23.

Loading the Dice

Even these relatively modest heritability figures may be exaggerations, artifacts of the somewhat convoluted way that heritabilities must be estimated in the real world. What a racehorse may really "inherit" from its ancestors is not so much its genes as its price. A high-performing sire will command a high price for its offspring, and nobody who pays $500,000 for a yearling is going to stint when it comes to care and training. This may explain in particular the apparent heritability of earnings of horses. High earning sires beget expensive foals, and the purchasers of expensive foals run them at tracks that have higher purses. Thus the performance of a sire can strongly affect the *environment* that its offspring will experience; there is a definite tendency for "class" in horses to be culturally transmitted, just as it is in human society.

Indeed, the paradoxical evidence that thoroughbreds are not getting any faster, and have not gotten any faster for almost a hundred years despite intensive breeding, has to cast some doubt on the assumption that racing ability is any longer heritable at all within the thoroughbred population. (Standardbreds, by contrast, continue to show improvement and regularly set new speed records.)

Several hypotheses have been proposed to explain the apparent paradox. The simplest is that breeders have just been fooling themselves all these years, for the reason just mentioned—that the ability to win races is not nearly as heritable as people have believed. The family lines of "great" racers may be nothing but a cultural artifact, perpetuated not by genes but by how much money people have been willing to pay for their offspring.

A second hypothesis is that while racing speed may well have a significant genetic basis, thoroughbreds have become so highly inbred since the stud books were closed in 1791 that there is simply no variation left to breed improvement from. Interestingly, this appears *not* to be the case. An exhaustive study of the performance ratings of thousands of three-year-old British thoroughbreds by two Irish scientists, B. Gaffney and E. P. Cunningham, found that performance is still improving and remains substantially heritable, at about 0.36. The measure they used is known as TIMEFORM, a rating that attempts to control for all the vagaries of actual races (distance, track condition, level of competition); TIMEFORM attempts to be a pure measure of the individual horse's racing merit, as expressed in the handicap weight that the horse would be assigned in a free handicap race. The researchers concluded that even though the winning times of races have not improved since the start of the twentieth century (and in some cases have declined), the TIMEFORM rating of British thoroughbreds improved by an average of 1 percent a year from 1952 to 1977.

What this suggests is that overall genetic improvement in the speed of thoroughbreds can still occur, and in fact still is occurring. That is, the *average* speed is improving, but the speed that the *best* horses can attain—which may always have been limited by the fundamental energetic factors discussed in the last chapter—is not.

A third possible explanation is that breeders have simply not been trying very hard (or very scientifically) to breed faster horses. Speed is arguably not even what breeders are in reality breeding for. Objective measures of a horse's intrinsic speed do not in fact correlate well with its actual performance in races. As handicappers always remind us, "class" is usually more important than raw speed in winning a race; horse A may run faster than horse B in a solo time trial but still come in second in a head-to-head competition. There is a strong element of equine social psychology at work in a race.

Speed probably correlates even less well with the price of foals at the yearling sales. Breeders choose to breed horses that win a lot of races, and for reasons we have already noted, that is a perfectly rational economic strategy for them to pursue (analogous to breeding the prize bull for his blue ribbons rather than for the milk production of his progeny). But it is not the way to bring about the most rapid improvement in the population. It may lead to no improvement whatever, but simply to the exchange of large sums of money; or it may lead to an improvement in factors that win races but do not relate directly to speed (such as temperament or mental toughness or social dominance).

Much the same confounding factor afflicts the breeding of performance horses in other sports. Many of the measures used to evaluate jumping horses or dressage horses or cutting horses by their very nature contain a lot of stuff jumbled together. They reflect not the action of a single gene or even several genes, but a mishmash of genetic and environmental factors. The low heritability of jumping ability, as measured by purses won, is hardly surprising. Breeding for more objective measures of a horse's intrinsic *genetic* abilities (such as the height of a free jump or maybe muscle fiber composition, or even some measure of temperament and trainability) would likely achieve faster *genetic* improvement. But again, horse breeders and horse buyers quite naturally choose to breed using the winners of contests—contests whose terms ensure that many, many confounding factors determine the winner. Designers of jumping courses, for example, try very hard *not* to follow a standardized template, but to put their individual stamp on the course; everything from the rider's ability and the time of day to whether the sun is casting a strange shadow at a particular fence and how far the horse was vanned the day before affects the outcome. In breeding it would make sense to try to isolate the purely genetic factors that go into a champion and make breeding decisions solely on that basis—rather than on the basis of the hodgepodge of genetic, environmental, and human factors that go into such measures as "winning." It is conceivable that by breeding intelligently using more losers and fewer winners, breeders could make faster progress than is currently the case.

Yet going back to Robertson's observation, horse breeders in the end really are not interested in improving the population as a whole. They are interested in getting the one great horse.

The Case for Mongrels

The obsession with pedigrees in the horse business, indeed even the word *thoroughbred,* reflects archaic ideas about nobility and bloodlines that we can thank British aristocrats of a bygone generation for saddling us with. Although the thoroughbred has its origins in cross-breeding between Arabian stallions and English mares, the breed has been closed to further cross-breeding ever since. The stud books of many other breeds are closed, too, condemning them to a restricted gene pool. Some breeds show even more striking inbreeding. Although standardbreds originated in crosses between thoroughbreds and various other breeds brought to America by European settlers in the eighteenth and early nineteenth centuries, and although standardbred registration was, until the stud book was closed in 1973, open to any horse that could trot a mile in 2 minutes and 30 seconds or pace at 2 minutes and 25 seconds, virtually every registered standardbred today traces its pedigree to a single nineteenth-century stallion, Hambletonian. All Morgan horses are descended from a single stallion of the late eighteenth century. The quarter-horse stud book was started in 1941 and for some time remained open to any horse, regardless of its ancestry, that had the basic characteristics and abilities of a stock horse, but the book is now closed (though cross-breeding with thoroughbreds is still allowed).

To be sure, inbreeding is not necessarily the evil that it is sometimes made out to be. Inbreeding is a rapid and effective way to expose and eliminate deleterious traits caused by recessive genes. Genes come in pairs as a rule, one inherited from each parent, and often a given gene can come in one of two possible types: one that instructs the body to manufacture a protein that performs a certain task (causing the eyes in humans to be brown, for instance) and one that for a variety of reasons fails to do so. The functional gene is said to be dominant, the nonfunctional one recessive. It only takes one of the pair to be functional for the trait in question to be expressed; thus a single dominant gene *dominates* the effect of the nonfunctional one. Someone with a gene for brown eyes and a gene for blue eyes has brown eyes, as does someone with two genes for brown eyes. Only if both genes are recessive, a state known as homozygous recessive is the recessive trait expressed (figure 10.1). (Homozygous means that both genes at a given site are the same, heterozygous that a given site carries one dominant and one recessive gene).

Someone with brown eyes can thus be a carrier of a recessive gene without realizing it. Many recessive traits are much

FIGURE 10.1 *The effect of dominance: bay-black coloration is dominant over chestnut coloration. Horses with one dominant (E) and one recessive gene (e) display the dominant trait (bay-black), but are "carriers" of the recessive trait that may show up in offspring when one gene from each parent is combined.*

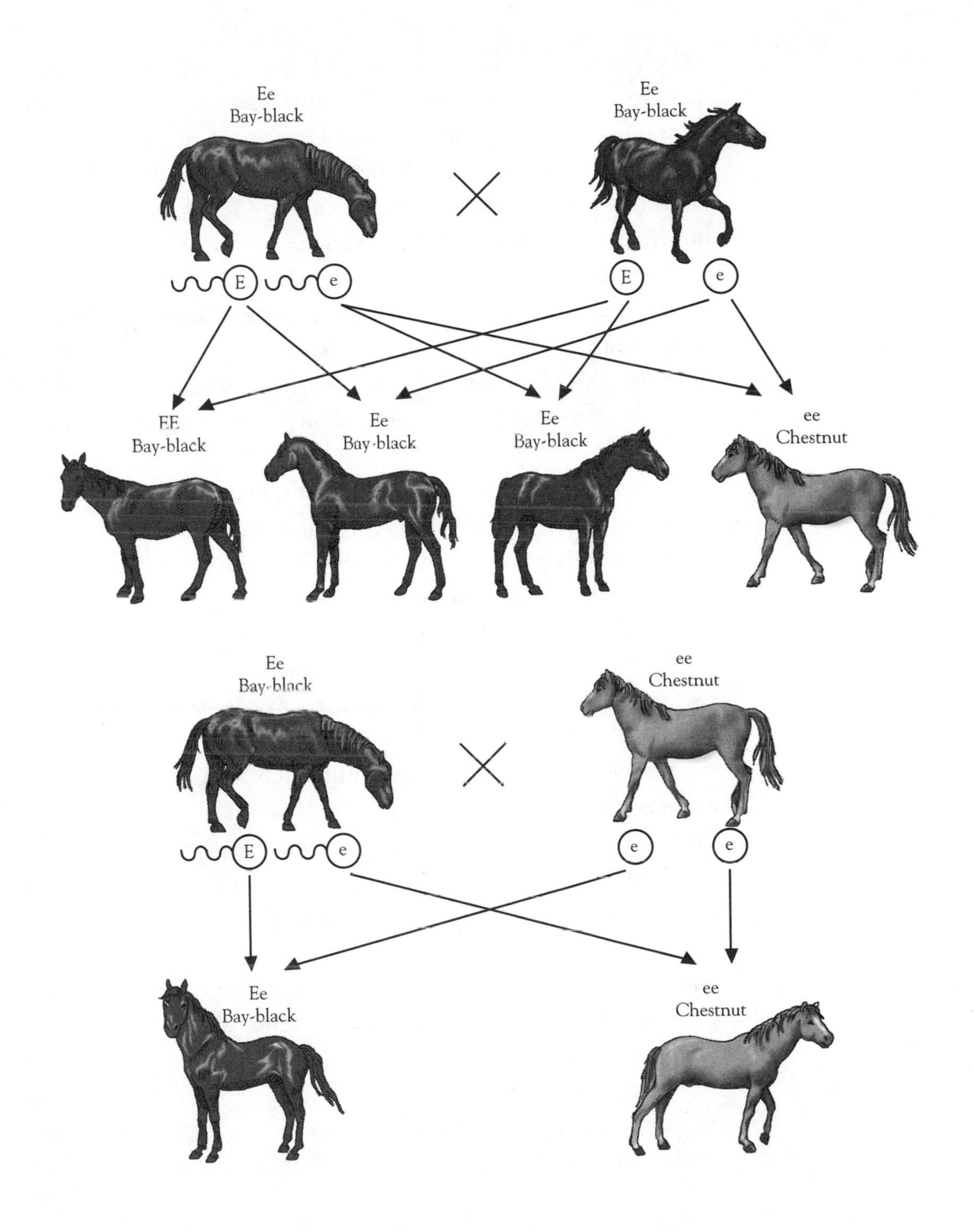
Ee
Bay-black
Ee
Bay-black
E
e
E
e
EE
Bay-black
Ee
Bay-black
Ee
Bay-black
ee
Chestnut
Ee
Bay-black
ee
Chestnut
E
e
e
e
Ee
Bay-black
ee
Chestnut

more deleterious than blue eye color, of course; if the gene in question is vital to some bodily function, an individual born with two recessive genes may suffer from an inborn disease. A breeding program that rigorously culled such individuals would help weed out the recessive gene from the population, but hidden carriers would still remain undetected.

Some inbreeding schemes can expose and eliminate these carriers. For example, a stallion can be tested by mating it either with a known homozygous recessive mare or with its own daughters. If any of these matings produces a homozygous recessive foal, then the stallion must be a carrier (figure 10.2).

Sometimes it is the dominant trait that is a disadvantage, however; in these cases inbreeding can work in a single generation to eliminate the trait, simply by excluding every individual that expresses the dominant trait.

But selective inbreeding aimed at fixing specific desirable traits can have the unintended consequence of also fixing certain undesirable homozygous recessive traits. Studies of standardbreds show that despite extensive inbreeding, none of the classic problems of inbreeding, such as a decline in fertility, have yet appeared in that population. On the other hand, thoroughbreds do show some problems that may suggest inbreeding degeneration. Any two thoroughbreds picked at random will on average have more than 13 percent of their genes in common, a degree of relatedness greater on average than that found between half-siblings (12.5 percent). More than 80 percent of yearlings show some signs of congenital cartilage deterioration at the joints, and more than 95 percent have upper respiratory problems that can affect breathing. These facts take on special significance in light of Howard Seeherman's clinical finding that the principal problems limit-

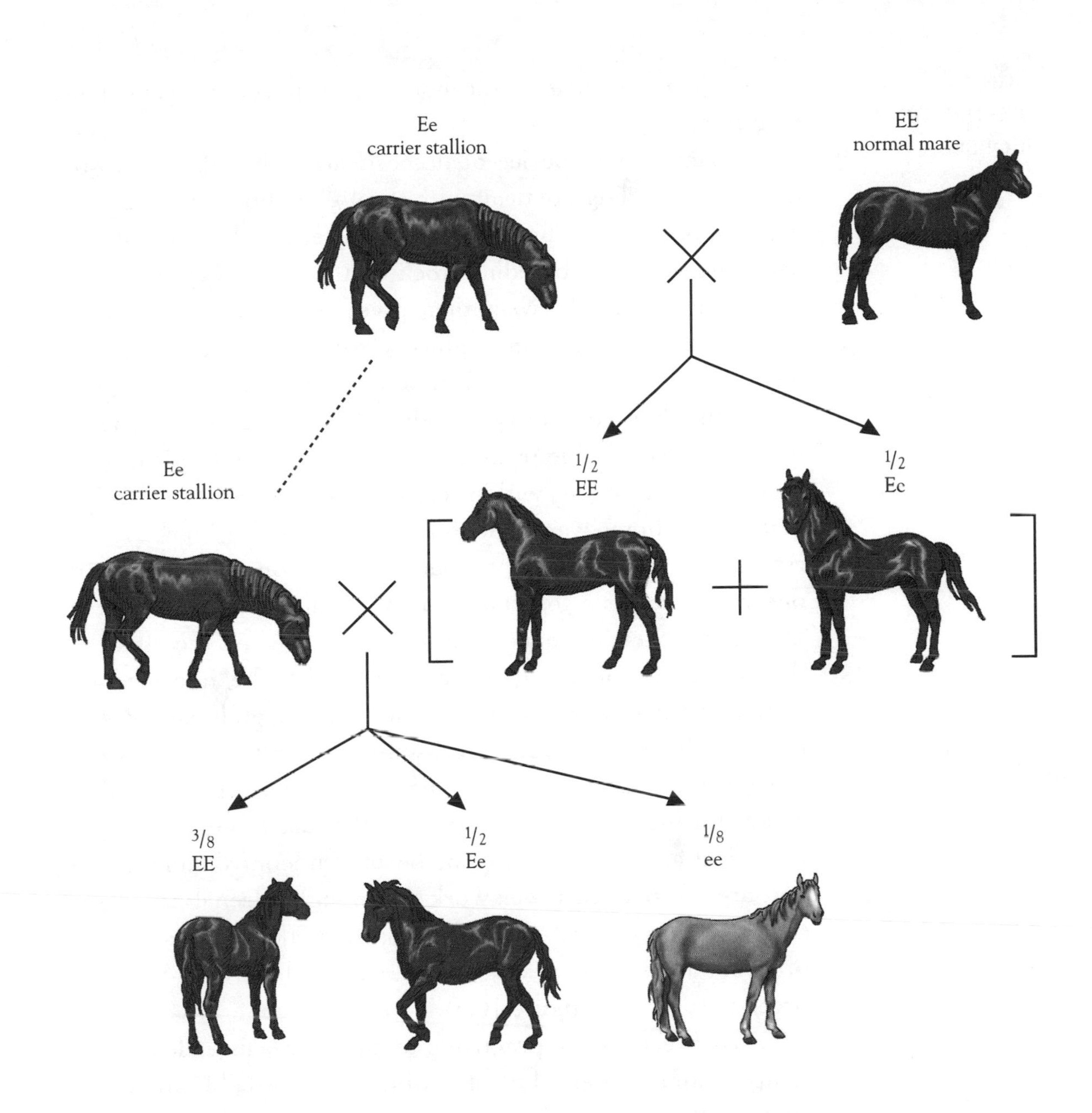

FIGURE 10.2 *Mating a stallion with its own daughters is one way to detect a carrier of a recessive trait; on average one in eight of the offspring of these crosses will express the recessive trait.*

ing the performance of racehorses are musculoskeletal and respiratory.

In many other species of domesticated animals the problems of inbreeding are dealt with through deliberate programs of cross-breeding. Inbred lines are still required to provide an adequate supply of breeding stock that excels in key desirable traits, but crossing between them gives an extra boost by eliminating some of the homozygous recessive traits of each that have inadvertently become fixed along the way.

Another benefit of cross-breeding, in fact the major benefit, is that some desirable traits simply *cannot* be bred for through systematic selection within closed lines. For these traits, neither the homozygous dominant trait nor the homozygous recessive is actually best; instead, a mix of one dominant and one recessive gene together proves optimal. This situation is known as "overdominance," and can occur when the effect of the two genes of a pair are additive, with the intermediate state being the most desirable. (There are several examples of this in color inheritance, discussed in the following section.) For instance, it may be that a moderate degree of excitability makes for the best racehorses; those that are too excitable get hysterical and waste energy or become uncontrollable, those that are too relaxed never work up enough adrenaline. It is a simple mathematical matter to prove that no selection program based on picking and breeding heterozygotes can breed true to type (figure 10.3).

Cross-breeding is practiced to an increasing degree in jumpers and hunters, but of course is not possible in sports such as thoroughbred racing that are restricted to a closed breed. It makes sense to maintain closed breeds for the production of breeding stock, as is done for sheep, cattle, pigs, and poultry throughout the world today. But it also

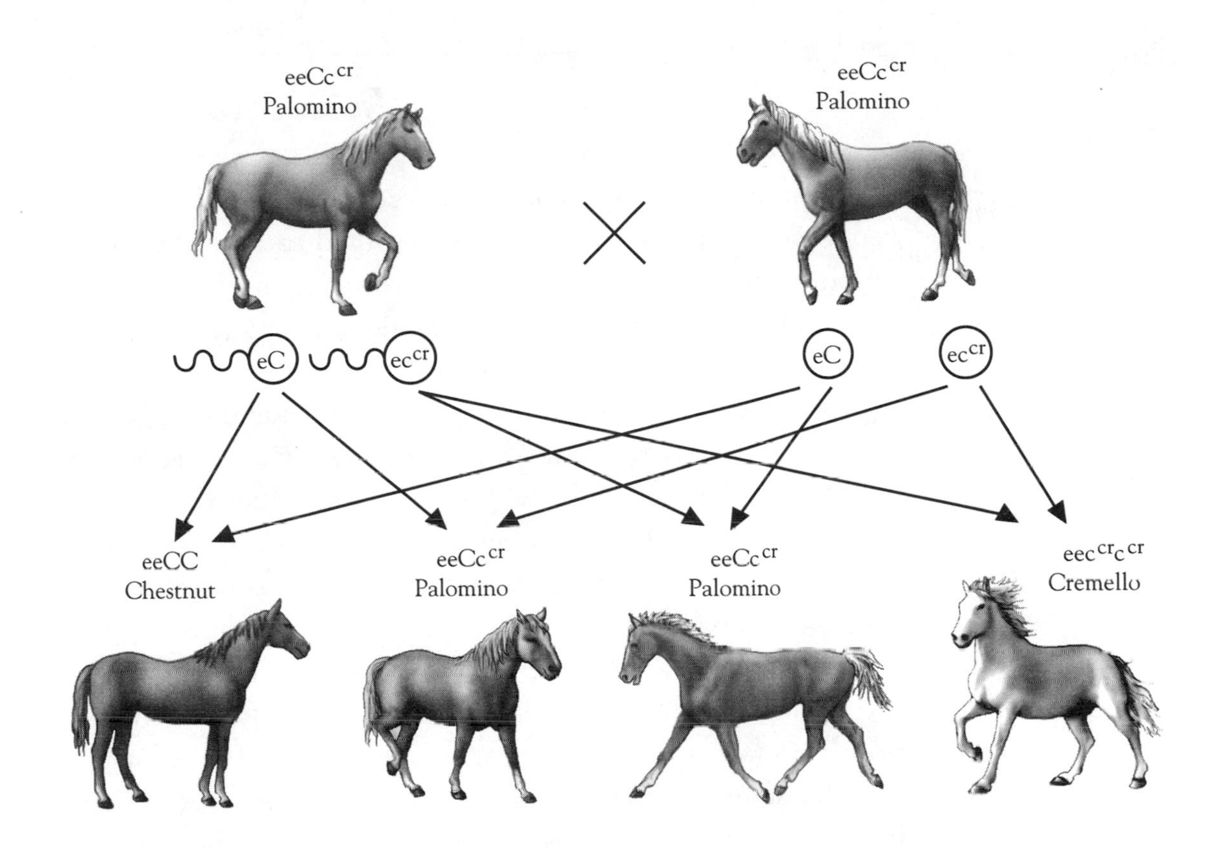

makes sense to separate breeding stock from performance stock. The livestock raised for market are usually not purebreds themselves, but rather cross-breeds of carefully selected purebred parent lines. Indeed, the breakthrough that has produced phenomenal crop yields through hybrid plants is based on this principle; inbred parental lines are grown only to produce the seed for the crosses that are actually sown each year by farmers. In a rational world, horse races would be open to all horses, regardless of breed. And it would be a good bet that before long some carefully chosen cross-breeds would start showing up in the winner's circles at such races.

FIGURE 10.3
Palominos do not breed true because their coloration is the result of heterozygosity — a mixture of a dominant (C) and a recessive (c^{cr}) gene, which produces a faded coat color. CC horses are full colored; $c^{cr}c^{cr}$ horses are a very pale color known as cremello.

An Example: Color Inheritance

The inheritance of coat color in horses is the one bit of horse genetics that has been extensively studied to date. It is interesting for its own sake, and indeed a proper understanding of color inheritance has huge economic importance for many breeders given the large premium that horse fanciers are willing to pay for certain desirable colors like palomino; it is interesting, too, as a paradigm of why naive selective breeding (the breeding of like with like or best with best) does not always work, even when the traits being selected for are unquestionably genetic—and why a more scientific approach is often necessary in practice.

There are basically two monkey wrenches that genetics throws at attempts to breed true. One is the above-mentioned problem of desirable traits that are the result of heterozygosity. The other is the considerable complexity introduced by the fact that most traits are *not* determined by a single gene, but rather by a complex interaction of multiple genes. Both situations arise in the color genetics of horses (plate 8).

Even the basic coat color of a horse is determined not by a single gene, but by the cumulative effect of several genes. In the first place, a gene designated *W* determines whether the coat has any coloration at all. The dominant *W* gene causes uniform white coloration, the recessive *w* allows other colors to be expressed. Thus only horses that are homozygous recessive for this gene—in other words, that carry two *w* genes, designated *ww*—can have color. Horses that are *Ww*—that carry one of the dominant genes—are white.

A peculiarity of this gene is that horses that inherit two dominants—those that are *WW*—suffer from a lethal defect that causes abortion very early in pregnancy. This lethal consequence is probably related to neural defects that appear at an early stage of the embryo's development. The cells responsible for skin pigment originate in an embryonic structure known as the neural crest, as do the cells that form the brain stem and spinal cord.

The nature of this side effect has created considerable pressure for this dominant gene to be eliminated through natural selection; it would disappear altogether if breeders never bred any true white horses. (Dominant-white coloration differs from other "whites" in horses in several ways: the skin is pink and the eyes are colored. Cremello and perlino horses, discussed below, are a very pale cream but have washed-out eye colors. Grays turn progressively whiter with age but are born colored.)

As it is, breeders who attempt to deliberately breed for this color are of necessity breeding a heterozygote with a heterozygote. Crossing a *Ww* with a *Ww* leads to four possible combinations, as each parent has an equal chance of contributing a *W* or a *w* to its offspring. This is exactly the same as the problem of how many different combinations of heads and tails can result from flipping two coins: there is an equal chance of the outcome's being *WW, Ww, wW,* or *ww*. The *WW,* however, dies before birth. Thus, two out of three of the live foals born have a dominant white gene and are white; the third is *ww* and is colored.

Colored horses are divided into two broad categories according to the action of the gene designated *E*. The dominant *E* results in a bay or black horse (which geneticists prefer to lump together and call "black"); the homozygous recessive *ee* results in a chestnut (or what geneticists prefer to call "red"). The final major color gene is the *A* gene, which in its dominant form codes for bay coloration (brown body with black mane and tail) and in its homozygous recessive *aa* form results in a black horse (black body with black mane and tail). The *A* gene has no effect on chestnut horses.

From this much it is readily apparent that a chestnut crossed with a chestnut (both homozygous recessives) will produce all chestnuts (just as two blue-eyed people will normally have all blue-eyed children). A black crossed with a black will produce only blacks among its black/bay offspring, but this cross may also produce up to one-quarter chestnuts if both parents are heterozygous for *E*—that is, if they both have the genotype *Ee,* there is a one in four chance that their offspring will be *ee,* and thus chestnut.

In all of these cases, selective breeding will consistently improve the odds of breeding true to type. That is not the case, however, with the genes responsible for palomino and buckskin coloration. These colors are the result of dilution genes that operate at the *C* site. The dominant *C* gene causes the full coat color to be expressed. But this is one of those cases where dominance is incomplete and intermediate effects occur. Horses that are homozygous for the dominant gene, *CC,* have regular coat colors. Horses that have a single recessive gene, designated c^{cr}, are partially washed out. Bays that carry the Cc^{cr} genotype are buckskins; chestnuts with the Cc^{cr} combination are palominos. If *both* of the genes of the pair are recessive, the dilution is even greater. A bay with this genotype is a perlino; a chestnut becomes a cremello. Both are a very light cream with blue eyes. This is why palominos and buckskins do not breed true—they are heterozygotes. Crossing a palomino with a palomino or a buckskin with a buckskin will, for every four foals born, yield on average one fully colored horse, two palominos or buckskins, and one cremello or perlino. (This ignores the complicating factor that some buckskin crosses may produce blacks as a result of heterozygosity at the *A* locus.)

A final complication results from the action of several dominant genes that further modify coat color: the dominant *D* gene results in dun coloration (grulla in black horses, dun in bay horses, and red dun in chestnuts); the dominant *R* gene is responsible for roaning, the interspersion of white hairs with colored hairs (bay roan in bays, blue roan in blacks, and strawberry roan in chestnuts); the dominant *G* gene overrides all other color coding to produce a coloration that becomes successively whiter with each shedding—a gray.

Many additional genes determine spotting patterns, dappling, flaxen coloration of points, and white marks on the face and legs.

The genes responsible for color traits that are expressed by homozygous recessive genotypes—such as the *∂∂* genotype of all nondun-colored horses—may well predate the domestication of the horse. It wasn't until selective breeding deliberately favored these recessive traits, however, that they began to appear with any frequency in the horse population. Wild horses were probably mostly dun-colored, a result of the dominant *D* gene. But because of its dominance, a mutation that produced a recessive *∂* gene would not automatically have been weeded out. True, the occasional full-colored, *∂∂* horse that showed up in the wild population would presumably have been at a competitive disadvantage, but horses with the *D∂* genotype would still be dun-colored and could act as carriers of the recessive gene, maintaining a small reservoir of the *∂* gene within the population.

Humans who valued interesting colors, by contrast, would quite naturally have seized on any *∂∂* horses that came along by chance—and because ∂ is recessive, breeding from full-colored, $\partial\partial$ horses would have given rise to nothing but more full-colored, $\partial\partial$ horses. The dominant D gene would rapidly dwindle in the population as a whole.

Colors that are expressed by a dominant gene, such as roaning or grays or certain spotting patterns, however, would logically seem to be the result of chance mutations that appeared only *after* domestication began. Had the genes for these colors appeared in the wild, they would have been quickly eliminated altogether through natural selection. (If a dominant trait X is unfavorable, then any horse carrying even a single X gene is at a disadvantage; thus all carriers, whether XX or Xx, are eliminated, and only the xx survives.)

The moral of the story, if there is one, is that the complexity of color genetics has to be but a shadow of the complexity of the genetics of traits that involve performance. Just because a characteristic is genetic does not guarantee that there is a simple or direct route to breeding for its consistent expression.

Breeding for More Than Just Looks

Most breeds are defined by remarkably modest, and remarkably superficial, criteria.

Many are nothing more than a standard of appearance—color, size, or body shape. Although racing ability in thoroughbreds and standardbreds, and to some extent in quarter horses and Arabians, has been consciously selected for (along with cutting ability in quarter horses), there is virtually no breed defined strictly on performance or behavioral grounds. Individual breeders, of course, will often make selections based on temperament and performance, but none of these standards serves to define breeds as a whole.

Perhaps the only consistent, real effort to breed for a specific behavioral trait is the differentiation within the standardbred between pacers and trotters. The recognition that a preference for trotting versus pacing is largely inherent, and the subsequent separation of the breeding lines accordingly, has led to separate strains that at present breed almost completely true to type. Pacers almost invariably produce pacers (98.5 percent), and although trotters sometimes produce pacers, the genetic influence still appears strong, with 80 percent of the offspring of trotting stallions racing as trotters. Genetic fingerprinting of blood factors in horses of various breeds has shown that the genetic distance between standardbred trotters and pacers is as great or greater than that between some distinct breeds (figure 10.4).

It is curious that a similar establishment of sub-breeds has not been attempted in thoroughbreds between sprinters and long-distance runners, especially given the apparent genetic difference in muscle types between these two specialties. Likewise, it would make more sense if, in place of the quarter-horse breed, there were several different breeds defined not by ancestry but by ability as a cutting, racing, or pleasure horse. A breed of endurance horses bred for an abundance of slow-twitch muscle fibers and stamina, a breed of pleasure horses selected for gentleness, and a breed of hunters selected for jumping ability and temperament are all eminently feasible and would be far more sensible than the current segregation of breeds defined primarily by history and physical appearance.

The example of dog breeds is instructive on this point. Most modern dog breeds have been defined for the last 150 years or so strictly on the basis of physical standards. As a result, many

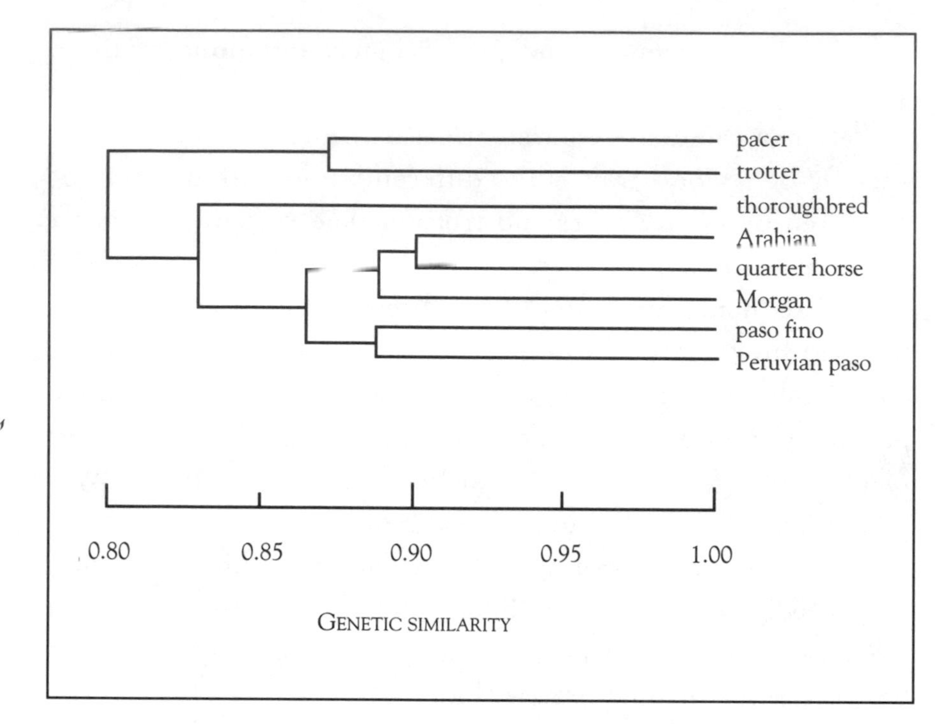

FIGURE 10.4
Standardbred trotters and pacers show a greater genetic difference from one another than do many distinct breeds, such as Arabians and quarter horses.

of the traditional behaviors associated with these breeds have been neglected or lost. In sharp contrast are Border collies, which are registered solely on their ability to herd sheep without regard to ancestry or physical appearance at all, and foxhounds and some other hunting dogs, which have been bred primarily for their scenting and field-working ability.

It is not impossible to breed for looks and brains simultaneously, but it requires a much larger pool of potential breeding animals to work with—which is why the efforts of single breeders to select for temperament or talent have relatively little macroscopic effect. (Consider a desirable physical trait that is found in 10 percent of the population and a desirable behavioral trait that is also found in 10 percent. Statistically, only 1 percent of the population will have both characteristics, which means that breeding for both traits simultaneously restricts dramatically the number of suitable sires and dams.)

There is clearly much untapped potential in breeding for behavioral traits in horses. It is far from clear, however, that the will exists to do so.

Male Chauvinist Pigs

The supreme importance of the stallion is part myth and part mathematical reality. The demographics of the thoroughbred population, and the obvious ability of one stallion to breed with many other mares during the year that any given mare is pregnant, allow breeders to select the top 5 percent or so of stallions for breeding; with mares they have to be far less selective: the top 50 percent are bred.

On the other hand, the belief in the prepotency of males has led to all sorts of foolishness that flies in the face of the genetic reality that half of a horse's genes come from its dam. The notion that an excellent stallion will somehow correct the faults of a mare is commonplace; yet, as animal geneticists point out, it is just as likely that the offspring of such a mating will inherit the worse characteristics of each.

If there is any bias in the relative contribution of sire and dam in a given mating, it is in favor of the female. The normal genes of the body are inherited equally from each parent. But the genes of one special part of the cell come solely from the mother. This is the organelle called the mitochondrion, a separate, self-contained part of the cell that is responsible for converting stored energy into work with the aid of oxygen. The evolution of mitochondria is curious, and some biologists believe it actually has its origins in a free-living organism that has evolved a symbiosis (it may even have begun in a parasitic role) with cells that allowed them to adapt to the oxygen-containing atmosphere that arose as plants evolved and began to produce oxygen as a waste product of photosynthesis.

Mitochondria are curious in another way, in that their DNA comes solely from the mother; there is no recombination of genes from both parents. This means that the rapid change that can be produced from one generation to another through the normal reassortment of parental genes does not occur in the mitochondria. Change occurs only by mutation, which takes place slowly. Moreover, any differences between female lines that arise from chance mutations will be persistent and passed on from mother to daughter—and from mother to son, too, though the sons will not pass those traits on to *their* offspring.

A study of female pedigree lines in thoroughbreds published in 1895 by Bruce Lowe identified 11 of 43 female families that seemed to produce a lot of exceptional racehorses. More exacting modern studies in dairy cattle have found that as much as 15 percent of the variance in milk production and butter-fat content can be traced to maternal lineage.

According to veterinarian and molecular biologist Acacia Alcivar-Warren, it makes sense that mitochondrial function would influence milk production in dairy cows—a cow that is producing 10,000 pounds of milk a year is surely converting an enormous amount of energy, and female lineages that happen to have locked in a chance mutation that improves the efficiency of mitochondria will be at an advantage. The same may well apply to racehorses.

Differences in mitochondrial DNA have been identified among horse breeds, though the significance of those differences is hard to know; further research hopes to pin down and identify specific markers for speed in thoroughbred mitochondrial DNA that could be used to guide breeding.

To date, genetic markers have played virtually no role in horse breeding and objective measures of performance have played only a limited role; looks, tradition, and money have carried the day. There is actually relatively little that individual breeders can do to buck this trend. The real change will come only when breed standards change, when cross-breeding becomes routine, and when breeding methods such as artificial insemination and embryo transfer are officially accepted.

CONCLUSION

THE FATE OF THE HORSE

It is a tribute to its fecundity and its adaptability that the horse has survived both near-extinction at the whims of nature and often harsh exploitation at the hand of man. For 6,000 years the horse was a creature of man's enthusiasm for warfare, his ever growing demand for motive and tractive power, and his anthropomorphic and romantic imaginings; for all three the horse has suffered misunderstanding, drudgery, and worse.

Mechanization and affluence are often bemoaned these days by the would be saviors of the planet, yet it is to mechanization and affluence that the horse, at least, owes its redemption. War is bloody enough without the blood of horses; farmwork is drudgery enough without the toil of draft animals. There is much to be said for tanks and tractors.

The 60 million horses in the world today are more pets than tools of war or work, and that is something unprecedented. It brings its own dangers, however—dangers of sentiment and indulgence. The sometimes overfed, underexercised, undertrained, and petted and coddled domestic animals of our age are not happy animals. The runaway populations of feral horses, once controlled by roundups and shooting, are a threat to many fragile ecosystems—and to their own survival, too, as starvation reaps a grim toll on overcrowded ranges.

The understanding of animal behavior that the more sensitive people of ages past acquired directly, through real-life experience, is being lost, even as affluence has made it possible for horses to enjoy a potentially better and more humane existence. But what experience can no longer provide science can, and that is one reason why scientific studies of the true nature of horses will be more important than ever in the future.

So too will be the increasing genetic control that man will come to exercise over the horse. The breeders of horses have so far managed to avoid the more drastic mistakes of dog and cat fanciers who, in pursuit of fads and fancies, have taken inbreeding to extremes and inadvertently bred for a number of congenital defects (such as hip dysplasia in several dog breeds). Yet, as we saw in chapter 10, the economics and less than scientific traditions of horse breeding have worked at times to resist innovations that could do much to preserve genetic diversity within breeds, while also selecting and refining the traits that make horses better adapted, physically and mentally, to the tasks we ask of them. Artificial insemination and embryo transfer are being used in some breeds today, but many breeders (those of thoroughbreds most notably) continue to block rule changes that would make these practices widespread.

Better understanding of the genetics and reproductive system of the horse is likely to benefit the species in other ways. Feral horses in the western United States and on the Atlantic barrier islands have caused severe damage to many ecosystems. For better or for worse, the western feral horses have been protected by federal law since 1971, and the eastern feral horses enjoy enormous sentimental support; yet with reproductive rates as high as 20 percent a year, they have in many areas severely overgrazed the range. On barrier islands such as Assateague, Maryland, they pose a threat to sensitive marsh habitats that are home to many small mammals and birds. A long-running research effort by Jay Kirkpatrick of the Deaconness Research Institute in Billings, Montana, aims to develop an immunocontraceptive that can be used to block conception in mares; the hope is to develop in effect a vaccine that causes the body to produce antibodies against the protein that coats its eggs. The antibodies then bind to and cover the coat, effectively blocking out sperm. Initial results in Nevada and at Assateague have been encouraging, if expensive; for feral populations where roundups and removal (or shooting) of excess horses are impossible, immunocontraceptives delivered by dart gun into the horse's rump are certainly an attractive alternative.

Finally, the tools that permit us to control the genetic fate of the species may also make it possible to successfully restore to the wild the only true wild horse, Przewalski's horse. Believed to be extinct in the wild since the 1960s but bred captively in zoos and private parks since the end of the nineteenth century, Przewalski's horse has already suffered the effects of inbreeding. All 1,100 Przewalski's horses in captivity today are the descendants of 13 animals; analysis of their pedigrees shows that, moreover, as much as two-thirds of the genetic diversity of those 13 parents has been lost in the last century. (Of the 26 genes carried by those original 13 horses at any given site on the chromosome, an average of 10.5 remain in the population today.)

Attempts to return Przewalski's horse to the wild as a free-ranging population within the species' historic range have begun in Mongolia and China. But experts such as Oliver Ryder of the San Diego Zoo note that successful reintroduction will require extensive coordination and genetic management using the populations of Przewalski's horse that now exist in zoos throughout the world—in order to ensure that the reintroduced population includes representation from the full range of the remaining gene pool.

Reintroduction of the horse to the very wilds from which it was domesticated 6,000 years ago will bring man and horse full circle. It will be a very modest but fitting repayment to a species that has given us so much. It is also a fitting note on which to end this book, for to return the wild horse to its home will be the truest sign that science has at last gained one small victory over the human nature and human ignorance that have not always served us, or the horse, well.

FURTHER READING

CHAPTER 1
THE IMPROBABILITY OF THE HORSE

Janis, Christine. "The evolutionary strategy of the equidae and the origins of rumen and cecal digestion." *Evolution* 30 (1976): 757–74.

———. "Evolution of horns in ungulates: ecology and paleoecology." *Biological Reviews* 57 (1982): 261–318.

MacFadden, Bruce. J. *Fossil Horses: Systematics, Paleobiology, and Evolution of the Family Equidae.* New York: Cambridge University Press, 1992.

McMahon, Thomas A., and John Tyler Bonner. *On Size and Life.* New York: Scientific American Library, 1983.

CHAPTER 2
FROM THE BRINK OF OBLIVION

Anthony, David W. "The domestication of the horse." In *Equids in the Ancient World,* vol. 2, Richard H. Meadow and Hans-Peter Uerpmann, eds. Wiesbaden: Reichert, 1991.

Anthony, David W., and Dorcas R. Brown. "The origins of horseback riding." *Antiquity* 65 (1991): 22–38.

Anthony, David, Dimitri Y. Telegin, and Dorcas Brown. "The origin of horseback riding." *Scientific American,* December 1991, pp. 94–99.

Levine, Marsha L. "Dereivka and the problem of horse domestication." *Antiquity* 64 (1990): 727–40.

Short, R. V. "The evolution of the horse." *Journal of Reproduction and Fertility, Supplement* 23 (1975): 1–6.

CHAPTER 3
EQUINE NATURE, HUMAN NATURE

Anderson, J. K. *Ancient Greek Horsemanship.* Berkeley: University of California Press, 1961.

Clutton-Brock, Juliet. *Horse Power: A History of the Horse and the Donkey in Human Societies.* Cambridge: Harvard University Press, 1992.

Littauer, Mary Aiken. "Bits and pieces." *Antiquity* 43 (1969): 289–300.

———. "Slit nostrils of equids." *Zeitschrift für Säugetierkunde* 34 (1969): 183–86.

Littauer, Vladimir S. *Commonsense Horsemanship,* rev. ed. New York: Arco, 1974.

Piggott, Stuart. *Wagon, Chariot and Carriage: Symbol and Status in the History of Transport.* New York: Thames and Hudson, 1992.

CHAPTER 4
SOCIOECOLOGY

Araba, B. D., and S. L. Crowell-Davis. "Dominance relationships and aggression of foals *(Equus caballus).*" *Applied Animal Behaviour Science* 41 (1994): 1–25.

Berger, Joel. "Organizational systems and dominance in feral horses in the Grand Canyon." *Behavioral Ecology and Sociobiology* 2 (1977): 131–46.

———. "Induced abortion and social factors in wild horses." *Nature* 303 (1983): 59–61.

Dodman, Nicholas H., et al. "Equine self-mutilation syndrome (57 cases)." *Journal of the American Veterinary Medical Association* 204 (1994): 1219–23.

Feh, Claudia, and Jeanne de Mazières. "Grooming at a preferred site reduces heart rate in horses." *Animal Behaviour* 46 (1993): 1191–94.

Fraser, Andrew F. *The Behaviour of the Horse.* Wallingford, U.K.: CAB International, 1992.

Houpt, Katherine A. *Domestic Animal Behavior for Veterinarians and Animal Scientists.* Ames: Iowa State University Press, 1991.

Houpt, Katherine A., and Andrew F. Fraser, eds. "Przewalski horses." *Applied Animal Behaviour Science* 21 (1988): 1–190.

Kilingel, H. "Social organization and reproduction in equids." *Journal of Reproduction and Fertility, Supplement* 23 (1975): 7–11.

Waring, George. *Horse Behavior: The Behavioral Traits and Adaptations of Domestic and Wild Horses, Including Ponies.* Park Ridge, N.J.: Noyes Publications, 1983.

CHAPTER 5
SEEING AND PERCEIVING

Pick, David F., et al. "Equine color perception revisited." *Applied Animal Behaviour Science* 42 (1994): 61–65.

Roberts, Steven M. "Equine vision and optics." *Veterinary Clinics of North America: Equine Practice* 8 (1992): 451–57.

Sivak, J. G., and D. B. Allen. "An evaluation of the 'ramp' retina of the horse eye." *Vision Research* 15 (1975): 1353–56.

CHAPTER 6
HORSE TALK

Dawkins, R., and J. R. Krebs. "Animal signals: information or manipulation?" In *Behavioural Ecology, An Evolutionary Approach,* J. R. Krebs and N. B. Davies, eds. Oxford: Blackwell, 1978.

Feist, James D., and Dale R. McCullough. "Behavior patterns and communication in feral horses." *Zeitschrift für Tierpsychologie* 41 (1976): 337–71.

Kiley, Marthe. "The vocalizations of ungulates, their causation and function." *Zeitschrift für Tierpsychologie* 31 (1972): 171–222.

Morton, Eugene S., and Jake Page. *Animal Talk: Science and the Voices of Nature.* New York: Random House, 1992.

CHAPTER 7
HORSE SENSE

Creel, Scott R., and Jack L. Albright. "Early experience." *Veterinary Clinics of North America: Food Animal Practice* 3 (1987): 251–67.

Hart, Benjamin L. *The Behavior of Domestic Animals.* New York: Freeman, 1985.

Kilgour, Ron. "Learning and the training of farm animals." *Veterinary Clinics of North America: Food Animal Practice* 3 (1987): 269–84.

Kratzer, D. D., et al. "Maze learning in quarter horses." *Journal of Animal Science* 46 (1977): 896–902.

McCall, C. A. "A review of learning behavior in horses and its application in horse training." *Journal of Animal Science* 68 (1990): 75–81.

McFarland, David, ed. *The Oxford Companion to Animal Behavior.* Entries under Imprinting and Navigation. New York: Oxford University Press, 1987.

Mader, D. R., and E. O. Price. "Discrimination learning in horses: effects of breed, age and social dominance." *Journal of Animal Science* 50 (1980): 962–65.

Marinier, S. L., and A. J. Alexander. "Coprophagy as an avenue for foals of the domestic horse to learn food preferences from their dams." *Journal of Theoretical Biology* 173 (1995): 121–24.

Miller, R. M. "Imprint training of the newborn foal." *Proceedings of the Thirty-sixth Annual Convention of the American Association of Equine Practitioners* 36 (1991): 661–66.

CHAPTER 8
THE MECHANICS OF MOVEMENT

Clayton, Hilary M., and David A. Barlow. "The effect of fence height and width on the limb placements of show jumping horses." *Equine Veterinary Science* 9 (1989): 179–85.

Farley, Claire T., and C. Richard Taylor. "A mechanical trigger for the trot-gallop transition in horses." *Science* 253 (1991): 306–8.

Gray, James. *Animal Locomotion.* New York: Norton, 1968.

Hildebrand, Milton. "The mechanics of horse legs." *American Scientist* 75 (1987): 594–601.

———. "The quadrupedal gaits of vertebrates." *BioScience* 39 (1989): 766–75.

Hoyt, Donald F., and C. Richard Taylor. "Gait and the energetics of locomotion in horses." *Nature* 292 (1981): 239–40.

Jones, William E., ed. *Equine Sports Medicine.* Philadelphia: Lea & Febiger, 1989.

Leach, D. H., and Anne I. Dagg. "Evolution of equine locomotion research." *Equine Veterinary Journal* 15 (1983): 87–92.

———. "A review of research on equine locomotion and biomechanics." *Equine Veterinary Journal* 15 (1983): 93–102.

Schamhardt, Henk C., et al. "External loads on the limbs of jumping horses at take-off and landing." *American Journal of Veterinary Research* 54 (1993): 675–80.

CHAPTER 9
ASSUME A SPHERICAL HORSE

Bruin, G., et al. "Adaptation and overtraining in horses subjected to increasing training loads." *Journal of Applied Physiology* 76 (1994): 1908–13.

Hintz, Harold F. "Nutrition and equine performance." *Journal of Nutrition, Supplement* 124 (1994): 2723S–29S.

Hodgson, D. R., R. E. Davis, and F. F. McConaghy. "Thermoregulation in the horse in response to exercise." *British Veterinary Journal* 150 (1994): 219–35.

Lambert, David H. "Practical experiences in the application of sports medicine." *Proceedings of the Thirty-sixth Annual Convention of the American Association of Equine Practitioners* 36 (1991): 477–84.

Rivero, José-Luis L., et al. "Muscle fiber type composition and fiber size in successfully and unsuccessfully endurance-raced horses." *Journal of Applied Physiology* 75 (1993): 1758–66.

Seeherman, Howard J., Elisabeth Morris, and Michael W. O'Callaghan. "Evaluation techniques" and "Comprehensive clinical evaluation of performance." In *Equine Surgery,* J. A. Auer, ed. Philadelphia: Saunders, 1992.

Von Wittke, P., et al. "Effects of training on blood lactate-running speed relationship in thoroughbred racehorses." *Journal of Applied Physiology* 77 (1994): 298–302.

CHAPTER 10
NATURE OR NURTURE?

Bowling, Ann Trommershausen. "Population genetics of Great Basin feral horses." *Animal Genetics* 25, supplement 1 (1994): 67–74.

Bowling, Ann Trommershausen, and Robert S. Clark. "Blood group and protein polymorphism gene frequencies for seven breeds of horses in the United States." *Animal Blood Groups and Biochemical Genetics* 16 (1985): 93–108.

Evans, J. Warren, et al. "Color inheritance, parentage testing, genetic lethals" and "Principles of selection for quantitative traits." Chaps. 13 and 15 in *The Horse.* New York: Freeman, 1990.

Cothran, E. G., et al. "Genetic differentiation associated with gait within American Standardbred horses." *Animal Genetics* 18 (1987): 285–96.

Hintz, Richard L. "Genetics of performance in the horse." *Journal of Animal Science* 51 (1980): 582–94.

Langlois, B. "Heritability of racing ability in thoroughbreds—a review." *Livestock Production Science* 7 (1980): 591–605.

Trommershausen-Smith, Ann [Ann Trommershausen Bowling]. "Coat color genetics." *Equine Practice,* November-December 1979, pp. 24–35.

Sponenberg, D. Phillip, and Bonnie V. Beaver. *Horse Color.* College Station: Texas A&M University Press, 1983.

CONCLUSION
THE FATE OF THE HORSE

Ryder, Oliver. "Przewalski's horse: prospects for reintroduction into the wild." *Conservation Biology* 7 (1993): 13–15.

ACKNOWLEDGMENTS

I am deeply indebted to the many scientists and veterinarians who freely shared with me their expertise, answered my many questions, and commented on draft chapters of this book. All responded with unfailing generosity, encouragement, and helpful suggestions. I would especially like to thank Franklin M. Loew of Cornell University; Howard J. Seeherman, Nicholas H. Dodman, Acacia Alcivar-Warren, Michael W. O'Callaghan, and Katrin Hinrichs of Tufts University; Bruce J. MacFadden of the Florida Museum of Natural History; David W. Anthony of Hartwick College; Eugene S. Morton of the National Zoological Park; Brian Timney of the University of Western Ontario; David F. Pick of Purdue University; Ann T. Bowling of the University of California at Davis; and Oliver A. Ryder of the San Diego Zoo. I would also like to pay tribute to C. Richard Taylor of Harvard University, a pioneering researcher in the study of animal locomotion, who died in 1995. He provided me with much invaluable assistance, taking the time to explain his research and putting me in touch with other key researchers.

I am also extremely grateful to Mary Taylor of Winchester, Virginia, a true horse professional, who read the entire manuscript at an early stage and helped steer me in the right direction with many crucial suggestions and perceptive criticisms; to Mark Godfrey for expert assistance with photo research; and to Martha Polkey, Katinka Matson, and Susan Arellano, who suggested countless improvements in the final manuscript, large and small.

And finally, this book could never have come about were it not for three great public institutions supported by the people of the United States—the National Library of Medicine, the National Agricultural Library, and the Library of Congress. Their doors, so far, remain open to all.

INDEX

Aborigines, Australian, 9
Abortion, 97–98
Accommodation, visual, 112–16
Adenosine triphosphate (ATP), 217–21
Aggression
  adaptive purpose of, 89–91, 95–98
  and appeasement, 86–87
  controlling, 84
  effect of castration on, 98
  frequency of, 89–90
  toward humans, 95–96, 98
Aids, artificial vs. natural, 3
Ainslie, Tom, 94
Akkadians, 72
Alarm calls, 134
Alcivar-Warren, Acacia, 260
Alexander, R. McNeill, 189, 198
Amphetamines, 104
Ancestry of the horse, 16–26, 35–38, 42–43, 56–59, pl. 1
Ancient peoples
  attitudes toward horses of, 71–77
  domestication of horse by, 20, 43, 45–57
  as hunters of horses, 20, 39–40, 45, 47–50
  use of horse in warfare by, 63–69
Andalusian horses, 42
Angular momentum, 184, pl. 6
Animal science, 3–4
Antelope, 9–10, 198
Anthony, David, 52, 53, 63
Anthropomorphism, 73, 79, 128–29
Appeasement, 86–87, 132
Arabian horses
  juvenile traits in, 100–101
  myths surrounding, 42
  relation to other breeds, 245, 258
Aristocratic associations of the horse, 71–74
Art, horses in, 64, pl. 3
  cave paintings, 40, 41, 57
  hunting prints, 186
  petroglyphs, 54, 55
  statues, 72, 75, 187
Artificial insemination (AI), 237–38, 264
Aryans, 63
Assateague, 52, 265
Asses
  bonding, 82–83
  diet, 29, 31
  domestication, 63
  evolution, 17, pl. 1
  learning ability, 153
  territorial behavior, 82–83, 145

Associative learning, 164–67
Assyria, 73
Atavistic traits, 57
Athens, 72
ATP (adenosine triphosphate), 217–21
d'Aure, Comte, 69
Aurochs, 40, 45
Avoidance behavior, 83, 86–87, 95, 145

Bachelor groups, 83
Baking soda. *See* Sodium bicarbonate
Balance, natural, 70
Ballistics of jumping, 205–8
Barks, 132–34
Bay-black color, 247, 253–54, pl. 8
Behavior
  abnormal, 102–7, 167
  breeding for, 257–59,
  defensive, 28
  effect of domestication on, 11–12, 99–101
  eliminatory, 142–45
  evolution of, 79, 81–83, 86–88, 90
  experimental study of, 119, 121–25, 150–54, 162–63
  homing, 168–71
  instinctive, 2–3, 105–6, 147, 158
  juvenile, 12, 80–81, 87, 99–101, 137, pl. 4
  play, 98–101, pl. 4
  in relation to humans, 3, 80–81, 84–85, 89, 95–96, 164–66
  sexual, 81–83, 97–98, 135–37, 143–44, pl. 4
  social, 37–38, 81–99, 139–42, pl. 4
  submissive, 12, 45
  territorial, 37–38, 82–83
Belmont Stakes, 213
Berger, Joel, 97–98
Bicarbonate of soda, 224
Biomechanics, 177. *See also* Energy; Gaits; Legs
Biting, 139. *See also* Threats
Bits
  primitive, 50, 51, 66–67, pl. 3
  and teeth wear, 51–54

Black Sea, 43, 45
Blind spots, 111–12. *See also* Vision
Blistering, 71
Blood, 214, 222, 224
Blow, 129–30, 134
Bluffing, 91–93
Bonding, 81–89
Bones
  cross–section area of, 13–14
  evolution of, 178–83
  injury to, 204–5, 209–10, 230–32
Border collies, 100, 154, 167, 258
Brain. *See also* Intelligence
  evolution of, 21
  and locomotion, 147, 149–50
  overheating of, 216–17
  size of, 21, 147
  and vision, 109–10, 121
Breakdowns, 210, 231–32
"Breaking"
  imprint training, 173
  lungeless, 93
  role of grooming in, 89
Breeding
  for appearance, 247, 251–56
  for behavior and performance, 236–38, 241, 256–59
  genetic factors in, 239–43, 248–50
  new technologies, 237–38, 264–65
  strategies for, 244–51, 256–60
  unscientific practices in, 236–39, 242, 244–45, 251
Breeds. *See also names of specific breeds*
  genetic differences in, 257–58, 260–61
  intelligence differences, 162–63
  neoteny in, 100–101
  origins of, 42
  registration practices, 238, 245–56, 251
Bridles, primitive, 67
British Isles, 40, 41
Buckskin color, 254, pl. 8
Burials, horses in, 50, 75, 77

Camouflage, 119–20

Cannon bone, 14, 182–83, 204–5, 231
Canter, 191. *See also* Gaits
Castillo Pocket (Colorado), 37
Castration, 66, 98
Cats, visual sense in, 114, 116, 122
Cave paintings, 40, 41, 57
Cavesson, 68
Cecum, 15, 29, 30
Cellulose, 15, 22–23, 28–34
Center of mass, 70, 186, 205
Central Asia, 40, 75
Centrifugal force, 198–99
Chariot, 53–54, 64, 66–68, 71–73
Cheek pieces, 50–51, 66–67
Cheetah, speed of, 15, 184–85, 195, 198
Chestnut color, 247, 251, 253–54, pl. 8
China, 64, 71, 75, 266
Chivalry, Age of, 72
Chromosome number, 57–59
Clades, 20–24
"Class," 92, 94–95, 242–43
Classical conditioning, 155
Clever Hans, 165–67
Climate change, 12, 22–24, 40
Coat color
  evolution of, 255–56
  genetics of, 247, 251–56, pl. 8
  and mate choice, 172
  primitive, 57–58, 255–56
Coevolution, 11, 61
Collar bone, 180
Color vision, 117–20
Columbus, Christopher, 40
Communication. *See also* Visual signals; Vocal signals
  and bluffing, 91–93
  evolution of, 87–88, 91–93, 127–28, 130–31, 139–42
  between horses and humans, 61, 161
  as manipulation, 131
  olfactory, 142–45
  semantic fallacy of, 128–31, 138
  tactile, 137
  visual, 127–28, 139–42
  vocal, 127–38
Conditioning, behavioral, 155–56
Cones (eye), 116, 117–20, pl. 5
Conservation of angular momentum, 184, pl. 6
Conservation of energy, 24, 183–86, 201, pl. 2
Contraception, 265
Coordination, 147, 149–50
Coprophagy, 172–73
Courtship. *See* Sexual behavior
Creatine, 218, 224
Cremello color, 251, 253, 254, pl. 8
Cribbing, 102, 103, 104–5, 163
Crimea, 75
Croesus, King of Lydia, 63
Cross-breeding, 245–51
"Cult stallion," 50–55, 75
Cunningham, E. P., 243
Cunningham-Graham, Robert Bontine, xii
Curvet, 3, 62
Cutting horses, heritability in, 241

Danube Valley, 43
Defecation behavior, 142–45
Deification of the horse, 74–77
Depth perception, 120–25
Dereivka, 46, 48–55, 56, 75
Diaphragm, 226, 227
Diastema, 15–16, 24
Diet
  and body size, 28–34
  evolution of, 18, 21–24, 32–33, 37–38
  needs of horses, 15
  and racehorse performance, 224–25
  of wild horses, 29, 31
Dinohippus, 19, 36
Direction finding, 168–71
Diseases, hereditary, 235, 248, 252–53. *See also* Inbreeding
Disobedience, 86
Dnieper River, 75
Dodman, Nicholas, 104, 106

Dogs
genetic diseases, 235
intelligence, 150, 154
metabolic rate, 33
play behavior, 99, 100
relation to humans, 80
visual sense, 114, 116
Domestication
behavioral changes under, 11, 99–101
effect on horse population of, 40–41, 47–50, 54
effect on human society of, 44, 54–55, 62–65
evolutionary advantages of, 39–41
initiated by hunting, 45, 47–50
place of, 40–43, 45, 56–59
"preadaptations" to, 10–11, 13–16, 22–24
Dominance, social. *See* Hierarchy, social
Dominant genes, 246–56
Dominant white color, 252–53, pl. 8
Dopamine, 104–5
Dorsal stripes, 57
Draft horses, heritability in, 241
Dressage, 70, 101
Drugs, in horse racing, 224–25
Dun color, 57, 255–56, pl. 8
Dung piles, 142–45

Ears, flattening of, 89, 93–94
Egret, cattle, 88
Egypt, ancient, 9, 10, 64, 68, 72
Embryo transfer, 237–38, 264
Endorphins, 104–6
Endurance, 176–77, 183–86
Endurance racing, 223, 257
Energy
conservation of, 24, 183–86, 201, pl. 2
consumption vs. speed, 202–4
dietary need vs. body size, 32
of standing, 36
utilization in muscle cells, 217–22
Eocene epoch, 21, 33
Eohippus. See *Hyracotherium*
Equitation
"high school," 3, 69–70
and jumping, 207
Estrous cycle, 97–98
Evolution. *See also* Domestication; Fossil horses
of behavior, 79, 81–83, 86–88, 90, 102–7
of coat color, 255–56
of communication, 86–88, 91–93, 127–28, 130–31
of gaits, 24–27
of intelligence, 21
misconceptions about, 16–21
of the modern horse, 10–19, 57–59, pl. 1
role of diet in, 15, 18, 21–24, 28–34
of social structure, 81–83
and "trap doors," 20–24
Exercise
and fatigue, 215–17, 220, 224–25, 228
and fitness, 214–15, 222, 229–34
and muscle composition, 223
and overheating, 215–17
Experiments
of intelligence, 150–54, 162–63
of visual perception, 119, 121–25
Extinction (evolution)
and body size, 13, 22
of browsing equids, 22
and domestication, 20
of horse in North America, 39–40
Extinction (learning), 157
Eye, 109–120. *See also* Vision

Fast-twitch fibers, 222–24
Fat in diet, 224
Fatigue, 215–17, 220, 224–25, 228
Fear, 156–57, 159, 167
Feet, force exerted by, 208–9
Feh, Claudia, 88
Feist, James, 138
Femur, pl. 2

Feral horses
color, 58
ecological damage by, 264–65
in Europe, 57
harem size, 83–84
in North America, 42, 264–65
reproductive rate, 265
social behavior, 86, 89, 138, 142–45
Fetlock, 182, 184, 186, 231, pl. 2
Fiber, dietary, 29, 33–34
Field of view, 110, 111–12
"Firing," 70–71
Fitness
aerobic, 214, 233–34
anaerobic, 214
and exercise, 214–15, 222
and racehorse performance, 229–34
Flaxen color, 255
Flehmen, 144, pl. 4
Foals. *See also* Juveniles
aggression toward, 96–97
behavior toward humans of, 80–81
imprinting in, 172–73
play behavior in, 99, pl. 4
recognition of mother by, 138
unilateral grooming by, 87
Foot, "springing," 24, 25, 184, pl. 2
Foraging behavior, 47. *See also* Diet; Time budgets of horses
Force of impact, on feet, 204–10
Fossil horses
brain size, 21
diet, 18, 21–22, 28, 33
evolution, 16–20
extinction, 22, 39–40
family tree (diagram), 19
footprints of, 24–26
lifespan, 35
in museums, 16–17
size, 18, 22
social structure, 37–38
speed, 27
teeth, 37–38
France, 40, 41, 57
Fraser, Andrew, 101
Frederick II, 73
Friendship. *See* Bonding
Froude number, 198–200

Gaffney, B., 243
"Gaited" horses, 25–26, 194
Gaits. *See also* Energy; Legs; Speed
asymmetrical, 194–98
and body size, 180
collected, 70–71
depiction of (illustration), 191
evolution of, 24–26
and force on legs, 204–5, 208–9
gait diagrams, Hildebrand, 190–94
historical study of, 186–89
optimum speed of, 201–4
and respiration, 225–29
selection of, 190–94, 198–205
stability of, 192–95, 198
symmetrical, 190–95
transitions between, 180, 199–205
Gallop. *See* Gaits
Gazelle, 9, 32
Genetics. *See also* Breeding
color, 247, 251–56, pl. 8
dominance, 246–56
hereditary diseases and inbreeding, 235, 239, 246, 248, 252–53
heritability, 239–41
horse family tree, 17, 257–59, pl. 1
markers, 260–61
overdominance, 250
of performance, 236, 239–41, 256–61
Germany, 56, 59
Gestation period, 13
Glycogen, 218–21, 224
Glycolysis. *See* Metabolism
Goat, domestication of, 43
Gods, horses as, 74–77
Gray color, 253, 255, 256
Grazing, 105. *See also* Diet
Greece, ancient, 62, 64, 66, 72–73, pl. 3
Greyhound, speed of, 26
Grooming, 85–89, pl. 4

Grulla color, 255, pl. 8

Habituation, 156–57, 173
Haldane, J. B. S., 14
Hambletonian, 245
"Handedness" in horses, 152
Harems, 37, 82–84, 96
Harness, chariot, 66–68
haute école, 3, 69–70
Heart, 222, 224
Heat loss, 32–33, 215–17
Hebrews, ancient, 73–74
Hecatombs, 75
Heritability, 236, 239–41
Herodotus, 75
Heterozygous genes, 246–56
Hierarchy, social
  dominance order in, 89–91
  evolutionary purpose of, 90–91
  and friendship bonds, 85
  and herd movement, 94–95
  relation to intelligence, 162
"High school" of equitation, 3, 69–70
Hildebrand, Milton, 179, 180, 183, 184, 190–91, 194
Hip, 182
Hipparion, 24–26
Hispaniola, 40
Hittites, 63, 71
Hock, 178, 182, pl. 2
Hodgson, David, 216
Homing, 168–71
Homozygous genes, 246–56
Horseback riding, origins of, 47–55
Horse gods, 74–77
Horse racing. *See* Racing
Horse sports, 101. *See also* Dressage; Endurance racing; Racing
Human genome project, 235
Human-horse relationship, 80–81, 84–85, 89, 95–96. *See also* Training
Humans
  athletic performance of, 211–12, 223
  lifespan, 35
  metabolic rate, 33
Human view of the horse, 2–3, 62, 68–69, 72–74
Humerus, 231
Hungary, 54
Hunters, breeding of, 257
Hunting
  and domestication of the horse, 45–50, 56
  and Ice Age extinctions, 12, 20, 39–40
  as status symbol, 72–73
Huxley, Elspeth, 43
Hyperactivity, 103
Hypothalamus, 217
Hyracotherium, 16–21
  diet, 33
  lifespan, 35
  social structure, 37
  speed, 27

Iberia, 56, 59
Ice Age (Pleistocene epoch), 12, 20, 24, 39, 50, 99
Icelandic pony, 26
Iliad, 72
Imitation, 163
Immunocontraception, 265
Imprinting, 171–74
Inbreeding, 239, 242–43, 246, 248–50, 265
Incest, 97
India, 64
Indians, 9, 39–40
Indo-European language, 63
Injuries, 13–14, 183, 204–5, 209–10, 231–32
Instinct, 2–3, 105, 106, 147, 158. *See also* Behavior; Hierarchy, social; Intelligence; Visual signals; Vocal signals
Intelligence
  cross–species comparisons, 147–51, 157–58
  evolution of, 21
  learning ability, 151–54

Intelligence *(cont.)*
memory, 153
and social dominance, 162
Ireland, 75, 77
Isaiah, 74
Islands, barrier, 42, 264–65

Janis, Christine, 31
Janzen, Daniel, 170
Japan, 47
Jockey Club, 238
Joints
design of, 24–25, 36, 179–80, 182, pl. 2
deterioration of, 248
Jumping, 205–8
breeding for, 241, 244, 250
impact of, 207, 208
as play behavior, 101
and visual perception, 112, 125
Juveniles. *See also* Foals
mortality of, 48
and racing, 231–32
tactile signals in, 137

Kassites, 63
Kentucky Derby, 213
Kicking, 89, 139. *See also* Threats
Kirkpatrick, Jay, 265
Kulan, pl. 1

Lactic acid, 218, 220, 224–25
Lady Wonder, 167
Language. *See* Communication; Vocal signals; Semantics
Leakey, Mary, 26
Learning, 150–59. *See also* Intelligence
and bad habits, 160–61
breed differences in, 162–63
imprinting, 171–74
"learning to learn," 153–54
Legs. *See also* Gaits
angular momentum of, 184, pl. 6
conservation of energy by, 24, 183–86, 201, pl. 2
defects in, 230–31
evolution of, 176, 178–79
in jumping, 205–8
moment of inertia of, 181
pendulum model of, 186, 198–99, 203
strength of, 13–14, 204–5
weight of, 181–83
Leopold, Aldo, 7
Levine, Marsha, 48, 50
Lifespan of mammals, 35
Ligaments, 183, 184, 226, pl. 2
Lips, sensitivity of, 21
Littauer, Mary Aiken, 66–67
Littauer, Vladimir, 68–69
Liver, 221
Locomotion. *See* Coordination; Energy; Gaits; Legs; Speed
Lorenz, Konrad, 171, 174
Lowe, Bruce, 260
Lungs, 214, 224
and cooling, 216
coupling to gait, 225–28
defects in, 230–32, 248–50
Lying down, 106

McCall, C. A., 160
McCullough, Dale, 138
MacFadden, Bruce, 17, 22, 35
McMahon, Thomas, 13, 35, 209
Manipulation, 131
Marathoners, 211, 212, 223
Marey, E. J., 187
Maze tests, 151–52, 159
de Mazières, Jeanne, 88
Megahippus, 19
Memory, 148, 153
Merychippus, 18, 19
Mesohippus, 18, 19
Mesopotamia, 71
Metabolism
aerobic, 218, 220–22
anaerobic, 218–22, 224–25
peak, 214
phosphocreatine reaction, 218, 219, 222, 224
rate vs. body size, 33

"Mind reading," 92–94, 140–42, 164–67
Miocene epoch, 22, 24, 38
Miohippus, 19
Mitanni, 63
Mitochondria, 218, 259–60
Mitochondrial DNA
  and horse family tree, 17, pl. 1
  of Przewalski's horse, 57
  and racehorse performance, 260–61
Moment of inertia, 181
Mongolia, 47, 266
Montaigne, 148
Morgan horses, 245–46, 258
Morphine, 104
Mortality rate, 47–50
Morton, Eugene, 131, 132, 134, 137
Motivational–structural rules, 132–34, 136
Muscles
  energy use by, 217–22
  fatigue in, 220, 224
  force exerted by, 175–76, 179–80
  heat generation by, 215–16
  types of, 222–24
Muybridge, Eadweard, 188–89, 198, 205
Myths about the horse, 62–63

Nannippus, 18
Napoleon, 69
National Cutting Horse Association Futurity, 241
Natural history of the horse. *See* Ancestry of the horse; Domestication; Evolution; Fossil horses
Navigation, 168–69
Neanderthals, 40
Near East, 63, 64, 67, 70, 73
Neocortex, 21
Neohipparion, 19
Neoteny, 12, 99–101
Nervous system. *See also* Brain; Intelligence
  and abnormal behavior, 103–4, 105–6
  and grooming, 87–88
  neurotransmitters, 104–6
Nicker, 129, 136–37
Night vision, 116–17
Nomads, Mongolian, 47
North America, 39–40, 42
Nosebands, 67–68
Nostrils, slit, 68
Nutrition, effect on performance of, 224–25. *See also* Diet

Obsessive-compulsive behavior, 103
Olympic games, 73, 211–12
Onager, pl. 1
Oocyte transfer, 238
Operant conditioning, 155–56
Opioids, 104–5
Optical illusions, 123–25
Orthogenesis, 16–18
Overdominance, 250
Overheating, 215–17
Oxygen, 219, 224, 227–28

Pace (gait), 191, 193–94
Pacers, 241, 257–58. *See also* Standardbreds; Trotters
Pain, 105, 135
Palomino color, 251, 254, pl. 8
Parahipparion, 19
Parahippus, 19
Parasites, 86
Passive stay apparatus, 36, pl. 2
Paso fino, 26, 194, 258
Patella, pl. 2
PC (phosphocreatine), 218, 219, 221, 224
Pecking order, 85. *See also* Hierarchy, social
Pendulum model of legs, 70, 186, 198–99, 203
Perception. *See* Smell; Vision
Performance
  genetic basis of, 236, 239–41, 256–61
  limiting factors in, 230–32, 241–43
  psychological factors in, 232–34
Perlino color, 253, 254, 255, pl. 8

Personal space, 83, 86–87, 95
Peruvian paso, 258
Petroglyphs, 54, 55
Phosphocreatine (PC), 218, 219, 221, 224
Photographs, stop action, 188–89
Phytoliths, 23
Pick, David, 119
Piggott, Stuart, 71, 75
Piston-pendulum model of lungs, 225–28
Play, 98–101
Pleistocene epoch (Ice Age), 12, 20, 24, 39–40, 99
Pliocene epoch, 36
Pliohippus, 19
Pogo sticks, 203–4
Poland, 56
Polygamy, evolution of, 37–38
Ponzo illusion, 124
Population of the horse
  global, 41
  U.S., xi
Porphyry, 54
Preferences
  food, 172–73
  side, 152
Prepotency, 259
Problem solving, 154
Protohippus, 35
Przewalski's horse
  in art, 41
  diet of, 31
  relation to domestic horse of, 56–59, 100–101
  social behavior of, pl. 4
  survival of, 40, 265–66
  time budgets of, 99, 105, 106
Psychology of racehorses, 232–34
Punishment, 157, 159
Pyruvic acid, 218, 220

Qin, Emperor of, 77
Quagga, 17
Quarter horse
  breeding and genetics, 246, 257, 258
  learning ability and intelligence, 152, 159, 162–63
  muscle fiber type, 223
  racing, 220

Racetracks, ideal design of, 209–10
Racing
  breeding for, 241, 256–57
  effect of drugs and nutrition, 224–25
  effect of dominance order, 94–95
  energy demands of, 219, 220–22
  history of, 72–73
  injuries in, 210, 231–32
  performance limitations, 214–15, 217, 220–21, 225, 229–32
  photo finish, 188
  as play behavior, 101
  two-year-olds, 231
Rack, 194. *See also* Gaits; Running walk
"Ramp retina," 114–15
Ramses IV, 72
Recessive genes, 246–56
Recognition ability, 85–86, 138
Reinforcement, 155, 157–59
Reins
  chariot, 66–68
  loose, 69
Resonant frequency of body, 203–4
Respiratory system, piston-pendulum model of, 225–28
Retina, 110, 112–15
Reward. *See* Learning; Reinforcement; Training
Rhinoceros, 15, 28, 29, 34
Riding, origins of, 47–55
Ritualization of behavior, 87–88, 139–42
Riva Ridge, 201
Roan color, 255, 256
Robertson, Alan, 236, 237, 238, 245
Rock carvings, 54, 55
Rods (eye), 116, 117–20
Romania, 54
Rome, ancient, 64, 72

Ruminants, 28–35
Running walk, 25–26, 192–194, 196. *See also* Gaits
Ryder, Oliver, 266

Scarne, John, 167
Scent marking, 142–45
Schooling. *See* Learning; Training
Scientific study of the horse, history of, 3–5, 186–89
Scotland, 64
Scythians, 66, 67, 75
Secretariat, 201
Seeherman, Howard, 230, 232, 248
Self-mutilation, 103, 105
Self-stimulation, 167
Semantics, 128–31, 138
Sesamoid bone, 231
Sexual behavior, 135, 143–44
  abnormal, 81
  aggressive, 97–98
  and evolution of social structure, 37–38, 81–83
  incest taboo, 97
Sexual dimorphism, 37–38
Sheep, domestication of, 43
Shoes, 208
Shoulder blade, 180–81
Shying
  at imaginary objects, 157
  role of vision in, 116
Size, body
  and diet, 28–34
  and domestication, 100–101
  and evolution, 18, 22, 36–38, pl. 2
  and heat loss, 32, 215–16
  and injury risk, 13–14
  and lifespan, 35
  and metabolic rate, 33
  and speed, 26–27, 175–83
  and vocalizations, 131–32
Skin, area of, 215–16
Skull, size of, 37
Slow gait, 194. *See also* Gaits; Running walk
Slow-twitch fibers, 222–24
Smell, 142–45, 169–71
Social signals. *See* Communication; Visual signals; Vocal signals
Social structure
  bachelor groups, 37
  evolution of, 81–83
Sodium bicarbonate, 224
Sonograms, 129–33
Spain, 40, 41
Speed
  of cheetah, 184
  as defense mechanism, 28
  of fossil horses, 26
  as function of size, 26–27, 175–83
  of gait transitions, 198–200, 203–5
  genetic basis of, 241, 243
  of horse, peak, 15, 26–27, 176, 201, 211–13
  of humans, 27, 211–12
  optimum, 201–4
Sports medicine, 211–13
"Springing" foot, 24, 25, 184, pl. 2
Sprinters, 220, 223
Squeal, 130, 135–36
Sredni Stog people, 45, 54, 55
Stallions
  aggression in, 95–98
  castration of, 66, 98
  courtship behavior in, 97–98, 135–37, 143–44, pl. 4
  dominance order among, 89, 91, 136, 145
  genetic contribution to offspring of, 238–39, 259
  mate preferences of, 58, 172
  scent marking in, 142–45
  squealing contests among, 135–36
Stall vices, 102–7, 163
Stance phase, 191–93
Standardbreds
  breeding, 245, 258
  energy demands of racing, 221
  fitness, 232, 233
  speed, 212, 242
  trotters vs. pacers, 257–58
Standing, 36, 106

Stanford, Leland, 189
Status symbol, horse as, 71–74
Stereograms, random-dot, 122
Stereotypic behavior, 102–7
Stifle joint, 182, pl. 2
Stimulus-response, 155–56, 160–61
Strabo, 66
Stress, 105–7
Stride
  frequency, 176–77, 179–81, 189, 200–205
  length, 175–79, 189, 198–200
  overlap, 200
Sumeria, 63
Surface area. *See* Size, body
Suspension phase, 191–93
Suspensory ligament, 203, pl. 2. *See also* "Springing" foot
Sweating, 216–17
Syria, 71

Tapetum, 116–17
Tapir, 15, 29, 134
Tarpan, 57
Taylor, C. Richard, 201–4
Teeth
  adaptations to diet, 22–24
  canine, 37–38
  clapping, 87, 96
  diastema, 15–16
  as evidence of domestication, 48–50
  sex differences in, 37
  wear patterns in, 51–54
Tendons, 24, 179, 183, 184, pl. 2
Tennessee walking horse, 26
Territoriality, 37–38, 82–83, 144–45
Thermoregulation, 215–17
Thoroughbreds
  breeding, 236, 241–43, 245, 258, 260
  energy demands of racing, 220–21
  fitness, 232, 233
  inbreeding, 242–43, 248
  intelligence, 162–63
  speed, 201, 212–13, 241–43
Threats, 89–90, 91–94, 132, 139–42
Tibia, pl. 2
Time budgets of horses, 99, 105, 106
TIMEFORM, 243
Timney, Brian, 121, 122, 123
Tourette's syndrome, 103
Trade, effect of horse on, 54
Training. *See also* Exercise; Fitness; Learning; Performance; Punishment; Reinforcement
  of aggressive horses, 84
  and bad habits, 160–61, 164–65
  of chariot horses, 71
  of juveniles, 89, 93, 173, 231–32
  physical conditioning, 214–15, 223, 229–34
  psychological factors in, 162–64, 232–34
  techniques in, 156–57, 160–62, 173
  of warhorses, 69–70
Treadmill studies, 202–5, pl. 7
Trojan War, 72
Trot. *See* Gaits
Trot–gallop transition, 180, 201–5
Trotters, 201, 241, 257–58. *See also* Standardbreds

Ugarit, 71
Ukraine, 40, 42, 46–57, 59

Veterinary medicine
  attitude toward horse of, 3–4
  drastic measures in, 70–71
Vision
  acuity, 116–17
  color, 117–20, pl. 5
  depth perception, 111–12, 120–25
  field of view, 110, 111–12
  focusing, 112–16
  night, 116–17
  optical illusions, 123–25
  species comparisons, 114, 116, 122–23
Visual signals, 139–42
Vocal signals
  acoustics of, 129–131, 136–37

Vocal signals *(cont.)*
ambiguity in, 132–34
evolution of, 128, 134–35
individual recognition of, 138
motivational-structural rules for, 132–34, 136
Von Osten, Wilhelm, 165

Walk. *See* Gaits
Walk, running, 25–26, 192–94, 196. *See also* Gaits
Walk-trot transition, 198–201
Warfare, horse in, 54, 55, 63–66, 69–73
Wheel, 54, 63
Whinny, 130, 137–38
White color, 252–53, pl. 8
Wild horses. *See* Feral horses; Przewalski's horse
Williams, Moyra, 170
Wolf, play behavior in, 98–99

Xenophon, 3, 6, 62, 69, 159, 161
Xian, 77

Zebras
behavior of, 28, 82–83, 94, 145
diet of, 29
evolution of 17, pl. 1
trainability of, 44, 153
vocalizations of, 134

ILLUSTRATION CREDITS

FIGURES

Figure 1.4. From Bruce McFadden in *Magnetite Biomineralization and Magnetoreception in Organisms: A New Biomagnetism,* Joseph L. Kirschvink et al., eds. New York: Plenum, 1985. Reproduced with permission.

Figure 1.5. Reprinted with the permission of Cambridge University Publishers, from Bruce MacFadden, *Fossil Horses: Systematics, Paleobiology and the Evolution of the Family Equidae,* 1992.

Figure 1.6. Basic data from MacFadden, *Fossil Horses,* 1992.

Figure 1.7. Basic data from Elise Renders, "The gait of *Hipparion* sp. from fossil footprints in Laetoli, Tanzania," *Nature* 308 (1984): 179–81.

Figure 1.8. Basic data from Thomas A. McMahon and John Tyler Bonner, *On Size and Life.* New York: Scientific American Library, 1983.

Figure 1.10. Basic data from McMahon and Bonner, *On Size and Life,* 1983.

Figure 2.2. Basic data from Marsha A. Levine, "Dereivka and the problem of horse domestication," *Antiquity* 64 (1990): 727–40.

Figure 2.3. Basic data from Levine, "Dereivka and the problem of horse domestication" (1990).

Figure 2.4. (a) Reprinted courtesy of David Anthony and Antiquity Publications Ltd., from David W. Anthony and Dorcas R. Brown, "The origins of horseback riding," *Antiquity* 65 (1991): 22–38.

Figure 2.5. Basic data from Anthony and Brown, "The origins of horseback riding" (1991).

Figure 2.6. Reproduced with permission of E.F. Brill, Leiden, The Netherlands.

Figure 3.1. Crown Copyright: Royal Commission on the Ancient and Historical Monuments of Scotland. Reproduced with permission.

Figure 3.2. Reprinted by permission of Mary Littauer and Antiquity Publications Ltd., from Mary Aiken Littauer, "Bits and pieces," *Antiquity* 43 (1969): 289–300.

Figure 3.3. The Granger Collection, New York.

Figure 3.4. © Earl Dibble/FPG International Corp., 1983.

Figure 3.5. Reprinted with permission of the Historical-Archaeological Experimental Centre, Lejre, Denmark.

Figure 4.1. Reprinted with permission of Noyes Publications, from George Waring, *Horse Behavior: The Behavioral Traits and Adaptations of Domestic and Wild Horses, Including Ponies,* 1983.

Figure 4.3. Animals Animals © Renee Stockdale.

Figure 4.4. Basic data from Katherine A. Houpt and Andrew F. Fraser, eds., "Przewalski horses," *Applied Animal Behaviour Science* 21 (1988): 1–190.

Figure 5.1. Basic data from Steven M. Roberts, "Equine vision and optics," *Veterinary Clinics of North America Equine Practice* 8 (1992): 451–57.

Figure 5.3. Basic data from J. G. Sivak and D. B. Allen, "An evaluation of the 'ramp' retina in the horse eye," *Vision Research* 15 (1975): 1353–56.

Figure 6.1. Courtesy of Eugene S. Morton.

Figure 6.2. Reprinted with permission of Blackwell Wissenschafts-Verlag GmbH, from James D. Feist and Dale R. McCullough, "Behavior patterns and communication in feral horses," *Zeitschrift für Tierpsychologie* 41, (1976): 337–71.

Figure 6.3. Reprinted with permission of Blackwell Wissenschafts-Verlag GmbH, from Feist and McCullough, "Behavior patterns and communication in feral horses" (1976).

Figure 7.1. Photo by Jack Bingham. © 1994 Marc Raibert/MIT Leg Lab.

Figure 7.2. Basic data from D. D. Kratzer et al., "Maze learning in quarter horses," *Journal of Animal Science* 46 (1977): 896–902.

Figure 7.3 Basic data from Waring, *Horse Behavior,* 1983.

Figure 7.5. Reprinted with permission of Holt, Rinehart and Winston, Inc., from Oskar Pfungst, *Clever Hans: The Horse of Mr. Von Osten,* 1965.

Figure 8.1. Reprinted with permission of Sigma XI, Scientific Research Society, from Milton Hildebrand, "The mechanics of horse legs," *American Scientist* 75 (1987): 594–601.

Figure 8.2. Basic data from McMahon and Bonner, *On Size and Life,* 1983.

Figure 8.3. Basic data from Milton Hildebrand, "Motions of the running cheetah and horse," *Journal of Mammalogy* 40 (1959): 481–95.

Figure 8.4. Basic data from Hildebrand, "Motions of the running cheetah and horse" (1959).

Figure 8.5. Culver Pictures.

Figure 8.6 William E. Jones, ed., *Equine Sports Medicine*. Philadelphia: Lea and Febiger, 1989. Reprinted with permission.

Figure 8.7. William E. Jones, ed., *Equine Sports Medicine,* 1989. Reprinted with permission.

Figure 8.8. Basic data from Milton Hildebrand, "The Quadrupedal gaits of vertebrates," *BioScience* 39 (1989): 766–75.

Figure 8.9. Basic data from James Gray, *Animal Locomotion.* New York: Norton, 1968.

Figure 8.10. Basic data from Jones, ed., *Equine Sports Medicine,* 1989.

Figure 8.11. Basic data from McMahon and Bonner, *On Size and Life,* 1983.

Figure 8.12. Reprinted with permission of Macmillan Magazines Limited, from Donald F. Hoyt and C. Richard Taylor, "Gait and the energetics of locomotion in horses," *Nature* 292 (1981): 239–40.

Figure 8.13. Basic data from D. H. Leach, K. Omrod, and H. M. Clayton, "Stride characteristics of horses competing in Grand Prix jumping," *American Journal of Veterinary Research* 45 (1984): 888–92.

Figure 8.14. Basic data from Jones, ed., *Equine Sports Medicine,* 1989.

Figure 9.1. Basic data from *1996 Information Please Sports Almanac.*

Figure 9.2. Basic data from Jones, ed., *Equine Sports Medicine,* 1989.

Figure 9.3. Basic data from Jones, ed., *Equine Sports Medicine,* 1989.

Figure 9.4. Basic data from Howard J. Seeherman, Elisabeth Morris, and Michael W. O'Callaghan, "Comprehensive clinical evaluation of performance" in *Equine Surgery,* J. A. Auer, ed. Philadelphia: Saunders, 1992.

Figure 10.1. Basic data from J. Warren Evans et al., *The Horse*. New York: Freeman, 1990.

Figure 10.2 Basic data from Evans et al., *The Horse*, 1990.

Figure 10.4. Basic data from E. G. Cothran, et al., "Genetic differentiation associated with gait within American standardbred horses," *Animal Genetics* 18 (1987): 285–96.

PLATES

Plate 1. Basic data from M. George and O. A. Ryder, *Molecular Biology and Evolution* 3 (1986): 535–46.

Plate 2. Basic data from Milton Hildebrand, "The mechanics of horse legs," *American Scientist* 75 (1987): 594–601.

Plate 3. (Scythian plaque) Werner Forman/Art Resource, NY; (Attic jug) The Granger Collection, New York; (horse bit) The Granger Collection, New York; (Egyptian tomb relief) Nimatallah, Museo Civico Archeologico, Bologna/Art Resource, NY.

Plate 4. (Camargue horses) Animals Animals © Henry Ausloos; ("last wild horses") © Sygma/Bernard Bisson; (foals playing) Animals Animals © Robert Maier.

Plate 6. Basic data from Hildebrand, "The mechanics of horse legs" (1987).

Plate 7. Photo courtesy of Howard J. Seeherman.

Plate 8. Basic data from D. Phillip Sponenberg and Bonnie V. Beaver, *Horse Color*. College Station: Texas A&M University Press, 1983.

ELKHART PUBLIC LIBRARY
3 3080 00674 2707